What readers are saying about *GIS for Web Developers*

This book is a perfect introduction to integrating robust mapping capabilities into your web applications, using highly maintainable, standards-compliant techniques. Scott manages to convey an enormous amount of GIS domain knowledge in a very succinct and understandable way.

▶ **Donald Marino**
  GIS Software Engineer, ITT Visual Information Solutions

The best published introduction to getting started with GeoServer quickly and effectively. Scott introduces all the concepts needed to get going and then puts these into action with clear examples. I highly recommend this book to any web developer looking to get up to speed with the geospatial world.

▶ **Chris Holmes**
  Chair, GeoServer Project Steering Committee

A friendly, informative guide through the wilderness of GIS tools and specifications. Scott has an upbeat, optimistic quality that comes through on almost on every page. His explanations are clear and understandable, and he never makes light of the complexities of the subject.

▶ **Kenneth A., Kousen, Ph.D.**
  President, Kousen IT, Inc.

Scott's conversational style is easy to read and well informed. I'm thrilled to see him opening up what he aptly refers to as "black boxes of geographical wonder." It reminds me of the whole reason I dove into open source in the first place. It's a good read and provides a handy introduction to fundamental concepts as well as several tools that have not be introduced in a book before.

▶ **Tyler Mitchell**
  Author, Web Mapping Illustrated

I really enjoyed the book, and I came from a background where I had no knowledge of GIS. I enjoyed the author's great sense of humor throughout the book. I feel I understand GIS a lot better now both in terms of what GIS is and the open source tools available for developers. The book has you implement a real-world application, which really helps you learn the material in a way that just reading about the tools cannot accomplish.

▶ **Greg Ostravich**
President, Denver Java Users Group

GIS for Web Developers

Adding *Where* to Your Web Applications

GIS for Web Developers

Adding *Where* to Your Web Applications

Scott Davis

The Pragmatic Bookshelf
Raleigh, North Carolina   Dallas, Texas

Pragmatic Bookshelf

Many of the designations used by manufacturers and sellers to distinguish their products are claimed as trademarks. Where those designations appear in this book, and The Pragmatic Programmers, LLC was aware of a trademark claim, the designations have been printed in initial capital letters or in all capitals. The Pragmatic Starter Kit, The Pragmatic Programmer, Pragmatic Programming, Pragmatic Bookshelf and the linking *g* device are trademarks of The Pragmatic Programmers, LLC.

Every precaution was taken in the preparation of this book. However, the publisher assumes no responsibility for errors or omissions, or for damages that may result from the use of information (including program listings) contained herein.

Our Pragmatic courses, workshops, and other products can help you and your team create better software and have more fun. For more information, as well as the latest Pragmatic titles, please visit us at

http://www.pragmaticprogrammer.com

Copyright © 2007 Scott Davis.

All rights reserved.

No part of this publication may be reproduced, stored in a retrieval system, or transmitted, in any form, or by any means, electronic, mechanical, photocopying, recording, or otherwise, without the prior consent of the publisher.

Printed in China.

ISBN-10: 0-9745140-9-8

ISBN-13: 978-0-9745140-9-3

Printed on acid-free paper.

First printing, October 2007

Version: 2007-7-13

Contents

Preface

We are on the edge of the next big wave of technology, and it has GIS written all over it. Soon every new cell phone will have GPS (or some form of location-based services) built in as a standard feature. Nearly every major database vendor now includes native geographic data types. Free sources of geographic data and free applications are just waiting for you to pull them together and do something clever. You might create a simple digital version of the pushpin map, or you might write the next Google Maps killer.

All of our lives we've asked "Where am I?" and "How do I get from here to there?"

You start by rolling over, then crawling, and then walking. You walked to school or were driven or took the bus. Maybe you eventually drove yourself. When you got older, you joined a society of people who use different modes of transportation every day. We ride subways to work. We take airplane flights to far-off places. We visit client locations. We attend conferences or night classes. We go shopping. We eat out at restaurants. Unless you spend your days physically tied to something large, heavy, and immobile, you probably spend a significant portion of your time thinking about how to get from here to there and back again.

And how does traditional geography make that easier? It offers you vector and raster data, orthographically rectified and portrayed in the Universal Transverse Mercator projection. (Don't you feel better already?)

Even asking a simple question like "What is your current latitude and longitude?" will likely cause most people to back away slowly, hands up, muttering, "That's OK—I'll ask someone else for directions."

In *GIS for Web Developers* we'll talk about GIS in simple terms and demonstrate its real-world uses.

We have always been awash in spatial data: houses and buildings have street addresses, customers cluster together in cities and states, you probably store your friends and family in one or more electronic address books. What has been missing up until now are tools targeted at developers without formal training in GIS. What was once a specialized field is now open to new class of technically savvy but untrained map hackers—neogeographers[1]. This book is squarely targeted at this new generation of mapmakers.

A word of warning to the faint of heart: you will be forced to wade through a quagmire of polysyllabic jargon. My apologies in advance. What you have to look forward to is that by the end of the book you'll be able to sling these phrases around with confidence, much like saying "instantiate" and "polymorphic" to your fellow software developers.

Every application and API presented in this book is free or open source. I have taken great pains to make sure that they are supported on all the major operating systems (Mac OS X, Linux, and Windows). You will have enough on your plate simply battling the obscure lingo and the incompatible file formats. The last things you need to worry about are platform-specific solutions, let alone expensive platform-specific solutions.

Thanks for your interest in *GIS for Web Developers*. Welcome to the brave new world of neogeography.

Acknowledgments

Big thanks go to Dave Thomas and Andy Hunt for creating the Pragmatic Bookshelf. It is truly a company that is "of the developer, by the developer, and for the developer." You have no idea how happy it makes me writing my prose in TextMate, using make to build the book, and using Subversion to keep track of the revisions. Or maybe you do, which is exactly my point.

Thanks also go to Daniel Steinberg, my editor, and all of the rest of the PragProggers who copy edited, indexed, and did all of the other behind-the-scenes machinations necessary to get this book from bits to atoms.

The crack team of tech reviewers went to extraordinary lengths to beat my factual and stylistic errors into submission: Schuyler Erle, Jody

---

1. http://news.nationalgeographic.com/news/2006/04/0425_060425_map_blogs.html

Garnett, Chris Holmes, Ken Kousen, Donald Marino, Tyler Mitchell, Greg Ostravich, Paul Ramsey, and Christopher Schmidt. I'd also like to thank the folks who read the manuscript *way* back when it was called Pragmatic GIS: Tom Bender, Erik Hatcher, Matthew Lipper, Garth Patil, Gary Sherman, Eitan Suez, Alex Viggio, and I'm sure many others whose names have been lost to the fog of time and/or the inadvertent deletion of ancient email. Much appreciation goes to everyone who purchased this book online when it was still in beta and submitted errata.

Many thanks to Jay Zimmerman for the No Fluff, Just Stuff symposium tour. Jay, along with Bruce Tate and Brian Sletten (also NoFluffers), made my transition from corporate developer to independent consultant not only possible but painless as well. Your support and advice throughout the process was more valuable than you'll ever know. As for the rest of the NoFluffers—David Bock, Scott Delap, Neal Ford, David Geary, Justin Gehtland, Andy Glover, Brian Goetz, Ben Hale, Stu Halloway, Jason Hunter, David Hussman, Ted Neward, Mark Richards, Jared Richardson, Nate Schutta, Howard Lewis Ship, Venkat Subramaniam, Glenn Vanderburg, and everyone else—let's just say that it is an ongoing honor and privilege to get to hang out with folks of your caliber 30 weekends out of the year. As for the heaping servings of grief you give me on the *rare occasions* I get us lost when I'm driving—"Nice job, MapGuy!"—remember that not all who wander are lost. Except me. I'm usually lost.

Finally, I'd like to thank my family. My wife, Kim, offered the same unique combination of supportive encouragement and taskmasterly discipline to this book that she does to our life in general. I had no idea there were so many subtle nuances to the seemingly innocent phrase, "So, how are things going?" My son, Christopher, has many maps up on his wall. He has toy compasses and knows the cardinal directions. With a bit of luck, the time he spends now drawing treasure maps will save him in the future from the genetic predisposition to getting lost that plagues his dad. And to Young Elizabeth, who joined us midway through the writing of this book, your snuggles and full-body smiles were just what I needed. Much love to each of you.

Chapter 1

Introduction

Developing geographic applications is far more complicated than it should be. I have several goals for this book. The first is to demystify *geographic information systems* (GIS) and teach you a bit of the lingo. The second goal is to help you download some free data and learn a programmatic API or two. These lead to the final goal of turning you into a GIS developer.

1.1 Demystifying GIS

Many popular websites have GIS underpinnings (and you don't need a PhD to use them). MapQuest[1] is perhaps one of the most well known. In the late 1990s, it virtually owned the online mapping market.

In the following years, additional players joined the game. All the major search engines now have GIS offerings. For example, take a look at Google Maps.[2] You simply enter a street address, and it shows you the location on a map. Yahoo[3] and MSN[4] offer similar functionality.

Although all these sites provide a valuable service, they do little to raise the geographic literacy of the general public. I can't criticize them too much for this—I'm sure that ease of use was their primary design goal. But by shielding us from the complexity of the GIS problems they solve, they don't help us build GIS solutions of our own. They are "black boxes" of geographical wonder.

---

1. http://www.mapquest.com
2. http://maps.google.com
3. http://maps.yahoo.com
4. http://maps.msn.com

Similarly, most consumer-grade *global positioning system* (GPS) devices are sold as black boxes as well. In-dash GPS is fast becoming the de rigueur option in high-end automobiles, but most drivers would no more consider customizing them than they would try to change the sound of their horn or the wiring of their radio.

I am not suggesting that everyone who drives a car should be a mechanic, or even want to be. But for those of us who are just the slightest bit curious, it would be nice to be able to crack open the hood and poke around. Maybe I've just been spoiled by my years as a web developer. When I come across a cool website, I can not only appreciate it as an end user but also choose View > Source to see how it was put together. To me, this is the best of all worlds—let it be a black box to those who don't care to look any further, but also cater to those who want to lift up the corner and nose around the insides a bit. I firmly believe that this democratic approach to the technology is one of the primary forces behind the Web's rapid growth and widespread adoption.

Unfortunately, this do-it-yourself, learn-from-others gestalt is missing from the GIS examples we've discussed so far. The fact that there isn't a baby step up to the next level of difficulty only compounds the problem. There seems to be very little middle ground when it comes to complexity in GIS applications. Compared to MapQuest, programs that expose their GIS underpinnings are a giant leap up in terms of complexity. The good news is even with just a little bit of industry knowledge, you can put together some impressive results with the free tools and data out there.

So, regarding my first goal for the book, the "blithely ignorant end user" segment and the "all-knowing industry veteran" segment are both well represented in the GIS space. My hope is that this book will allow you to join the small but growing middle class of GIS users—those who "know more than some but not as much as others." (The cool kids are calling these folks *neogeographers*.)

1.2 Finding Free Data Sources and Applications

With only a little bit of vernacular, you can access significantly more "white-box" GIS resources. The trick is finding them. The second goal of the book is to show you where they are and how to assemble them into a meaningful application.

You should be reasonably comfortable downloading and configuring popular open source programs. Java developers pull down Ant, JUnit, and the JDK all the time. Rubyists install MySQL and Rails regularly. These are not niche applications; they are core to the development process.

The GIS domain is no different. A number of free and open source applications are crucial to your success as a GIS developer. In fact, some open source desktop GIS applications rival the capabilities of their commercial counterparts. There are standards-based web frameworks that allow you to display GIS data in a browser. There are GIS databases and command-line utilities—all free and released under the usual assortment of open source licenses.

The one area that might seem a bit more foreign to nonmapping programmers is the quest for downloadable free GIS data. Unlike traditional programs where the majority of the data is generated by the application itself, most GIS applications need to be seeded with some preexisting data.

For example, consider a GPS application. As you hike up a path or drive along a road, your GPS unit can be configured to periodically drop digital bread crumbs called *waypoints*. This allows you to see where you've been and backtrack along the same path if necessary. Although the waypoints are a major part of the application, they are only part of the picture (literally!). If the screen simply shows a series of black dots floating on a white background, it doesn't do you much good. In other words, showing only the generated data isn't enough. Showing those points in relation to a *basemap* (a map showing the roads or hiking trails in the area) is where the real value comes into play.

There is a vast amount of free basemap data on the Web. The problem is it isn't gathered together in one place, and the popular search engines don't have targeted searches for geographic data like they do for web pages, images, music files, and so forth. Finding the right basemap data for your application is often more of a challenge than using it once you have it.

Sometimes simply combining existing map data in a unique and meaningful way is all you need to do. For example, you might choose to display all cities in the United States over a basemap of state boundaries. This data is available and requires no further manipulation. Your job is to bring it together and display it.

Other times the data your application generates needs to appear in the context of a known set of data. You might decide to display cities with populations over a certain number and then overlay that data with sales regions where profit margins exceed a certain percentage. The combinations of generated data and basemap data are endless, and the tools to help you display and manipulate them are out there just waiting to be used.

So, as I mentioned, the second goal of this book is to give you a guided tour of the Internet, showing you where all the best nooks and crannies are for finding free GIS applications and data sets. (Check out the companion site for this book—http://www.mapmap.org—for up-to-date links to all the data and applications mentioned here.)

1.3 Becoming a GIS Programmer

The third goal of the book is to show you how to become a GIS programmer. Once you have the vocabulary, the applications, and the basemap data in place, you are going to want to generate and customize your own sources of data.

For example, the free data you download will rarely be in the format you'd like it to be. You'll learn how to convert it among different file formats and move it in and out of a database freely. You'll learn how to query certain pieces of it and use the tools to create entirely new data sets.

If the second goal of the book is to show you how to be a consumer of the data, the third goal is to show you how to become a producer of the data.

1.4 What Are You Getting Yourself Into?

With these three goals in mind, let's see how this book is laid out.

The first half of the book lets you get your feet wet and your hands dirty. We download common GIS applications and free basemap data. In the second half we get several samples working to show you how everything comes together.

Chapter 1—Introduction

You're reading it right now—need I say more?

Chapter 2—Vectors

This chapter offers you your first taste of assembling maps from the freely available geodata out there. Vector maps are line maps (as opposed to maps that use satellite or aerial imagery). We'll pull down vector data from a variety of different sources, learn some basic file formats, and pull them all together in a free viewer.

Chapter 3—Projections

The previous chapter ends on a bit of a cliff-hanger: sometimes map data gathered from disparate sources just snaps together; other times it doesn't. The main culprit for "snap-together failure" is when the base layers are in different projections. This chapter explains what projections are, covers why data ends up in different projections in the first place, and shows you how to reproject your data layers to restore the "snap-together" magic that you were promised in the previous chapter.

Chapter 4—Rasters

Once you get comfortable with vector data, you might be interested in adding some photographic data layers to your map as well. In this chapter, you see the ins and outs of dealing with raster (photographic) data, including where to find it, how to view it, and, most important, how to get at the hidden metadata that moves it from being simply pretty pixels to true geographic data.

Chapter 5—Spatial Databases

You're probably going to want to store your geodata in a database for all of the same reasons you typically store your plain old nonmapping data in a database: speed, security, queries, and remote users. In some cases, your database supports geodata natively. Other times you have to spatially enable it. This chapter shows you how to take PostgreSQL— a popular open source database—and spatially enable it using PostGIS so that you can centralize the storage of all of your newfound vector data.

Chapter 6—Creating OGC Web Services

Whether you're interested in publishing a finished map in a web browser or want to provide access to the raw data via a web service, there is no denying that putting your geodata on a web server is the quickest way to reach the broadest audience. This chapter introduces the standard interfaces provided by the Open Geospatial Consortium (OGC) that allow you to do both.

You'll install and configure GeoServer, a Java servlet–based OGC server. GeoServer allows you to share your shapefiles and PostGIS data sets via the Web in a standardized way.

Chapter 7—Using OGC Web Services

This chapter digs deeper into two of the most popular OGC services—Web Map Service (WMS) and Web Feature Service (WFS). WMS services allow you to create viewable maps suitable for a web browser from disparate sources across the Web. WFS services give you access to the raw data as Geographic Markup Language (GML). Now that GeoServer is fully installed and configured, you'll start reaping the benefits of your standards-based infrastructure. You'll combine data from your local GeoServer installation with remote OGC services from NASA and others. These remote services aren't running GeoServer, but you (and your users) won't be able to tell the difference.

Chapter 8—OGC Clients

As a reward for wading through the low-level OGC APIs in the previous chapter, this chapter shows you how to take advantage of your new-found knowledge at a much higher level. We look at three client-side applications that consume OGC data with great aplomb while hiding much of the complexity. Mapbuilder is an OGC Ajax web framework that comes with GeoServer. OpenLayers is another web-based slippy map interface that not only supports OGC services but also allows you to mix in data from proprietary interfaces such as Google Maps. And finally, we'll look at uDig, a rich desktop client that offers strong OGC support alongside the other data formats such as shapefiles and Post-GIS.

Chapter 9—Bringing It All Together

In this chapter, you see a real-world use of everything you've learned. You take a data set that contains addresses but no geodata and spatially enable it. You combine it with existing basemap layers culled from across the Web. You store it in a database, expose it as an OGC web service, and ultimately create a interactive web map.

Now that you know what to expect out of this book, let's get started.

Chapter 2

Vectors

In this chapter we talk about getting your hands on vector basemap data. Prepare yourself for a bit of a scavenger hunt—there isn't a single place where you can download everything you need. Once you have it, you'll probably want to see it as well. We download a free viewer so that you can gaze lovingly at the hard-earned results of your work.

2.1   Raw Materials

Most traditional software development projects start from bare dirt— clean, pristine, empty database tables... sketches of screens and work-flow diagrams on notebook paper and cocktail napkins... nothing but hope and potential.

Data is rarely a consideration during the early stages of development. Sure, one of the first steps you generally take is to plan your data structures. You might even create a sample or two of how the data will look for prototyping and testing purposes. But the bulk of the production data is usually generated by the software once it goes live.

GIS projects are unique in that they depend on having some existing data in place. Thankfully you are not expected to draw the outline of the United States or sketch in the highways and cities to the best of your recollection. This preexisting data, called *basemap data*, is generally created and maintained by someone else. Your job as a GIS developer is to find it and incorporate it into the finished product.

For example, let's say you are creating a new system to keep track of your customers. If your goal is to eventually display your customers' locations on a map, you'll need to create a *spatial* field to store their geographic locations in addition to the usual assortment of string and integer fields. The term *spatial* means "the space around you." (I would have voted for calling it a "location" field, but no one had the foresight to ask me.)

But the spatial field alone is not enough. If the only layer in the finished application is the customer spatial data, all you'll see is a bunch of black dots floating in space over a white background. Although there is *some* information you could glean from this—seeing how your customers are clustered together might be vaguely interesting—seeing your customers in relation to known landmarks such as state boundaries, roads, and airports is probably more valuable. Layering your data over the basemap data puts it in context and gives it meaning. Are you looking at a city block? A county? A state? A country? Even if you really *did* just want to see how tightly clustered your customers are, adding this additional reference information will help.

If you've ever watched the weather report on the evening news, you should be familiar with the idea of map layers. (See Figure 2.1, on the facing page.) The newscaster stands in front of a whirling storm system (the data layer) superimposed over a map of the United States (the basemap layer). When the newscaster zooms in for your local forecast, the basemap layers change to counties, cities, and roads.

To put it in programming terms, GIS applications are a series of loosely coupled, highly cohesive map layers. You might say that the rest of this book, and for that matter a large part of the GIS industry, is about combining map layers in new and interesting ways. (Granted, the most interesting data layers will probably end up being the ones you create yourself through data collection or analysis.)

2.2 Raster Data

When it comes to map layers, you need to consider two primary types of data: raster data and vector data.

Raster data is nothing more than a top-down photograph of the earth. It can be an image from a satellite or an aerial photo. Cartographers call it raster data strictly for the intimidation factor—it keeps us from clapping our hands in the middle of a business meeting and saying giddily, "Ohhhh, let's add a pretty picture to the map."

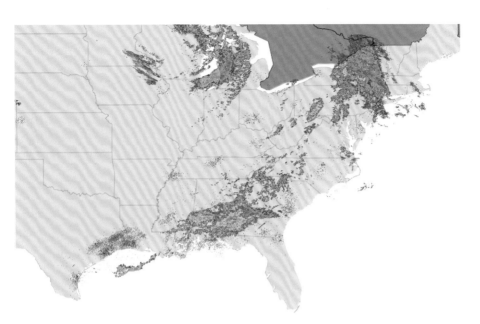

Figure 2.1: A WEATHER MAP WITH MULTIPLE MAP LAYERS

What, you want a more precise description than that? OK—the technical definition of a raster is a file that stores its data in discrete cells organized into rows and columns. Think of it as a spreadsheet; however, in this case, the individual cells are the pixels of the photo.

The information stored in the cells could simply be the portrayal information—the red, green, and blue values for each pixel that tells the rendering software how to display it. But it could also be data such as the historical yield of a corn field in bushels per acre. Instead of color information, each pixel contains a value that corresponds to the yield of a specific area on the ground. In that case, the file isn't a photograph at all, even though it's stored in TIFF, which you normally associate with viewable images. You wouldn't ever try to view it directly.

Instead, you'd hand it off to a piece of GIS software for further analysis. Or maybe you'd upload it to your tractor so that it could lay down additional fertilizer in precisely the areas where your field underperformed in the past. (Don't laugh! Do a web search on *precision agriculture* to read case studies about this sort of thing.) Regardless, we're simply using a well-known image file format as a convenient series of buckets to transport our data. So, to be annoyingly precise, all photos are rasters, but not all rasters are photos.

Are you sorry you asked? Don't worry if all of this raster/photo non-sense is confusing right now. It should become clearer when we get to Chapter 4, *Rasters*, on page 59. Why not talk more about it now? Because I said so.

OK, the real reason I'm putting off rasters until later is that often-times photographic data is simply not needed. Consider the weather map mentioned earlier. The newscaster probably started with a satel-lite image of a big cloud, but few people would understand what they were looking at without additional hints. It's only when the newscaster draws big arrows on the screen showing the direction of the storm that we can clearly see what the newscaster is trying to convey.

Similarly, roads are pretty tough to tell apart from the air. And even if you can distinguish one from the other, they might be obscured by clouds or hidden under a canopy of trees. So, the newscaster super-imposes the name of the road over the raster layer and outlines it in a bright color to help you get oriented. At this point, the line drawings almost become more important than the photograph itself.

The meteorologist frequently draws in data that doesn't show up at all in photographs, such as wind direction and temperature. Meteorolo-gists even draw in data that doesn't exist for *temporal* (time-related) reasons, such as expected high temperatures and predicted snowfall.

As you can see, the raster data layer plays a minor role in modern weather reporting. It is the raw source of much of the data, but the important stuff (in terms of the finished report) happens in the non-raster layers.

For all of these reasons, we can safely ignore raster data until later chapters. There is no raster data on the road maps in your glove com-partment. There is no raster data on the home page of today's most popular mapping websites. (Don't believe me? Go to any of the websites I mentioned at the beginning of Chapter 1, *Introduction*, on page 1.) I'm not saying that raster data is unimportant; I'm saying that we can con-vey a whole bunch of information without showing actual photographs.

Now, am I saying that satellite imagery isn't an unbearably cool aspect of those websites? Of course not. But after you get over the initial "gee whiz" factor, tell me honestly which view you use more often to get your driving directions. Which view do you print and take with you in the car: the vector or raster view? (It's OK—I knew the answer before I even asked it.)

Getting Oriented

Have you ever stopped to think about what the phrase "getting oriented" really means? When you pull a road map out of your glove compartment, you first generally orient it so that it is "right side up." But the choice of north as up is fairly arbitrary. When you live on a round planet, any side of your map could be considered "right side up."

Early Roman maps used east as their up or orientation direction. Since the sun always rises in the east, it was a natural choice for getting your paper map lined up with the real world. (The English word *orient* comes from the Latin verb *oriens*—to rise.)

Later in Europe, churches were built facing east toward the holy city of Jerusalem. Religious reasons notwithstanding, this established a convenient set of landmarks to help line up their maps at night or on a cloudy day.

So, what was the most obvious choice of names for the Asian countries located to the east of Europe? The Orient, of course.

Once magnetic compasses came into common use, north became the natural direction to orient your map. Here is a tiny device that always points in the same direction—rain or shine, day or night, independent of religious affiliation. What better reason to change the way you line up your map, even if you can't be bothered with changing the description of what you're doing?

For an exercise in disorientation, take a look at some south-side-up maps.* They are quite popular with tourists "down under" in Australia and New Zealand.

*. http://www.flourish.org/upsidedownmap

2.3 Vector Data

The arrows, lines, and dots used by the television meteorologist are all examples of *vector data*, which is nonphotographic line-based data. The earliest maps were comprised of nothing but vector data. The caveman who scratched lines in the sand with a stick was using vector data. Much as painted portraits predate photographs by thousands of years, vector map data predates satellite images.

The question of whether to use raster or vector data on a map is not a question of which is qualitatively better than the other—it is a question of which is more appropriate for the story you are trying to tell.

Earlier we said that raster data stores values in discrete cells. Each pixel in a photograph holds a specific value. Vector data differs in that it stores only *vertices*. In other words, it stores each corner point rather than the entire line. This makes for a much more compact data format, but it is appropriate only for data where discrete values are not required. Think of it this way: vector data is generally appropriate for storing outlines of objects, while raster data is more suited for expressing the content of objects.

A vector outline of a farmer's field is appropriate for showing where it is located in the county. Raster data is more appropriate for doing scientific analysis of the crops growing in the field that year. Showing the results of that analysis, such as areas of the field that yielded significantly more or less than the average, might again be a better candidate for a vector data layer. Neither format is intrinsically better or worse than the other, but one is certainly more appropriate than the other depending on the intended use of the application.

Another important consideration in the raster vs. vector discussion is that vector data is an interpretation or generalization of natural phenomena. It is an abstraction of reality. A photograph of a river shows every twist and turn; a vector representation of the river can be generalized to the point where it is represented by a straight line.

2.4 Types of Vector Data

Three basic types of vector data exist: point, line, and polygon.

Points are the simplest form of vector data. They are dots on a map layer. On a two-dimensional map, points are represented by an (X,Y) coordinate pair. 3D points add a Z coordinate.

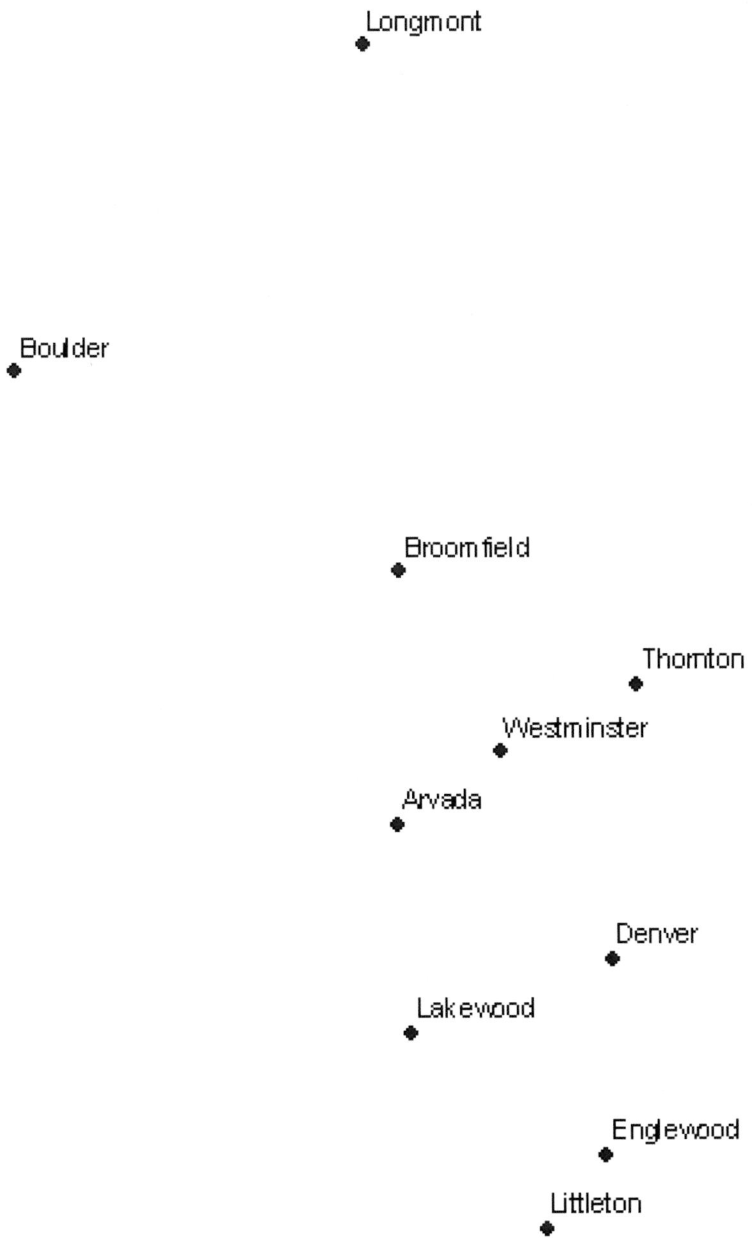

Longmont
•

Boulder
•

Broomfield
•

Thornton
•

Westminster
•

Arvada
•

Denver
•

Lakewood
•

Englewood
•

Littleton
•

Figure 2.2: VECTOR POINTS (CITIES IN COLORADO)

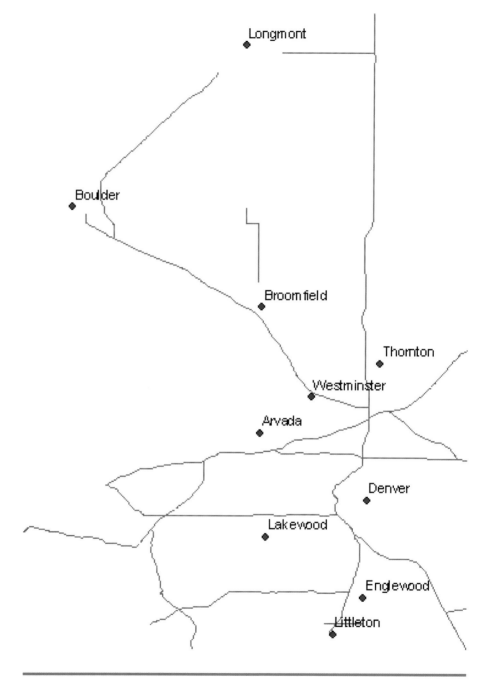

Figure 2.3: VECTOR LINES (HIGHWAYS IN COLORADO)

You can use point data to visualize cities, restaurants, airports, and so on. In reality these entities are more accurately squares, rectangles, or oddly shaped polygons, but oftentimes the data you are trying to portray on the map is a simplifying assumption.

In some applications an accurate outline of a city is required. Other times a simple "X marks the spot" does the trick. Of course, both might be important depending on the zoom level of your map. Looking at a country- or state-level map, cities are probably best represented as dots. As you zoom in to the street level, the outline of the city becomes a better representation of the feature. (See Figure 2.2, on page 13.)

Lines are the next step up the vector food chain. At least two points are required to define a line. Each point is now called an *endpoint* or vertex. Lines can have as many vertices as necessary. The number of points can be *densified* or *generalized* (increased or decreased) depending on the level of detail required.

Line data is often used to represent static phenomena such as roads and rivers, but it can also be used as a data layer to help visualize dynamic data: driving routes of buses or delivery vehicles, driving directions between two addresses, flight paths, and so on. Notice how adding a basemap layer of roads helps ground the city points? (See Figure 2.3, on the facing page.) It gives the cities context and a sense of place.

Our final stop in the grand tour of vector data types is the *polygon*, which is Greek for "many gons"—OK, OK: "many angles." To me, the defining characteristic of a polygon is the many *lines*, not the many *angles*. Then again, I'm not Greek, and I didn't invent geometry. (Geography and geometry—so close and yet so far apart....) Just as a line is made up of many points, a polygon is made up of many lines. Another way to differentiate between lines and polygons is that lines are open ended and polygons form closed shapes. Many GIS applications require the first point and the last point of a polygon to be identical, emphasizing that they must be closed shapes in order to be considered well-formed.

Polygons are most commonly used to represent boundaries: continents, countries, states, and the like. Adding county boundaries to our Colorado map completes the picture for now. (See Figure 2.4, on the next page.)

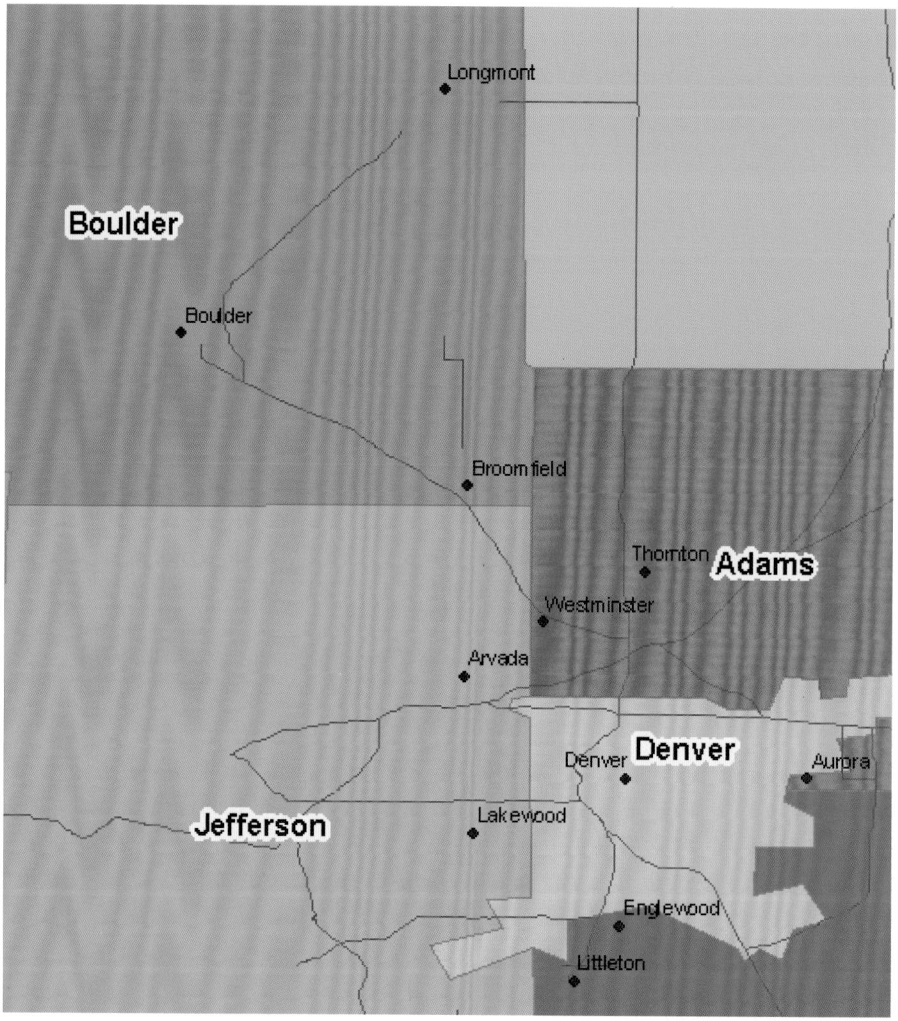

Figure 2.4: VECTOR POLYGONS (COUNTIES IN COLORADO)

2.5 What Data Is Available?

We've covered some good ground so far. We know the difference between raster and vector data. We know that we're on the hunt for good vector basemap data. Let's start downloading.

If you're a Milquetoast weenie with no sense of adventure, you can download all the basemap data used in this chapter from http://www. mapmap.org/g4wd. Keep in mind that I'm not going be able to hold your hand each time you need to find new basemap data. The hunt is almost as important as the catch in this chapter. I recommend that you cozy up to the search engine of your choice and follow along in the next few sections.

In America, we are fortunate that many government agencies are not only tasked with creating and maintaining geographic data but that they are also compelled by law to make that data freely available. In past years, seeing the data generally involved making a trip down to the local courthouse and checking out large pieces of paper. With the advent of the World Wide Web, getting this data is now easier than ever.

When it comes to looking for data outside of the United States, your mileage may vary. The Canadian government has a nice website[1] that offers downloadable data for free. Other national governments are less forthcoming with free data. They cite reasons ranging from potential national security risks to high maintenance costs for keeping their points, lines, and polygons private. Some countries allow commercial entities to gather and sell geodata for them. Others maintain a government-controlled monopoly. Grassroots organizations such as Open-StreetMaps[2] tap into the Wikipedia[3] phenomenon with a uniquely geospatial angle—anyone with a personal GPS unit is encouraged to upload their waypoints to create open source maps of their hometown.

If you purchase a commercial GIS product such as ESRI ArcGIS or MapInfo Professional, it usually includes several DVDs worth of international basemap data. Also, some companies specialize in selling geographic data. (Do a web search for *commercial map data*.) Bear in mind that this data is usually licensed for internal use only. If you'd like to publish this data on the Web, expect to pay a premium or face the very real possibility of not being able to use it at all.

---

1. http://www.geobase.ca/
2. http://www.openstreetmap.org/
3. http://wikipedia.org

Free vs. Accurate

The unfortunate reality of vector data is that someone has to create it and keep it up-to-date. This costs money.

Government agencies in the United States provide geodata for free because it has been paid for by tax dollars. But since each state, county, and municipality creates and maintains its own data sets independently, pulling the disparate data together from different locations presents its own set of challenges.

Commercial data vendors can eliminate much of that pain by aggregating the data for you. They also create their own custom data sets that oftentimes are more accurate and up-to-date than the free data you can find floating around (if you can find it at all). But understandably, these companies expect to be well paid for the added value they provide.

I'm neither suggesting that the free data is always out-of-date or inaccurate nor suggesting that the commercial data is 100% free from errors.

For the purposes of this book, more than enough free data is available to get you up and running. But when you create the budget for your production application, be sure to allocate enough resources to research, scrub, and assemble the free geodata, or make plans to purchase the data sets you'll need.

Free business data, like the locations of popular retail stores and restaurants, is especially tough to find. It would be nice if fast food chains and national stores made this information freely available as spatial data sets. That would certainly add more value to my life than the silly games and the rehashed TV commercials you usually find on their websites. I can't think of a better form of free advertising ("Find all Starbucks locations near you—click here to download them for use in your own maps"), but companies with more paranoid worldviews might see it as sharing valuable corporate data that could potentially be used against them by their competitors. The bottom line is that if you need map data of local businesses, expect to buy it from a third-party reseller.

2.6   Know Your File Formats

Some government data, even though it is free, isn't exactly map friendly. For instance, the *CIA World Factbook*[4] is a great public domain resource for international information. It provides all kinds of interesting facts about every country in the world: the population, the currency, even a map of the country. Unfortunately, this data doesn't do us much good as neogeographers. The maps are provided as PDFs or JPEGs. They lack any sort of geospatial metadata, making them essentially impossible to incorporate into your own map. The textual data is in HTML instead of XML, so parsing it is an exercise in screen scraping. As you can see, even though some data is free, it also needs to be in a format that we can use.

Once you find free data that *can* be used in a map (which we'll do in just a moment), the next problem emerges: there isn't an international standard for file formats. The data can be in one of any number of potentially incompatible binary flavors. Thankfully, many utilities exist to convert the data from one format to the next. We explore one such utility, ogr2org, in Section 3.8, *Reprojection Utilities*, on page 55. Another, GPSBabel,[5] supports more than 100 file formats. The name alone should give you an idea of what you are up against when it comes to battling proprietary file types.

One of the most common file formats in the wild is the ESRI *shapefile*. The shapefile format is not an open standard, but it is well documented[6] and widely used. Like Adobe PDF, many applications, both commercial and open source, can effortlessly read and write shapefiles.

Geographic Markup Language (GML) is an XML dialect that is growing in popularity. It's attractive because it is an open standard and text files are generally easier to create than binary files. Currently, GML is more commonly used in web services than static files, but this may change as more desktop applications add support for it. We examine GML in greater detail in Chapter 6, *Creating OGC Web Services*, on page 123, as well as in Chapter 7, *Using OGC Web Services*, on page 147. In the meantime, let's take a closer look at the shapefile format.

---

4.   https://www.cia.gov/cia/publications/factbook/index.html
5.   http://www.gpsbabel.org/
6.   http://www.esri.com/library/whitepapers/pdfs/shapefile.pdf

2.7 Anatomy of a Shapefile

The word *shapefile* is a bit of a misnomer—a well-formed shapefile is really at bare minimum three separate but related files. When you download a shapefile, there should be a file ending in .shp, another ending with .shx, and a third ending in .dbf. Most GIS applications balk at opening shapefiles that don't have all three files present.

The .shp file contains the vector geometries. Shapefiles must contain homogenous geographic data; in other words, you cannot mix points and polygons in the same file. (It is the job of the GIS viewer to superimpose map layers of different types on top of one another.) There is no way of telling which geometry type is stored in a shapefile without opening it up in a viewer, but rest assured that the first geometry type you see in the shapefile will be the same as the last.

The .shx file is an index file. For each record in the .shp file, there is a corresponding entry in the .shx that gives the offset and the record length.

The .dbf file contains all of the nonspatial attributes. If your shapefile contains state boundaries, the .dbf file might contain fields for the full name of the state, the abbreviated name, the population, and so on. Those of you who have fond memories of the ancient DOS-based database dBASE should really keep those sentiments to yourself. You will, however, feel right at home opening this file and nosing around with your beloved application in all of its 16-bit glory...late at night...when no one else is around. (You could also pull it up in Microsoft Excel just for grins.)

The fourth most popular shapefile appendage is the optional .prj file. It tells you what projection the data is in. We talk about projections in Chapter 3, *Projections*, on page 33.

2.8 The Downloadable States of America

The U.S. Census Bureau is a great source for downloadable basemap data in shapefile format. Let's take a quick tour of its website.[7]

The U.S. Census Bureau calls its data set the *TIGER* database, which stands for Topologically Integrated Geographic Encoding and Referencing, although it isn't a database in the traditional sense of the word at

---

7. http://www.census.gov/geo/www/cob/index.html

Figure 2.5: DOWNLOAD SHAPEFILE BASEMAP DATA FROM THE U.S. CENSUS BUREAU.

all. The actual TIGER data files are stored in a custom ASCII format, so working with them can be a challenge. (The TIGER data set predates the XML revolution, but not offering a SQL version of the data set is a curious omission.) Adding insult to injury, the information is spread across multiple files in a pseudorelational database way. Thankfully, you aren't stuck with working with the TIGER data set in its funky native format. The U.S. Census Bureau provides the data as shapefiles as well. Click the Download Boundary Files link. (See Figure 2.5.)

To begin, let's pull down a file that contains the outline of the states:

1. Click State and State Equivalent Areas: 2000.
2. Scroll down to the shapefile section.
3. Click All 50 States, D.C., and Puerto Rico.[8]

---

8. http://www.census.gov/geo/cob/bdy/st/st00shp/st99_d00_shp.zip

After the 2MB download is complete, unzip st99_d00.zip. You should see the three associated files that make up the shapefile: st99_d00.shp, st99_d00.shx, and st99_d00.dbf. Congratulations! You now have the outlines of all 50 U.S. states on your hard drive.

A vast amount of data is available to you from this website. I encourage you to look around a bit. Download whatever else looks interesting. Don't worry about me—I've got nothing but time.

2.9 Downloading a Viewer

We're not done downloading yet. We have the data but nothing to view it with. We need an application that will help us see the contents of our new shapefiles. Since ESRI created the shapefile format, it's not surprising that they offer a free viewer as well. ArcExplorer[9] is written in Java, so it will run on Windows, Linux, and Mac OS X. Download ArcExplorer, and follow the instructions on the website to install it.

This isn't the only desktop application we'll download. We'll have quite a collection in place by the end of the book. Each will have its own strengths and weaknesses, but strong shapefile support will be the common characteristic shared among all of them. We're starting with ESRI's viewer purely for poetic reasons. It seems only fitting, don't you think? (OK, the truth is ArcExplorer is a bit of a one-trick pony—it *only* knows how to display shapefiles. I chose it for our first example so that you wouldn't wander off, distracted by other shiny knobs and buttons.)

Viewing Data in ArcExplorer

Let's take a look at the shapefile of the United States (see Figure 2.6, on page 24):

1. Start ArcExplorer.
2. Right-click Layers, and choose Add Data.
3. Navigate to the st99_d00 directory, and choose the shapefile. You should see a familiar set of polygons appear on your screen.

ArcExplorer offers a set of map tools that is common to almost every GIS application:

- To zoom in, click the Zoom In button (the magnifying glass with the plus sign), and lasso an area of the map.

---

9. http://www.esri.com/software/arcexplorer/download.html

Free vs. Open Source

All of the applications we use in this book are free, but not all of them are open source. For example, ArcExplorer is a free download. It isn't a trial version or shareware; ESRI gives away the application at no charge.

What keeps it from being called *open source* is that you can download only a compiled or binary distribution. ESRI does not provide the source code that was used to create the program. In simple terms, you get the cake for free (the program), but you don't get the recipe (the source).

At first blush this doesn't seem to be a big deal, but bear in mind that this prevents you from using the same View > Source menu command you might use for a web page. In other words, if you like the way ArcExplorer zooms in and out, you cannot see how it is implemented by looking at the source code. We are back to dealing with a black box.

Some folks take the distinction between free and open source very seriously. As the name of this book's publisher suggests, I take a more pragmatic approach when choosing software. I tend to use the tool that best does the job, and I encourage you to do the same. I won't avoid using a tool that is free if the source code isn't provided, but given the choice between two utilities that are equally capable in all other aspects, I will generally choose the open source alternative.

Free tools give you a proverbial fish. Open source tools *teach* you how to fish. In the long run, the latter approach is a more beneficial and sustainable approach to software development.

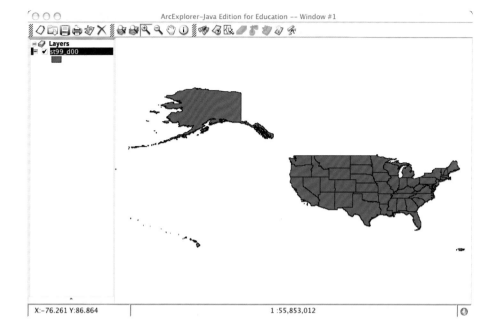

Figure 2.6: VIEWING THE U.S. SHAPEFILE WITH ARCEXPLORER

- To zoom out, click the Zoom Out button (the magnifying glass with the minus sign), and lasso an area of the map.
- To move the map around on the screen, click the Pan button (the white hand), and drag the map.

Viewing Feature Attributes

Each state is a polygon, but we can also say that each state is a *feature*. Shapefiles are sometimes generically called *feature collections*. Features can have both spatial and nonspatial attributes.

The spatial attributes of the features are easy to see—they are the polygons on the screen. To see the nonspatial attributes, click the Information button (the i button), and click a feature. A new window pops up showing nonspatial data such as the name of the state.

Having to click each feature to see its attributes would be pretty annoying, not to mention time-consuming. To see all of the nonspatial attributes at once, right-click the st99_d00 layer in the Layers list, and choose

Attribute Table. A separate window appears showing the nonspatial attributes for all 273 states.

What, you haven't been keeping up with your American geography? Don't tell me that you can name only 50 states.

The truth is that many states, especially the landlocked ones, are represented by a single polygon. The states along the coast are a different story. They tend to have many islands. Each of those polygons is stored as a separate record in the shapefile. To verify the single-polygon-per-record theory, do the following:

1. Zoom in on Washington state. (It's the state in the upper-northwest corner. Please tell me that you already knew that. Sigh....)
2. Scroll in the attribute table down to the grouping of Washington records.
3. As you click each record, notice the highlighting on the map pane: a different polygon is highlighted for each record.

This "one shape/one record" data type is called a *simple polygon*. In Section 5.3, *Adding Geometric Columns by Hand*, on page 102, we discuss the notion of *multipolygons*. (We also show you how to group simple polygons into multipolygons to get back to the expected 50 state/50 record database table.) Not surprisingly, there are multipoints and multilines as well as multipolygons.

There is really no right or wrong answer when it comes to simple shapes vs. multishapes. The historical argument for using simple shapes is that they were the lowest common denominator and therefore the most widely usable data type across programs. This distinction isn't as important as it used to be. All of the popular tools nowadays can handle multishapes. The argument for using one over the other should be purely semantic at this point. If you want to treat all of the polygons as a single state, use a multipolygon. If you want to treat each polygon as an individual entity (for island research, for example), then use a simple polygon data type. You should let the business case determine the data type for you.

2.10 Styling Your Layers

Let's talk about changing the appearance of the feature collection. This is called *styling* the layer, or changing its *portrayal* rules.

Right-click st99_d00, and choose Properties:

- On the Symbols tab, you can change the fill and outline colors of the feature.
- The Labels tab allows you to display one of the nonspatial attributes on the screen. Choose Name from the combo box to have each state's name appear inside the polygon.
- The General tab is the miscellaneous bucket. You can change the layer name to US States. This affects the label that appears in the Layers list. Note that you can also set layers to appear and disappear based on your zoom level. For example, displaying a detailed city street layer when you are zoomed out to see the entire world doesn't make much sense—it will slow down your application with extraneous data that cannot be displayed.

Click OK to get out of the Properties dialog box. Your map should reflect the changes you made.

2.11 Viewing Multiple Basemap Layers

Let's add a second data layer. This time we'll show the counties of Colorado superimposed over the U.S. state boundaries. (See Figure 2.7, on the next page.)

1. Return to the U.S. Census Bureau site, and download the County and County Equivalent Areas data for Colorado:[10]
2. Unzip co08_d00.zip.
3. Right-click the Layers list in ArcExplorer, and choose Add Data.
4. Navigate to the co08_d00 directory, and click the shapefile.
5. Zoom in on Colorado. You should now be able to see both the states layer and the counties layer.

Layer Ordering

Notice that you can change the order of the map layers by dragging them up and down in the list. If one layer is opaque and higher in the list than another layer, the higher layer might obscure the lower layer completely. Chances are good that if the state layer is first on the list, it will completely hide the counties layer.

---

10. http://www.census.gov/geo/cob/bdy/co/co00e00/co08_d00_e00.zip

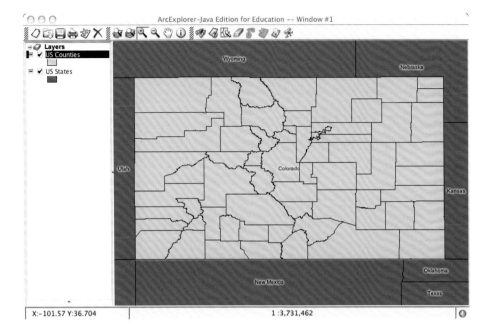

Figure 2.7: ARCEXPLORER DISPLAYING BOTH THE STATES AND COUNTIES LAYERS

This is a common problem when dealing with multiple map layers. Point-based data layers will rarely obscure other layers, so they are commonly moved to the top of the list. Lines are often treated the same way. Polygon layers, on the other hand, tend to be the worst culprit when it comes to inadvertently hiding other layers. Thankfully, you can employ a couple of strategies. One common practice is to adjust the transparency of the features. Rather than making them 100% opaque (which is often the default setting), you can adjust the value down to allow lower layers to fade through. (This transparency value is sometimes called the *alpha* value.)

ArcExplorer doesn't allow you to adjust the transparency of a polygon layer, but we can do something else to achieve the same effect:

- Right-click the state layer, and choose Properties.
- Change the style to Transparent Fill.
- Change the outline color to red, and increase the width to 2.
- Click the OK button to see your changes.

By just showing the outline of the polygons, you can be sure that your other layers will show up regardless of their order in the list.

2.12 More Data, Please

The U.S. Census Bureau data is a good start, but some of the information contained in the files is a bit dated. For instance, Broomfield County in Colorado came into existence after the 2000 census. The city of Centennial, Colorado, was formed after the census as well.

To get our hands on a more up-to-date shapefile, we can visit the United States Geological Service (USGS) National Atlas.[11] The National Atlas contains both raster and vector data.

If you click the Boundaries link and scroll down a bit, you'll come across County Boundaries 2001.[12] Despite the label, this shapefile was last updated in 2004. It contains the newly created Broomfield County, among others. Download it, and add it to the map. While you're here, feel free to download other interesting layers as well—cities, airports, roads, railroads, even volcanoes.

The map is getting pretty busy, isn't it? Notice that you can hide layers by simply unchecking them in the Layers list. If you want to remove a layer completely, right-click it, and choose Remove.

2.13 More International Data, Please

As mentioned earlier, the Canadian government has a great website[13] for downloading Great White North feature collections. Canada will even let you download the features in French if you'd like.

Let's download the Canadian Provinces boundary file:

1. On the Geobase website, click Administrative Boundaries (well hidden under the Data drop-down menu).

2. Click the Download Data link.

3. Click the ESRI Shapefile link.

---

11. http://www.nationalatlas.gov/atlasftp.html
12. http://edcftp.cr.usgs.gov/pub/data/nationalatlas/countyp020.tar.gz
13. http://www.geobase.ca/

Once the data is safely on your hard drive and unzipped, you can add it to the map in ArcExplorer. Right-click Layers, navigate to the directory where you unzipped the data, and choose the prov_ab_p_geo83_e shapefile. Notice how it snaps right in along the northern border of the United States? Zoom in on the U.S./Canadian border. Turn the Canadian layer on and off. It fits perfectly, even though it was produced independently of the U.S. data layers.

Do you see how you can mix and match data from completely different sources? Does it seem too good to be true? (Cue the ominous music.)

2.14   When Good Data Goes Bad

As easy as things have been thus far, sometimes bad things happen to good maps. We added the Colorado counties to our map successfully. Let's add the Colorado highways next and see what happens.

Each state generally has one or more departments that make GIS data available. The Department of Roads and/or Transportation is always a good place to start. State universities are also good candidates for free geodata.

If you're brave-hearted, you can try to enter the URL for the Colorado Department of Transportation website.[14] Or you can do a web search on *cdot shapefile*. It's up to you.

Let's download the statewide highways shapefile:

1. Select Statewide Data Set.

2. Choose Highways from the combo box that appears.

3. Click the Download button.

When you add the highways layer to the map, your newfound spirit of adventure should be crushed: the highways are nowhere to be seen. Yet the highways layer is right there in the Layers list. If you right-click the highways layer and choose Zoom to Layer, you should see a spiderweb appear with Denver roughly in the middle. If you right-click the Colorado counties layer and choose Zoom to Layer, the counties appear, but the highways disappear again. What is going on here?

---

14. http://www.dot.state.co.us/App_DTD_DataAccess/GeoData/index.cfm?fuseaction=GeoDataMain\&MenuType=GeoData

Here's a clue. Move your mouse around the Colorado counties layer, and note the X/Y coordinates at the lower left. X should be in the low -100s; Y should be in the upper 30s to lower 40s. Now zoom to the highways layer. X is in the 200,000s? Y is in the 4,000,000 range? That's a neat trick, isn't it? What we have here, friends, is a failure to communicate. More specifically, we have data in two different projections.

In the next chapter I'll show you how to get your highways to line up with all the other map layers. Reprojecting your data is reasonably easy once you understand the basics.

2.15 Saving Your Map in ArcExplorer

The last task we'll do in this chapter is save your map. The obvious way to do this is to choose File > Save and enter a filename. You've probably done this thousands of times in other applications. So, why am I about to belabor the point? (It's certainly not because I get paid by the word....)

I want you to consider what we're actually saving here. We're not saving individual basemap layers. Technically we haven't changed the data in any of the layers. What we created was a composite map. We gathered data from a variety of sources, layered it in a specific order, styled each layer to our liking, and zoomed in on a specific geographic area. So, what we are saving are the instructions for how to re-create the map. What we are saving is the current state of the map.

This is an important concept that you'll see come up over and over again in GIS applications. Realistically you'll download the U.S. state boundaries only once, but you'll reuse them countless times. Saving the state of your map will happen far more often than saving actual data.

When you saved the map, you might have noticed that the file had an .axl file extension. ArcExplorer uses a proprietary XML format to save map state called ArcXML. Although ArcXML is not as widely adopted as the shapefile format, many GIS applications use XML to save their states. In Section 8.1, *The OGC Web Map Context File*, on page 173, we look at the open standards–based Context file format that does exactly for OGC web applications what ArcXML does for ArcExplorer.

If you open your saved ArcXML file in a standard text editor, you should see the basemap layers you added to the map and portrayal information

```
 1   <!--Extended version of ArcXML generated by MapObjects - Java Edition v2.0.1 Build 454.100 -->
 2   <?xml version="1.0" encoding="UTF-8" ?>
 3   <ARCXML version="1.1">
 4       <CONFIG>
 5           <ENVIRONMENT>
 6               <LOCALE language="en" country="US"/>
 7               <UIFONT name="Dialog"/>
 8               <SCREEN dpi="72"/>
 9               <SEPARATORS/>
10           </ENVIRONMENT>
11           <LAYOUT>
12               <DATAFRAME>
13                   <MAPELEMENT active="true" id="1">
14                       <PROPERTIES position="0" dominant="false" shownames="false"
15                                   preserveaspectratio="false"/>
16                       <ENVELOPE x="60.0" y="60.0" width="100.0" height="100.0"/>
17                       <MAP>
18                           <PROPERTIES>
19                               <ENVELOPE minx="-111.90820586031226" miny="35.30703382616093"
20                                         maxx="-100.9594147098727" maxy="43.252174307010876"
21                                         reaspect="false"/>
22                               <MAPUNITS units="decimal_degrees"/>
23                           </PROPERTIES>
24                           <FOLDERS>
25                               <FOLDER name="ws-0" type="shapefile">
26                                   <ATTRIBUTE name="directory"
27                                              value="/Users/sdavis/gisData/census/allStates"/>
28                               </FOLDER>
29                               <FOLDER name="ws-1" type="shapefile">
30                                   <ATTRIBUTE name="directory"
31                                              value="/Users/sdavis/gisData/census/colorado-counties"/>
32                               </FOLDER>
33                           </FOLDERS>
34                           <LAYER name="st99_d00" id="0" type="featureclass">
35                               <DATASET workspace="ws-0" name="st99_d00" type="polygon"/>
36                               <SIMPLERENDERER>
37                                   <SIMPLEPOLYGONSYMBOL fillcolor="192,205,202"
38                                                        boundarycaptype="round"/>
39                               </SIMPLERENDERER>
40                           </LAYER>
41                           <LAYER name="co08_d00" id="1" type="featureclass">
42                               <DATASET workspace="ws-1" name="co08_d00" type="polygon"/>
43                               <SIMPLERENDERER>
44                                   <SIMPLEPOLYGONSYMBOL fillcolor="199,212,174"
45                                                        boundarycaptype="round"/>
46                               </SIMPLERENDERER>
47                           </LAYER>
48                       </MAP>
49                   </MAPELEMENT>
50               </DATAFRAME>
51           </LAYOUT>
52       </CONFIG>
53   </ARCXML>
54
```

Figure 2.8: ARCXML SAVES MAP STATE IN ARCEXPLORER.

for each layer. (See Figure 2.8.) Since this is a plain-text file, you should have no problem manually editing it. You could even programmatically create it if the need arises.

2.16 Conclusion

You are well on your way to becoming a GIS expert. You should feel a bit more comfortable talking about spatial data, both vector and raster. We talked about the three basic types of vector data: point, line, and polygon. You learned about shapefiles and various sources to download free data. You downloaded a free GIS viewer, styled your map layers, and saved map state in an XML file.

The next chapter will introduce you to more new geographic terminology as we discuss map projections. As a bonus, we'll get those pesky Colorado highways to line up with the other basemap layers in your map.

Chapter 3

Projections

Getting spherical earth data to display nicely on a two-dimensional screen or piece of paper requires a bit of cleverness and some compromises. In this chapter, we learn what it means to project our map data. We also talk about how to merge disparate data sets into a common file format and projection.

The end of the previous chapter was a bit of a cliffhanger. If you just want to get your Colorado highways to line up with your other map layers, skip to Section 8.1, *The OGC Web Map Context File*, on page 173. If you want some background information on why they didn't line up in the first place, read on....

3.1 The Round Earth

Our jobs as cartographers would be much easier if we were all members of the Flat Earth Society.[1] Having to map a spherical object onto a flat surface introduces all sorts of problems—problems that we'll discuss in this chapter. (Being a Flat Earther actually greatly simplifies the field of science. How does gravity work? It doesn't—it's a hoax. Why don't the oceans spill off the edge of the world? Mountain ranges rim the earth. See? Easy....)

If we can all agree that the earth is round, then let's talk about the different ways to model our planet: globes and maps.

---

1. http://www.theflatearthsociety.org/

Are You Sure That the Earth Is Round?

Although the Flat Earthers have had good company through-out history, many early societies hinted that the earth is round.

Watching a ship disappear over the horizon is pretty good empirical proof that the earth is round. If the earth were flat, the ship would gradually recede into the distance instead of slowly "sinking" below the visible horizon.

The ancient Greek mathematician Pythagoras hypothesized in 500 BCE that the earth was spherical because the phases of the moon are crescent shaped instead of straight lines. Only a round earth would cast curved shadows on the moon.

In 350 BCE Aristotle suggested that the earth was round because sailors' views of the stars and constellations changed as they got farther away from the equator.

Then in about 230 BCE, Eratosthenes gave us our first mathematical estimate of the circumference of the earth. Based on the length of the shadows in two different cities during the summer solstice, he calculated the circumference of the earth to be roughly 46,270 km (28,750 miles). Modern calculations place it at 40,074 km (24,902 miles) at the equator. Not too shabby for an ancient guy, eh?

Even the story that Columbus set out to prove that the earth is round in 1492 CE is a bit off.

(Continued...)

Globes

A globe is the best approximation of the earth we have. However, it has several problems—it isn't exactly portable, and to get to the level of detail we need for a city map, the globe would have to be ridiculously large. The circumference of the world at the equator is about 40,000 km (25,000 miles). The United States is about 10% percent of that, or about 4,000 km (2,500 miles) coast to coast. The width of an average state is about 400 km (250 miles) across, or 1% of that. The width of an typical city is about 40 km (25 miles) across, or 0.1% of the circumference of the world.

If we start with a globe the size of a basketball, it has a diameter of about 24 cm (9.5 inches). If you hold up a standard piece of paper in

Are You Sure That the Earth Is Round? (cont.)

From Europe, India was a desirable trade destination for its exotic spices. The route east from Spain involved either land travel through hostile territories or a long boat trip around the tip of Africa.

Columbus suggested that sailing west from Spain would bypass these challenges and establish a new, more efficient route to India. His detractors didn't suggest that he would "fall off the face of the earth"—they simply thought his estimate of the earth's circumference was too small and that the journey would be too long to be efficient.

Here are some modern measurements to back up his contemporary naysayers: Spain to India heading east as the crow flies is about 8,000 km (5,000 miles). The trip around the tip of Africa to India is about 19,000 km (12,000 miles). Spain to India taking the western route is about 32,000 km (20,000 miles).

He might not have realized it, but Columbus was pretty lucky that 6,500 km (4,000 miles) into his westward trip he ran into a little island called America. The fact that he called the indigenous people there "Indians" gives you a bit of insight into where he thought he had landed.

"landscape" mode, your paper map is able to show one half of the world with just a bit of each pole cut off.

To see the United States on a map of the same size, our globe would have to be five times larger, or just less than 1.2 m (4 feet) across. To see a state on that same map, our globe would end up being just under 12 m (40 feet) across. If we wanted to see a city on the map, our globe would end up being just less than 120 m (400 feet) in diameter, or more than four times the length of the basketball court.

"I want to get a tattoo of myself on my entire body—only 2 inches taller."
—Steven Wright, comedian.

Mr. Wright isn't talking about geography, but his absurdist point is valid here. Admittedly the best model of the earth is an earth-sized globe, but the more accurate it becomes, the less usable it becomes as well. Our hypothetical globe—even just zoomed to the U.S. level—quickly turns into an unwieldy instrument.

Paper Maps

Paper maps are great: they can efficiently display great amounts of detail in a small space. A bound Atlas on your bookshelf can display orders of magnitude more information than a globe in a fraction of the space, but there are drawbacks to maps as well.

"Writing about music is like dancing about architecture." —Elvis Costello, musician.

To paraphrase Mr. Costello: portraying spherical, three-dimensional data on a two-dimensional piece of paper introduces its own set of inaccuracies. Something gets lost in the translation, much like "dancing about architecture." Until real-time holography becomes commonplace in the computing world, displaying maps on a computer monitor will be cursed with the same set of limitations as their paper-map cousins.

3.2 Cartesian Planes

Every time you look at a graph, you have the mathematician René Descartes (1596 CE–1650 CE) to thank. He is credited with merging algebra and Euclidean geometry. He's the one who codified the practice of describing points using X, Y, and Z coordinates. A two-dimensional plane with the X axis along the horizontal and the Y axis along the vertical is called a *Cartesian plane*[2] in his honor. (See Figure 3.1, on the next page.)

Thinking of things in terms of a grid is so ingrained in us that it's hard to imagine a time or a situation where it's not useful. In geography, though, it's not useful at all. In fact, it's downright misleading.

Basic Mapping Terminology

Maps commonly present a *graticule*, or grid of X and Y lines. In geography, the X axis is called a line of *latitude*. The Y axis is called a line of *longitude*.

On a globe the lines of latitude are often called *parallels*. Like rungs on a ladder, they never cross each other or vary in relation to one another.

The zero-degree parallel is called the *equator*. Latitude lines moving north from the equator are numbered positively, 0 through 90 degrees. Moving south, they are negative numbers, 0 through -90 degrees.

---

2. http://en.wikipedia.org/wiki/Cartesian_plane

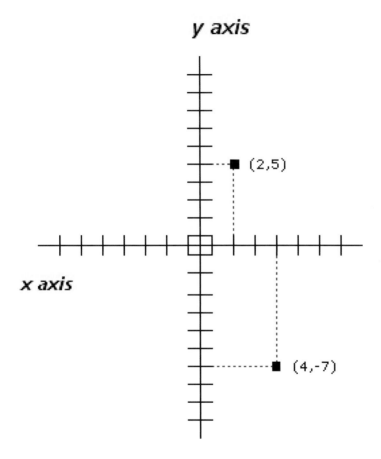

Figure 3.1: THE CARTESIAN PLANE

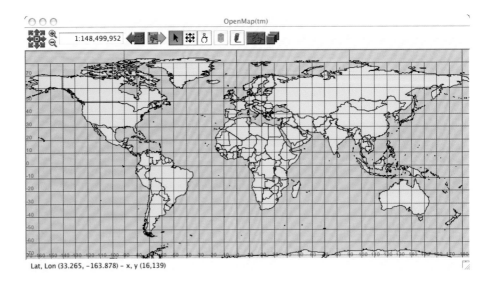

Figure 3.2: THE WORLD MAPPED ONTO A CARTESIAN PLANE

It is the lines of longitude, or *meridians*, that cause the Cartesian plane to break down in terms of mapping accuracy. On the globe the meridians converge on a single point at the north and south poles. On a Cartesian plane they are parallel like the lines of latitude. This, as we'll see in a moment, introduces a huge amount of mapping inaccuracy as you move farther away from the equator. This is why Cartesian planes are rarely used in anything but the simplest maps.

The zero-degree meridian, called the *Prime Meridian*, runs through England. All lines of longitude east of the Prime Meridian are numbered positively, 0 through 180 degrees. All meridians to the west are negative numbers, 0 through -180 degrees. The International Date Line zigzags along the 180-degree line of longitude in an attempt to avoid bisecting land masses.

Cartesian Mapping Errors

As you can see, projecting spherical data onto a Cartesian plane causes great distortion, especially as you approach the poles. (See Figure 3.2.) Each grid cell on the earth is not a perfect square—it is a trapezoid that ultimately turns into a triangle when you reach the poles. (See Figure 3.3, on the next page.) By stretching the side of the cell

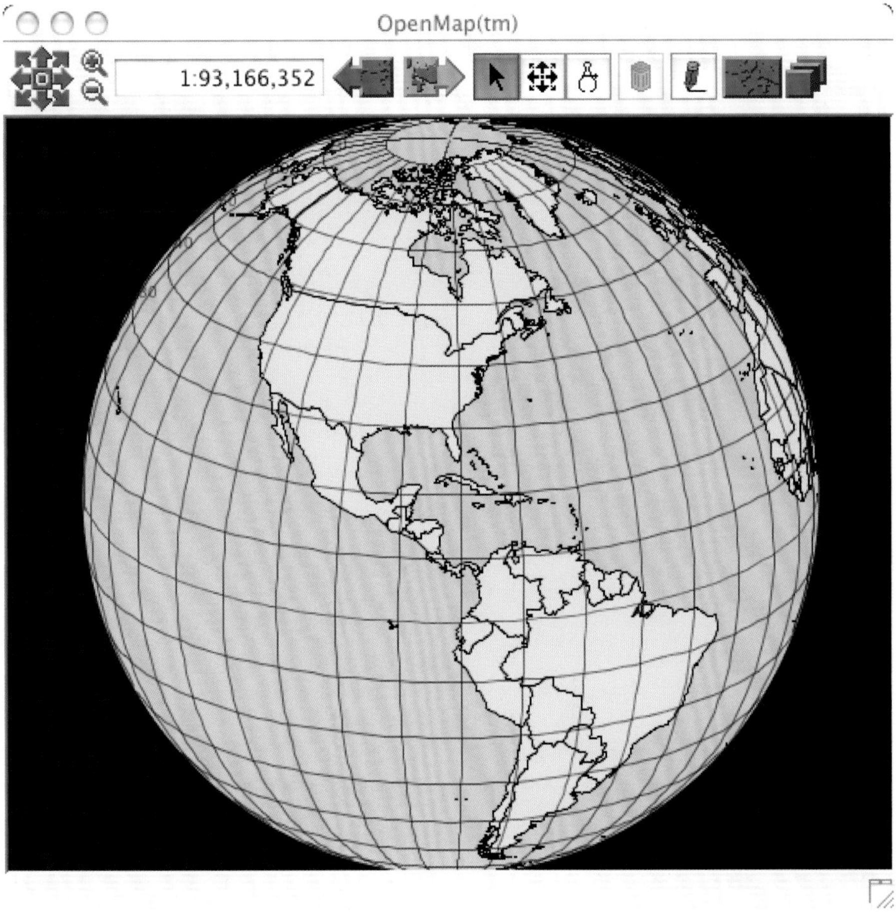

Figure 3.3: THE WORLD MAPPED ONTO A SPHERE

opposite the equator to make it perfectly square, your view of the world is subjected to the dreaded "Silly Putty" effect.

Think of it this way: the very top and bottom lines of latitude on the Cartesian plane—the ones that span the entire width of the map—are in fact a single point on the earth. To see the effect this has, look at the relative size of Greenland compared to South America on both maps. On the Cartesian map, Greenland's size is greatly exaggerated.

3.3 What Is a Projection?

As you've probably figured out by now, portraying the round earth on a flat surface is called a *projection.*

I've always thought that the term *map projection* was evocative of what really occurs when you look at a paper map. A movie projector shoots an image onto a flat screen. The actors and the set are all three-dimensional when the filming takes place, but the resulting movie is a two-dimensional portrayal of the events. Wearing funny paper glasses with red and blue lenses really doesn't change this—it tries to compensate for the lack of a third dimension with varying degrees of success.

Map projections are really no different from the movie on the flat screen. They try to compensate for the lack of a third dimension in a variety of clever ways, but invariably they end up introducing some form of distortion.

Types of Mapping Distortion

Four basic types of mapping distortion exist: distance, direction, shape, and area.

The Cartesian map preserves direction (north is up, south is down), but it distorts distance, shape, and area. It distorts distance because of the "Silly Putty" effect we discussed earlier—at the poles objects appear to be much farther apart from each other than they actually are. It distorts shape and area for the same reason—by stretching a trapezoid into a square, it distorts the shape of the countries and their corresponding areas.

This really is a vexing problem. No two-dimensional projection can minimize all four types of distortion. Think of it this way: if you peel an orange and press the peel flat on the table, the results inevitably will look different from how they originally looked when they were still on the fruit. The best you can do when it comes to map projections is to recognize that all maps, no matter how well put together, will always have some inaccuracies.

Types of Projections

Cartographers throughout the ages have tried a variety of clever projection hacks. In addition to a perfectly square grid, they use cones and cylinders for projection surfaces as well. Each type of projection is meant to minimize a different type of distortion.

Much like the argument over whether to use vector or raster data, the question of which projection to use isn't one of right or wrong—it is the question of which does the best job of minimizing the distortion you are most interested in viewing. For example, a common projection is the Mercator projection. It was the projection used for most of the world maps hanging in classrooms during the twentieth century. It is also essentially (although not *exactly*) the projection that Google Maps uses.

The Mercator projection is a slightly modified Cartesian plane created in the mid-1500s by Gerardus Mercator. Mercator wanted to create a map that would be useful for sailors—the cardinal directions of the compass matched up with the map so that they always knew which direction to sail. His map couldn't tell them how far it was between locations, but in that day and age distance wasn't as important as direction. Traveling by sea could take as long as necessary provided you didn't get lost along the way.

The Mercator projection fell out of favor in the late twentieth century as the default projection for world maps hanging on the walls in classrooms because of its area distortions. Its critics said that it exaggerates the size of first-world countries compared to third-world countries. The Peters projection briefly was suggested as a replacement, but by better representing areas it distorted the basic shape of the continents.

Most of the maps on the National Geographic website[3] use oval projections such as the Winkel Tripel projection. North isn't truly up anymore since the lines of longitude are curved, but it better preserves the relative size and shape of the continents.[4]

---

3. See http://www.nationalgeographic.com.
4. For an interesting perspective on mapping distortions, see http://www.perrygeo.net/wordpress/?p=4.

OpenMap

You might have noticed that I use an application other than ArcExplorer for some of the figures in this chapter. The world maps are courtesy of an open source Java application called OpenMap.* OpenMap doesn't have all of the styling capabilities of ArcExplorer, but I like having it around because it has the world boundaries and graticule baked in. I often recommend it to people who want to download a single program and begin working immediately.

It doesn't have nearly the projection support that ArcExplorer has. It supports only five projections, whereas ArcExplorer offers hundreds. But OpenMap is the application I reach for when I need a two-dimensional globe. After I fire it up, I almost immediately choose Navigation > Projections > Orthographic. You can then use the eight arrows in the upper-left corner to spin your virtual globe in any direction.

The moral of this story is each application has strengths and weaknesses. Having more than one application at your fingertips allows you to play "best of breed" when it comes to business requirements. And since all of the applications mentioned in this book are free and cross-platform, your software budget doesn't have to bear the brunt of your fickle tastes.

*. http://openmap.bbn.com/

3.4 Changing Projections in ArcExplorer

ArcExplorer allows you to change the on-screen projection of your map, but it still won't solve our miscreant Colorado highways problem. It can only reproject the composite map, not the map layers individually. When using ArcExplorer, you need to ensure that all of your data layers are in a common projection before you add them to the map. We'll show you how to do that in the last section of this chapter. (Be patient! We're almost there....)

To best see how each projection gives you a distinctly different view of the world, let's download a world boundary shapefile.[5] Create a new map in ArcExplorer, and add the world layer.

---

5. http://www.cipotato.org/DIVA/data/MoreData.htm

> ### You Say "Tomato," I Say "Ellipsoid"
>
> A *sphere* is a three-dimensional circle whose X, Y, and Z radii are all the same. According to the strict mathematical definition, if you shorten or lengthen one radius of a sphere, you get a spheroid. If all three radii are different lengths, you get an ellipsoid.
>
> Even though they are mathematically different, you'll see spheroid and ellipsoid used interchangeably by many geographers. And can you blame them for being confused? Webster's Dictionary lists a synonym for spheroid as "ellipsoid of revolution."

To change the map projection, choose Tools > Projections. We are currently looking at unprojected data. (This is also commonly called *geographic* or simply *lat/long* data.) Take a moment to apply some of the other projections and see how it changes the way your map looks.

3.5 What Does *Round* Really Mean, Anyway?

As if dealing with imperfect projections isn't difficult enough, we also have to deal with the fact that the earth isn't truly round. If it were a perfect sphere, we could use PI and all of that good math to calculate distances. But *that* would make our jobs too easy, now wouldn't it?

A more accurate representation of the earth is a *spheroid*. Because it rotates on an axis running through the poles, the earth bulges a bit at the equator. The radius of the earth at the equator is 6,372 km (3,960 miles). The radius from core to pole is 6,350 km (3,946 miles). This means that the earth is about 44 km (27 miles) wider around the middle than it is tall. (If you suffer from the same problem, try that argument the next time you see your family doctor: "Honest, Doc, I'm not fat—it's the centrifugal force....")

So, a spheroid is a better way to model the shape of the earth than a simple sphere. That is, it would be if the earth were completely covered with water. The surface of the earth is much more complicated than simple sea-level measurements. It isn't perfectly smooth by any account. The *topography*—elevations in the land—varies greatly from place to place because of mountains, plains, and valleys.

There is a mathematical average of sea level and topography called a *geoid*. It undulates with the terrain on the earth, but it only approximates true elevation. A geoid is a more accurate elevation model than a spheroid since it roughly accounts for topography. (For a nice visual aid and the nasty mathematical equations behind it, see the geoid article[6] on Wikipedia.)

More accurate than a geoid is a true *digital elevation model* (DEM). A DEM isn't a mathematical approximation of elevation; it is a true measurement of height at regular intervals along the surface of the earth. The Shuttle Radar Topology Mission (SRTM) DEM[7] is produced by NASA. It is a raster product that offers actual elevation points every 30 m (100 feet) over the United States and every 90 m (300 feet) over the rest of the world. Many commercial data vendors can sell you DEMs at an even higher level of accuracy than the SRTM data.

So, you can see that cartographers have a wide variety of elevation models they can use when creating map projections. The more accurate the elevation model, the less the missing third dimension will affect the accuracy of the projection.

Ellipsoids and Projections

Most projections use an ellipsoid. The question is, *which* ellipsoid? There are almost as many ellipsoids as there are projections.

A popular nineteenth century ellipsoid still used in many map projections today is the Clarke 1886 ellipsoid. It was created by English cartographer Alexander Ross Clarke. Even though he never visited the United States, his model of the world was used for North American projections for more than 100 years.

More recent (and more accurate) ellipsoids used for North America projections include the Geodetic Reference System of 1980 (GRS80) and the World Geodetic System of 1984 (WGS-84). The adjective *geodetic* lets people know that the models are based on a spheroid rather than a simple planar (two-dimensional) model.

Datum and Projections

Further mathematical refinements to the geodetic model are called *datum*. For instance, the North American Datum of 1927 (NAD27)

---

6. http://en.wikipedia.org/wiki/Geoid
7. http://www2.jpl.nasa.gov/srtm

datum is based on the Clarke 1886 ellipsoid. The North American Datum of 1983 (NAD83) datum further refines the GRS80 ellipsoid.

If you are working with international data, you will most certainly come across different ellipsoids and datum. Each continent, each country, and each state generally uses a different mathematical model that best approximates its locality.

You don't need to know how the datum and ellipsoids interact at a mathematical level to be an effective geographer. You do, however, need to pay attention to which are being used to ensure that you don't run into the Missing Colorado Highway Syndrome.

3.6 Coordinate Reference Systems

Stick with me here. We started out wondering why our roads in Colorado didn't match up with our county boundaries. We are almost ready to fix the problem.

The last piece of the puzzle for us to decipher is the *coordinate reference system* (CRS) used by the data layer. We've talked about a point on the earth being referenced by a coordinate pair in degrees latitude and longitude. But we can express an (X,Y) pair in many ways.

Degrees, Minutes, Seconds

All of this talk about spheroids and PI probably got you thinking about 360 degrees. If you were paying close attention, you may have noticed that -180 through +180 degrees longitude adds up to 360, the same number of degrees in a circle. -90 degrees through +90 degrees latitude equals 180 degrees, exactly half of a circle.

So even though we know that the earth isn't a perfect sphere, degrees are still a useful unit of measure when it comes to specifying the location of a point. Of course, the order of the points can be a bit confusing. Here's where Cartesian terminology messes up geographers once again. Cartesian coordinate pairs are always expressed as (X,Y). Geographers traditionally talk about latitude/longitude points. Therein lies the rub—longitude corresponds to the X coordinate, latitude to the Y. If you aren't paying attention, it is ridiculously easy to accidentally transpose the values. (Does it sound like I'm speaking from *personal* experience here?)

So when you're slinging coordinate pairs around, be absolutely sure that you understand who you are slinging them at—mathematicians and cartographers will be endlessly confused if you are not specific.

If you're dealing with U.S. coordinates, here's a quick sanity check: latitude values will always be positive, and longitude values will always be negative. This is because the United States is north of the equator and west of Greenwich, England. Of course, this trick breaks down when you are dealing with international locations.

To further muddy the waters, whole degrees are far too coarse-grained to express location to the typical level of precision we need. The distance between each degree of longitude at the equator is 111.3 km (69 miles). Recall that the lines of longitude converge at the north and south poles, so the distance between each degree of longitude at the poles is 0.

The United States borders Mexico at roughly 30 degrees latitude. It borders Canada at roughly 49 degrees latitude. The distance between each degree of longitude at the Mexican border is 96.5 km (60 miles). The distance at the Canadian border is 71.7 km (44.6 miles).

The point I'm trying to make here is that Google Maps wouldn't be as popular as it is today if it gave you door-to-door directions with a 50-mile margin of error. So, how can we break a degree up into smaller units?

A common way to express subdegree measurements is by using "degrees, minutes, seconds" notation. We said earlier that there are 360 degrees in a circle. Each degree can be subdivided into 60 minutes. Each minute can be broken up into 60 seconds. Now we have a way to give more precise locations. The distance between minutes at the equator is 1.85 km (1.15 miles). The distance between each second is 31 m (102 feet).

So to give the precise location of the White House (1600 Pennsylvania Avenue, Washington D.C.), we can say that it is at 38 degrees, 53 minutes, 55 seconds north and 77 degrees, 2 minutes, 16 seconds west. In shorthand DMS, it is (38 53' 55", -77 2' 16").

If you really want to get fancy, you can say that you are expressing sub-degree measurements using *sexagesimal* notation. If a decimal system is base-10, then a sexagesimal system...is...base-60, of course. We have 60 minutes, 60 seconds—you get the idea. (This is a great term to drop in meetings if you want to sound especially intelligent.)

Do I Really Need to Know Sexagesimal Notation?

It's no coincidence that the number 60 comes up with surprising frequency in this chapter. Believe it or not, the first recorded numbering system in history was sexagesimal. The Babylonians in roughly 2,000 BCE created a base-60 numbering system that echoes throughout our society today.

So, why did they decide on base-60 instead of base-10? Conventional wisdom suggests that humans are hardwired to understand a decimal numbering system because of our ten fingers and toes. Did the Babylonians have 59 fingers and a vestigial tail that made it more natural for them to choose a base-60 numbering system?

Not exactly. What makes a base-60 system unique is how many even divisors it has. The number 10 can be evenly divided only in half or into fifths using integer math. The number 60 can be divided by 2, 3, 4, 5, 6, 10, 12, 15, 20, and 30 with no remainder. Using a sexagesimal system, you can easily break things into halves, thirds, fourths, fifths, sixths, and so on.

Here's where the base-60 conspiracy gets interesting. There are 360 degrees in a circle and 360 days in a year. (Of course, this was before the Roman emperors starting messing around with the calendar.) There are 12 months in a year. There are 30 days in a month. There are two 12-hour periods of daylight and darkness in a day. There are 60 minutes in an hour. There are 60 seconds in a minute. How are all of these numbers related? They are all sexagesimal, of course. (This is the sort of thing that keeps numerologists up at night.)

The fact that we live on a round planet in a circular orbit around the sun makes all of these 360s a bit easier to swallow. Cyclical patterns can be easily described using sexagesimal values.

(Continued...)

Do I Really Need to Know Sexagesimal Notation? (cont.)

Fast-forward to modern times. The USGS uses sexagesimal notation to describe many of its maps. For example, to find free satellite imagery on the Web, use the word *DOQQ* in your web search. A Digital Orthographic Quarter-Quadrangle (DOQQ) is a standard USGS imagery product.

Let's parse that monstrosity. *Digital* is the easy part—this isn't a paper map; it's a digital file that you can use in a GIS application. *Orthographic* means basically that it is a top-down view. (Orthogonal means "composed of right angles.") So far, the USGS is telling us that this is a digital, top-down view of the earth.

Let's consider the last half now—*Quarter-Quadrangle*. In its inimitable way, the USGS is trying to tell us how much of the earth the map covers. Each angle (or degree) is divided into quads (or fourths). Given sixty minutes to a degree, a quadrangle (quarter degree) is fifteen minutes. A quarter quadrangle further divides each fifteen-minute length into fourths, giving you 3.75 minutes. So, the USGS is telling us that each of these maps are 3.75 minutes to the side. At U.S. latitudes, this means each image is roughly 8 km (5 miles) to a side.

In summary, each DOQQ is a digital image that is a top-down view of the earth that is 3.75 minutes to a side. See? It's intuitively obvious to the most casual observer...who knows sexagesimal notation, that is.

Decimal Degrees

Sexagesimal notation might have some historical precedent when it comes to describing locations on the earth, but as a computer programmer it probably made you break out into a cold sweat, thinking "Sheesh, how am I going to parse out all of those base-60 numbers and the tick marks?" Thankfully DMS is only one way of expressing (X,Y) pairs. Decimal degrees is another popular way of expressing location coordinates, especially in computer-based GIS systems. Rather than saying something is at 1 degree 30 minutes, you can say that it is at 1.5 degrees. In addition to being more computer-friendly, decimal degree notation is a bit more compact as well. The White House's location in decimal degrees is (38.898748, -77.037684). (When describing a geographic point in decimal degrees, you should use at least six places to the right of the decimal point to ensure the same level of accuracy as a full DMS coordinate.)

Converting DMS to DD is a piece of cake. There are various websites[8] that do this for you "automagically," or you can do the math yourself: simply divide the minutes by 60; divide the seconds by 3,600; and then sum the degrees, minutes, and seconds.

Meters

Projections that use lat/long points are generally most useful for showing the absolute location of a feature. Although you can certainly derive the distance between two lat/long points, latitude and longitude are not good units for measuring distance. It even sounds funny: "I drove more than 3.5 degrees on vacation last summer."

The main reason for avoiding the use of degrees as a unit of measure is they change depending on where you are in the world. Degrees of latitude can vary by up to 21.5 km (13.4 miles) between the equator and the poles. Degrees of longitude can vary by more than 100 km (63 miles) from equator to pole. Trying to use a nonstandard, inconsistent measurement unit to describe the distance between two features is probably not the best strategy to pursue.

The good news is we've already got some popular distance units that have a constant value and are widely accepted—meters and feet, kilometers and miles. If you'd like to create a map that allows you to measure distances easily, using distance units instead of location units is perfectly acceptable.

UTM

The *Universal Transverse Mercator* (UTM) projection is a popular distance-preserving projection. Its (X,Y) coordinates are expressed in meters instead of degrees. It has a reasonably square graticule, which means you can use a ruler to measure straight line distances between two points on a map. It preserves area and shape, and although the directions it portrays aren't absolute, they fall into the basic "up is up" category.

---

8. http://www.jeeep.com/details/coord

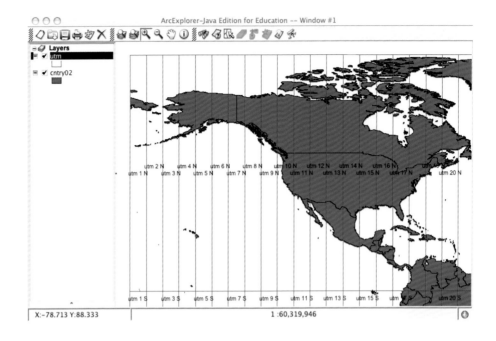

Figure 3.4: UTM ZONES

So why does this Cartesian plane work when others have failed? It's primarily because it isn't a single projection. Rather, it is a collection of 120 projections.

Huh?

It's actually quite clever. The world is broken up into grids that are 6 degrees of longitude wide. There are 60 northern UTM zones and 60 southern. (Six times 60? Yup—360 degrees....)

UTM zone 1N starts at the International Date Line. UTM 2N is 6 degrees east. UTM 2S is the same zone, only south of the equator. (See Figure 3.4.) The continental United States is covered by nine UTM zones: UTM 10N in California to UTM 19N in Maine.

But still, how does UTM magically help us preserve distance, direction, and everything else that the previous projections couldn't? Recall our basketball globe at the beginning of the chapter: zoomed out to the full extent of the globe, you are looking at a distinctly round object. As you zoom into the state and city level, your field of vision becomes distinctly more planar. When looking at areas that small, the curvature of the earth can effectively be ignored.

Rather than trying to accurately represent the entire globe using a single projection, UTM breaks the globe down to manageable portions that can be reasonably portrayed as a simple Cartesian plane. UTM attempts to preserve distance, shape, and area by sacrificing the amount of information it presents at once. Small map extents but high accuracy—I'd say that's an altogether reasonable compromise.

The U.S. Army adopted the UTM grid in 1947. For battlefield maps, the *area of interest* (AOI) was small enough to be accurately portrayed on a simple grid with minimal distortions. So, east/west measurements were the same as north/south. Area and shape were reasonably well preserved. The map sacrificed true cardinal directions for a square grid, but there was usually an indicator showing the difference between *map north* and *magnetic north*. In other words, "up" was more or less "up."

Dealing with UTM projections has some other interesting quirks. For one, UTM coordinates are not unique across the globe. They are certainly unique within the zone, but the same address can exist in *each* UTM zone.

Let's look at this idea further. The lat/long point (0,0) describes a unique place on the earth: the point where the equator and the Prime Meridian intersect. But as we've discussed, there are some aspects of using lat/long that can be potentially confusing. The longitude of the White House could be described as either -77 or 77 degrees west. The latitude of 38 degrees north could be easily transposed with longitude value, thereby describing an entirely different point on the globe.

UTM remedies this in several ways. First, no UTM coordinate will ever be negative. For northern UTM zones, the equator is given a value of 0. For southern UTM zones, the equator is given a *false northing* value of 10,000,000. (The definition of a meter is discussed in the sidebar on the next page. It might be handy in understanding why the false northing works. The south pole is effectively 0; every measurement northward from that point is guaranteed to be a positive value.)

When considering east/west coordinates, UTM doesn't use the Prime Meridian as a starting point. Each UTM zone has a *central meridian* that is given a *false easting* of 500,000. So all coordinates west of the zone's central meridian are generally in the 200k–400k range. All coordinates to the east of it are in the 500k–700k range.

Why Meters Instead of Feet?

You've probably noticed that whenever I mention measurements I express them in meters instead of feet. Why is that? This is primarily for the same reason that I generally describe lat/long points using decimal degrees instead of degrees, minutes, seconds. As a programmer, you'll find working with decimals and base-10 numbers infinitely easier to work with.

The metric system, although it was created after the French Revolution in the late eighteenth century, is *ideal* for programmers. Because it is base-10, moving from meters to kilometers is a trivial equation. If you were hard-pressed, you could even do metric conversions using string manipulation by simply appending or lopping off zeros as appropriate.

Contrast that with using the traditional English units of measure. There are 12 inches to a foot and 5,280 feet to a mile, and don't even get me started with yards and furlongs. The math certainly isn't impossible, but it requires a bit more thought than simple decimal place twiddling.

Of course, the fact that the metric system was founded on geographic principles makes it even more appropriate for us to use. Looking for a new standard unit of measure based on scientific truth, the meter was defined as 1/10,000,000th the distance from the equator to the pole.

Since a UTM zone is limited to 6 degrees, no zone will ever be wider than about 675k meters. The false easting of 500k ensures that all east/west coordinates will be measured in hundreds of thousands.

Map distortions are minimized along the central meridian. As you move farther away from it into adjacent zones, the lines of latitude begin to curve up for the northern zones. This is called the *UTM smile*. In my mind, it only makes sense that a projection that guarantees positive coordinate values should smile as well. Of course, this theory breaks down for southern UTM zones. In the southern hemisphere the coordinates are still positive, but the UTM lines curve down giving you a *UTM frown*. (I haven't come up with a clever explanation for that one yet, but just give me some time....)

In addition to always being positive, X and Y coordinates in the middle latitudes are generally different orders of magnitude. Eastings are always in the hundreds of thousands. Northings are generally in the millions. This gives you another sanity check to make sure that you haven't accidentally transposed the X and Y values.

So, we now have yet *another* way to describe the location of the White House. It is in UTM zone 18N, 323,294 E, 4,307,514 N.

3.7 Getting Your Data Layers Aligned

What is the practical purpose of all of this mumbo jumbo? The bottom line is that you need to know the projection, the ellipsoid, the datum, and the CRS of each of your data layers. If each map layer uses the same artifacts, they magically align themselves in your map window. If they don't, they show up in odd locations. It's as simple as that.

How do you find out what projection your map layers are in? Let's start by examining the Canadian data set we downloaded. Included with the .shp, .shx, and .dbf files is another file with a .prj extension. .Prj files are plain ASCII text files that contain the secret information expressed in *well-known text* (WKT).

WKT formats are defined by the Open Geospatial Consortium (OGC).[9] This is not the last time you'll hear the OGC mentioned; it is a standards body that has defined specifications that play a key role in almost every chapter of this book. For a more detailed description of the WKT format, see the Simple Feature Specification for SQL.[10]

Open the .prj file in a text editor. You should see the following:

```
GEOGCS["GCS_North_American_1983",
  DATUM["D_North_American_1983",
    SPHEROID["GRS_1980",6378137.0,298.257222101]],
  PRIMEM["Greenwich",0.0],
  UNIT["Degree",0.0174532925199433]
]
```

This tells you (after you squint a bit) that the data is in the Geographic Coordinate System (GEOGCS); it uses the NAD83 datum and the GRS80 spheroid; and finally, the map units are expressed in degrees. Recall that GCS means that the data is unprojected. So, any other unprojected data that uses the same spheroid, datum, and units should line up with this map layer perfectly.

---

9. http://www.opengis.org
10. http://portal.opengeospatial.org/files/?artifact_id=829

The U.S. Census Bureau data doesn't include a .prj file, but we can assume that it uses the same artifacts since it snapped right in with the Canadian data set.

What, that's not enough proof?

OK, go back to the U.S. Census Bureau website. Instead of clicking the Download Boundary Files link, click Descriptions and Metadata. Now click State and State Equivalent Areas.[11] Scroll down to the first metadata table. As you can see, the projection for our US States layer is Geographic (Lat/Long), and the datum is NAD83.

Yeah, I agree—it would've been nice of them to include a .prj file. The assumption (and this is a weak assumption) is that if you don't tell someone otherwise, they should assume that your data is in simple unprojected lat/long. There is still no guarantee that you are using the same ellipsoid, datum, and units, so the lack of projection information really means that you are guessing about all of the other artifacts. Not the most robust system, eh?

Click the link labeled For Further Information at the bottom of the table. Then click the Projection Information link.[12] With any luck, this junk should begin to make sense.

And what of our misunderstood Colorado highway data? Will we ever learn why it didn't line up with our other map layers? Open its .prj file in a text editor:

```
PROJCS["NAD_1983_UTM_Zone_13N",
    GEOGCS["GCS_North_American_1983",
    DATUM["D_North_American_1983",
    SPHEROID["GRS_1980",6378137,298.257222101]],
    PRIMEM["Greenwich",0],
    UNIT["Degree",0.0174532925199943295]],
PROJECTION["Transverse_Mercator"],
    PARAMETER["False_Easting",500000],
    PARAMETER["False_Northing",0],
    PARAMETER["Central_Meridian",-105],
    PARAMETER["Scale_Factor",0.9996],
    PARAMETER["Latitude_Of_Origin",0],
    UNIT["Meter",1]]
```

The projection file tells us that the data is in a Projected Coordinate System as opposed to GCS. The data is in the "NAD 1983 UTM Zone 13N" projection. Although it is based on the same GEOGCS as our other map layers, the projection and units mismatch causes the data to appear in a completely different location on the map.

Even if you don't remember all the minute details of this chapter, I hope you'll remember that your .prj files should be identical for all of the data layers of your map. And, no, simply copying one .prj file around to all of your data layers won't magically reproject your data. This file contains metadata about your data's projection—it doesn't *cause* your data to be projected; it describes *how* it is projected.

So, the question remains: if your data isn't in the right projection, how do you reproject it to get it to play nicely with the other layers?

3.8 Reprojection Utilities

Three tools form the foundation of nearly every open source GIS project: Proj, GEOS, and GDAL. These tools are the key to getting Colorado highways to show up in the right place on our map.

Two of the three (GDAL and Proj) are maintained by Frank Warmerdam. He is arguably one of the most prolific developers in the open source GIS community today.[13]

In Appendix A, on page 235, you'll find instructions for building these tools from source. I highly recommend it—each is a reasonably easy to compile if you have a basic GNU build environment in place. For the purposes of this chapter, downloading the precompiled binaries will be sufficient. Visit http://fwtools.maptools.org/ for Linux and Windows binaries. (FWTools? You probably already beat me to it—Frank Warmerdam Tools.) http://fink.sourceforge.net/ doesn't provide FWTools for Mac users, but it does contain binaries for the individual applications.

Proj[14] is a reprojection library. You won't often invoke it directly, but it is at the core of a number of open source GIS utilities.

GEOS[15] is short for Geometry Engine Open Source. GEOS allows applications to define geographic objects (points, lines, and polygons) in a standard way, as well as read and write WKT. GEOS wasn't written by Mr. Warmerdam. It was written by another major contributor to the open source GIS community: Refractions Research. Paul Ramsey and crew have their hands in a number of different projects, but they are

---

13. http://home.gdal.org/projects/

14. http://www.remotesensing.org/proj

15. http://geos.refractions.net

probably best known for creating and maintaining the leading spatially enabled open source database—PostGIS.

Once we know how to define geometric objects and reproject them, Geospatial Data Abstraction Library (GDAL)[16] gives us an easy-to-use command-line interface wrapper. GDAL is used to reproject raster files, but it includes a subproject named OGR that is used to reproject vector data. OGR technically stands for nothing at this point. It got folded into the GDAL project only because it is really convenient to have a single set of tools that you can use to reproject both raster and vector data. http://ogr.maptools.org will give you more insight into the origin of the name and its current set of capabilities.

Now that we have all of the tools in place, let's reproject our Colorado highways shapefile. Change to the directory that contains the Colorado highways shapefile, and enter the following command:

```
ogr2ogr -t_srs EPSG:4269 co-hw.shp highways.shp
```

We'll parse the command-line arguments in just a minute. For right now, why don't you create a new map with the Colorado counties data layer and your newly reprojected Colorado highways shapefile. Savor a brief moment of them lining up perfectly.

See? All is well in the world. Your data layers are all lined up perfectly, and your faith is restored in your ability to assemble maps using free data sources. OK, now let's talk about how you got it accomplished.

ogr2ogr is really a Swiss Army knife of vector file manipulation. Type ogr2ogr -h to get the full listing of command-line switches:

```
Usage: ogr2ogr [-skipfailures] [-append] [-update] [-f format_name]
               [-select field_list] [-where restricted_where]
               [-sql <sql statement>]
               [-spat xmin ymin xmax ymax] [-preserve_fid] [-fid FID]
               [-a_srs srs_def] [-t_srs srs_def] [-s_srs srs_def]
               [[-dsco NAME=VALUE] ...] dst_datasource_name
               src_datasource_name
               [-lco NAME=VALUE] [-nln name] [-nlt type] layer [layer ...]]

  -f format_name: output file format name, possible values are:
     -f "ESRI Shapefile"
     -f "TIGER"
     -f "S57"
     -f "MapInfo File"
     -f "DGN"
     -f "Memory"
```

---

16. http://www.remotesensing.org/gdal

```
    -f "CSV"
    -f "GML"
    -f "PostgreSQL"
-append: Append to existing layer instead of creating new
-update: Open existing output datasource in update mode
-select field_list: Comma-delimited list of fields from input layer to
                    copy to the new layer (defaults to all)
-where restricted_where: Attribute query (like SQL WHERE)
-sql statement: Execute given SQL statement and save result.
-skipfailures: skip features or layers that fail to convert
-spat xmin ymin xmax ymax: spatial query extents
-dsco NAME=VALUE: Dataset creation option (format specific)
-lco  NAME=VALUE: Layer creation option (format specific)
-nln name: Assign an alternate name to the new layer
-nlt type: Force a geometry type for new layer.  One of NONE, GEOMETRY,
      POINT, LINESTRING, POLYGON, GEOMETRYCOLLECTION, MULTIPOINT, MULTILINE,
      MULTIPOLYGON, or MULTILINESTRING.  Add "25D" for 3D layers.
      Default is type of source layer.
-a_srs srs_def: Assign an output SRS
-t_srs srs_def: Reproject/transform to this SRS on output
-s_srs srs_def: Override source SRS


Srs_def can be a full WKT definition (hard to escape properly),
or a well known definition (ie. EPSG:4326) or a file with a WKT
definition.
```

We used ogr2ogr here to simply reproject the data. You can also use it to change file formats. It can even dynamically query data out of a spatial database. We'll use it much more in Chapter 5, *Spatial Databases*, on page 97.

The -t_srs argument specifies the target Spatial Reference System (SRS), or simply the target projection. We didn't need to use the -s_srs (Source SRS) argument since the .prj file was present.

So, what does EPSG:4269 mean? It should come as no surprise that it's a bit of syntactic shorthand for Unprojected (Lat/Long) NAD83. Everything else was in that projection, wasn't it? Compare co-hw.prj to the other .prj files. They should match up.

If you look at the bottom of the ogr2org help output, notice that you can specify projections using the full WKT description. Typing that stuff out doesn't seem very efficient, so you can also store the WKT in a text file and specify a fully qualified path to the file. But the simplest way to specify a projection is to use the *European Petroleum Survey Group* (EPSG)[17] SRID. Recall that the OGC created the WKT format. The EPSG's claim to fame is creating a standard numbering scheme to

---

17. http://www.epsg.org

describe each projection. It would be nice if the EPSG code showed up somewhere in the WTK, but these are two different standards created by two different groups at two different times.

For a full listing of all of the EPSG codes, you can download a Microsoft Access file from the Web. For a more vendor-neutral way to get at these codes, a table is included in the standard PostGIS installation.

The good news is pretty soon all of these different ways to describe a projection will become second nature. EPSG:4326 is the same as plain old lat/long WGS84. UTM 13 N based on NAD83 is EPSG:26915. UTM 13 N based on NAD27 is EPSG:26713. We will continue to work with the EPSG codes throughout the rest of the book.

3.9 Conclusion

Yes, this was a long chapter. Yes, there is *lots* to learn when it comes to map projections. You might be exhausted, but this chapter was by no means exhaustive. We covered the basics here, but this is a topic you'll revisit over and over again in your GIS travels.

We talked about the challenge of getting three-dimensional data portrayed on a two-dimensional computer screen. We talked about how Cartesian planes are both a blessing and a curse to cartographers. We talked about several projections and the four types of map distortions they attempt to minimize (direction, distance, area, and shape). We talked about the types of ellipsoids, datum, and coordinate reference systems.

Once you understood those basic building blocks, you were introduced to several ways to describe a projection. There is the WKT representation. There is also the EPSG code.

Finally, we talked about the three basic tools of the open source GIS trade: Proj, GEOS, and GDAL. Our use of ogr2ogr to reproject our shape-file is only the beginning. We will use these tools throughout the rest of the book to get our data lined up and ready to use.

In the next chapter, we'll talk about raster images. If you are going to use them as a map layer, they need to be projected just like your vector layers. GDAL will come back to save the day once again.

Chapter 4

Rasters

In this chapter, we'll discuss the specifics of raster imagery: where to download free images, where to download free viewers, and how to use free utilities such as GDAL to reproject and convert file formats.

4.1 Getting Started with Raster Data

After talking about vector data and projections, you're still hanging around. You've heard me say that vector data is where most of the real work gets done in GIS, but here you are saying "When can we see the pretty pictures?" OK, I admit that it's one thing to find your house on a vector map. It's another thing altogether to see an actual picture of your house taken from space—undeniably cool.

A great place to start looking at raster imagery is http://maps.google. com. Notice that Google starts you out with a vector view of the United States. Google has taken care of assembling the various data layers, styling them, and ensuring that they are all in the same projection. Google didn't cobble together the free layers that we've been playing with—you can tell by the copyright notice in the lower-right corner that the company purchased commercial data sets from NAVTEQ and Tele Atlas, two of the major players in the industry.

Things really get fun when you click the Satellite link in the upper-right corner. You are now presented with a raster view of the same extent. Looking at the copyrights in the lower-right corner, you can see that Google purchased the imagery from DigitalGlobe and EarthSat. In this chapter, we'll find the same type of imagery available for free on the Web.

Zoomed out at this level, the satellite imagery is really nothing more than window dressing. You can't get much useful information from the photograph. But when you're zoomed in closer, the contrast is more striking. For example, let's take a look at the Colorado State Capitol building. Type 200 E. Colfax Ave Denver CO in the query box.

I'm sorry. How silly of me. First type in your home address and look around. You're going to be totally distracted and worthless to me until you get it out of your system. Go ahead—I'll be right here when you're finished.

OK, now that I have your undivided attention, type 200 E. Colfax Ave Denver CO in the query box. If you zoom in on the vector view, you can see all sorts of detail. The streets, parks, and major buildings are all clearly labeled. The blue arrows tell you which direction the one-way streets go.

Now click over to the satellite view. You can see cars in the parking lots. You can see trees and grass and sidewalks. You can even count the number of lanes in the streets. This is undeniably cool, but if you were new to Denver and trying to find your way around, which view would be more helpful?

I think the answer is most likely the vector layer, although the raster layer does show you a greater level of detail. In it, you can see parking lots and actual buildings, while the vector layer simply shows gray rectangles for most blocks.

This perfectly illustrates the ideas I first put forth in Chapter 2, *Vectors*, on page 7. Vector data is an abstract representation of reality. In the case of Google Maps, by showing less detail in the vector layer, you actually get more information. The map designer has effectively eliminated much of the "noise" and boiled the vector layer down to its bare essentials. The primary purpose of Google Maps is to give driving directions, so the elements that don't aid in that endeavor (sidewalks, trees, and so on) are removed. Although this version of the software doesn't do it, it could quite easily remove roads from the map that are closed for construction or even remove all roads that aren't on your route from point A to point B. This perfectly illustrates the ideas I first put forth in Chapter 2, *Vectors*, on page 7. Vector data is an abstract representation of reality. In the case of Google Maps, by showing less detail in the vector layer, you actually get more information. The map designer has effectively eliminated much of the "noise" and boiled the vector layer down to its bare essentials. The primary purpose of Google Maps is to give driving directions, so the elements that don't aid in that endeavor (sidewalks, trees, and so on) are removed. Although this version of the software doesn't do it, it could quite easily remove roads from the map that are closed for construction or even remove all roads that aren't on your route from point A to point B.

For some mapping use cases, vector data is wholly inappropriate. Google did a good job of stripping out all of the temporal artifacts from the vector layer like the cars in the street and parking lots. But what if that was what you were trying to study? Analysis of traffic patterns is absolutely dependent on the noise that was removed for clarity in the other application. Someone trying to create a vegetation index for downtown Denver is far more interested in the trees and grass than the sidewalks and streets. The shadows in the imagery don't show up in the vector layer, but without them our ancient friend Eratosthenes wouldn't be able to estimate the circumference of the world. You get the idea.

Cartographers vs. Photogrammetrists

At this point it's probably worth introducing a couple of relevant job titles. We've mentioned cartography several times already. Cartographers are mapmakers. (The origin of the word is Greek: the suffix *graphy* means "to write," and *carto* means "maps.") Historically, cartographers have focused on assembling vector layers (often drawing them by hand). Modern job descriptions often loosen the constraints to include working with imagery as well.

Photogrammetry, on the other hand, focuses more closely on the imagery side of things. A photogrammetrist might just ensure that a raster image is geographically and geometrically correct. A broader interpretation of the job title might also include analyzing photographs looking for patterns (such as traffic patterns or vegetation indexes) and *feature extraction* (creating vector layers out of the imagery). For example, a photogrammetrist could create a road layer by extracting the roads out of the raster image. Another common type of output is a Land Use/Land Cover report. Local governments can use imagery to create vector layers of how the land is being used—streets, buildings, residential housing. Even knowing where cement and asphalt is vs. dirt, grass, and crops is useful: it can help city planners figure out where to place sewers to accommodate rainwater runoff.

So, a photogrammetrist might start with a raster image and extract features to create vector layers. The cartographer then takes the resulting vector layers and assembles them into a map. For more information about these job titles and some real-world examples,[1] do a web search on the terms.

4.2 Terraserver-USA: Another Source of Free Raster Imagery

Google is a really useful web application, but it is a black box of GIS. You cannot turn data layers on and off. You cannot add your own data layers. You cannot change the styling of the layers. And you certainly can't download the data layers for use in a desktop GIS application.

Don't get me wrong—I have a great deal of respect for Google's interface design (so much so that I wrote a book on it).[2] Google's goal was to create an application easy enough for Grandma to use, and it hits its mark perfectly. (Notice that lat/long coordinates are nowhere to be found in the user interface?) But we're going to need a little more flexibility and horsepower in order to move on, even at the expense of added complexity. Let's turn our attention to another web application that can supply us with some raw materials for our own use.

Terraserver-USA[3] looks an awful lot like Google Maps at first glance. (See Figure 4.1, on the facing page.) You can zoom into an area by entering an address, clicking the map, or entering a lat/long coordinate. The green areas of the map show where they have raster data available for viewing. (The dark green areas indicate color imagery; the light green areas are black and white.)

Terraserver-USA is a joint research project between the USGS and Microsoft. It came online in June 1998. It gave Microsoft an opportunity to work with a huge data set and stress-test its software in a real-world scenario. It gave the USGS an opportunity to put its entire archive online.

One of the biggest differences between Terraserver-USA and Google Maps is that Terraserver-USA allows you to download the base imagery for use in your own application. (The website says, "The images are from

---

1. http://www.iseek.org/sv/13000.jsp?id=100031
2. http://www.pragmaticprogrammer.com/titles/sdgmapi/
3. http://terraserver-usa.com

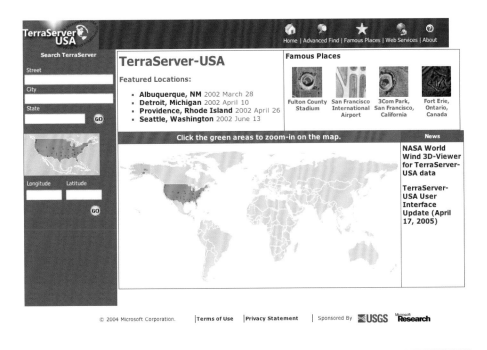

Figure 4.1: TERRASERVER-USA, ANOTHER SOURCE FOR RASTER DATA

the U.S. Geological Survey and are freely available for you to download, use, and redistribute. The TerraServer team and the USGS appreciate credit for their work on this project by displaying the message 'Image courtesy of the USGS.'") This, of course, brings with it its own set of challenges: there is more than 6 terabytes of imagery available for download. As a matter of fact, the name of the site has a bit of a double meaning: *terra* for world and *tera* for trillions of bytes.

We'll revisit the Colorado State Capitol building in just a moment. For now, take a moment to look around Famous Places: click the link in the upper-right corner. One of my favorites is the one labeled "B-52 Aircraft, Davis-Monthan AFB, Tucson, Arizona." This is the "boneyard" where the U.S. Air Force parks all of its decommissioned aircrafts. Zoom in and out. Pan around. Get familiar with the navigation tools and the different locations. This chapter will resume in five minutes.

4.3 Mosaics and Tessellation

The Terraserver-USA data set is a coast-to-coast *mosaic* of USGS imagery. As mentioned earlier, the USGS has a standard imagery product called a DOQQ. These are photographs of the continental United States that are roughly 8 km by 8 km (5 miles by 5 miles). It takes about 500 of these DOQQs to cover a strip of the United States from the east coast to the west; 325 of them cover a straight line from the North Dakota border to the southern tip of Texas. Terraserver-USA blends them all together (more than 150,000 individual scenes) to make them appear as one seamless data set.

When most people think of a mosaic, they probably envision a piece of art made up of tiny fragments of glass or pottery arranged together to make a bigger picture. The artist usually emphasizes the individual pieces by leaving a gap between them, letting the plaster or mortar show through. (For some beautiful examples of historic mosaics, see the Joy of Shards.[4])

When GIS folks create mosaics, they usually try to avoid bringing attention to the seams between the individual images. This can be done by choosing your *cut lines* very carefully. If you stitch the imagery together along a road or a river, you can usually make the seams virtually undetectable.

Since the Terraserver-USA folks had such an avalanche of pixels to deal with, they weren't able to handcraft their mosaic. In some areas, the boundaries between individual images are quite noticeable. Since the images were taken at different times, the colors and shadows might not quite match up. There might be seasonality differences. (It's common to hear GIS professionals talk about scenes taken during *leaf-on* and *leaf-off* seasons.) The images might have *pixel misregistration* issues— positional inaccuracies that happen when the pixels aren't assigned to the correct lat/long points on the ground. If you're dealing with a single image, misregistration can be tough to catch, but if you are dealing with two or more images, misregistration can cause roads and rivers to shift suddenly between scenes. (See Figure 4.2, on the next page.)

The flip side of mosaicking is *tessellation*, or breaking an image up into smaller tiles. Both Google Maps and Terraserver-USA serve up tiles instead of the entire data set at once. If you've got a slow Internet con-

---

4. http://www.thejoyofshards.co.uk/history

Figure 4.2: AN EXAMPLE OF MISREGISTRATION

nection, you can see the individual tiles of the map show up as they are downloaded. The map area in both applications is chopped up into roughly a three-by-three grid.

So, wait just a gosh darn second here—you mean to tell me that Microsoft took 150,000 individual scenes, mosaicked them together, and then turned around and broke them back up into tiles again?! Well, um, "yes" is the short answer, but it's a bit more complicated than that. As much as I would like to make a Microsoft joke at this point (I'm an Apple user), this is a pretty common practice. Tessellation and mosaicking are almost always done on the same data set. Mosaicking is done for presentation purposes; tessellation is done for distribution purposes. An individual DOQQ is about 8,000 pixels by 8,000 pixels. That is far too big a hunk of data to send across the Internet comfortably, so the countrywide mosaic was created for artistic purposes and then tiled back down into smaller pieces for easy distribution over the network.

4.4 Temporal Analysis

Let's see what Terraserver-USA brings to the table when it comes to the Colorado State Capitol building. (Leave the Google Maps view of the capitol building up in another tab or another browser window if you can.) Enter the address 200 E. Colfax Ave, Denver, CO, and click Go. On the results page you'll see links to three types of raster imagery. First, don't be fooled into clicking the Topo map link. Really. Don't click it. Trust me, you'll be disappointed.

You clicked it anyway, didn't you? Well, as long as we're here, let's talk about it. Ironically, the topo map is a vector map in raster's clothing. A topographical map is a vector map that shows terrain and elevation. They are quite common. Hikers and campers seem to enjoy using them, but otherwise as nearly as I can tell, they exist only to clutter up your search results with files that aren't really what we wanted. They are technically rasters, but they aren't photographs. I'd be more impressed with them if they were distributed as a true vector layer—then I could style them, adjust their transparency, offer them as an additional map layer, and so on. Instead, they are fully opaque line drawings that usually date back to the 1970s and earlier. Click your browser's back button in disgust, and look at the other two results.

Both the Urban Areas and Aerial photos are closer to what we want. Click the Aerial link to see a black-and-white photograph of the capitol building. (Not all aerial photos are black and white. *Aerial* just tells us that it was taken from an airplane as opposed to a satellite.) This doesn't look like the capitol building to you? Pan one click to the south and one click to the west to center it on your screen. (See Figure 4.3, on the facing page.) Ahh, that's much better. Choose the Urban Areas tab to see a color photo of the same scene. (See Figure 4.4, on page 68.)

Let's put on our photogrammetrists pants and analyze these two images. It's trivial to turn a color image into a black-and-white one, but several clues tell us that these are in fact two distinct images. (Yes, you're right: one pretty good clue is that each image is clearly dated under the ZIP code in the address, but let's pretend for a moment that you aren't a complete killjoy.) Notice the temporal differences? The trees and foliage are much fuller in the black-and-white image than they are in the color one.

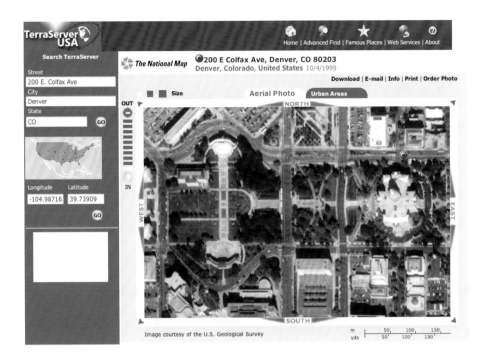

Figure 4.3: TERRASERVER-USA, COLORADO STATE CAPITOL BUILDING IN BLACK AND WHITE

This is a perfect example of leaf-on/leaf-off scenes. The black-and-white photo was taken in October; the plants are still in full bloom after the growing season. The color photo was taken in April; the grass hasn't quite come back in from the winter dormancy, and the trees haven't put up a full set of leaves yet.

Another clue is that the shadows are at different angles. This can potentially show seasonal differences, but at the very least it shows us that the two pictures were taken at different times of the day. Shorter shadows tell us that the sun is directly overhead. Longer shadows mean that the sun is closer to the horizon.

The biggest giveaway that the photos were taken at two different times are the cars in the streets and parking lots. If you look closely at the major intersections, different cars are passing through the same intersection. Cars, people, boats, trains, you name it—anything that moves, when captured in a still photograph, is a great temporal artifact to use when it comes to image analysis.

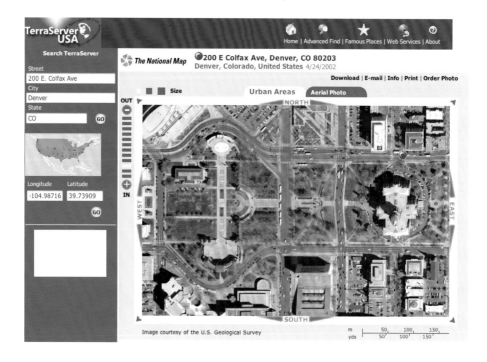

Figure 4.4: TERRASERVER-USA, COLORADO STATE CAPITOL BUILDING IN COLOR

Even things that change more slowly over time—such as buildings and housing developments—can be used in image analysis. Municipal governments are often very interested in new construction because it directly affects their taxable base. *Change detection* or *change queues* are vector reports that compare the temporal differences between two images of the same spatial extent. By comparing year-over-year differences, you can see how a given AOI has changed over time.

Just for grins, go back and compare the Terraserver-USA scenes to the Google Maps one. It should be fairly evident that Google Maps scene is the same as the Terraserver-USA Urban Areas scene (at least it was at the time of this writing—Google is constantly upgrading its imagery).

For a more dramatic example of change detection, leave these windows open, and fire up a new browser window or tab. Go to http:// terraserver-usa.com, and enter 1701 Bryant St Denver, CO. Notice that you get a long list of possible hits. This happens when the *geocoder* can't resolve a street address to an exact lat/long coordinate.

Figure 4.5: TERRASERVER-USA, MILE HIGH STADIUM AS A STADIUM

I've been saying all along that mapping is an inexact science, and here is yet another example of it.

The link that comes closest to what we are looking for is the second in the list: Bryant St, Denver, CO 80204. Click Aerial Photo. Click one zoom level out, and then pan three clicks north. Ah, good old Mile High Stadium and its nascent successor, Invesco Field at Mile High. (See Figure 4.5.) In 1999, Mile High Stadium was still in full operation while Invesco Field was under construction.

Now click the Urban Areas tab. (See Figure 4.6, on the next page.) By 2002, Mile High Stadium had been converted into a first-class parking lot. Invesco Field is now the official host to the Denver Broncos football team.

4.5 Panchromatic vs. Multispectral

I hope you're getting more comfortable looking at raster images. If you'd like a nice generic phrase to describe what we've been doing, *remote*

Figure 4.6: TERRASERVER-USA, MILE HIGH STADIUM AS A PARKING LOT

sensing is the common industry term for it. In a nutshell, we've been looking at things close up from a sensor that was far away when it took the picture. The sensor might have been mounted on a satellite or on the bottom of a specially outfitted airplane—*remote* by any definition of the word.

Let's dig a bit deeper into the types of images we've been viewing. Clearly the USGS has two distinct product lines: DOQQs are black-and-white photos available for any area in the United States, and Urban Areas (as the name implies) are color photos taken over metropolitan areas. However, the phrases *black and white* and *color* are positively too simple, too unambiguous, and too easy to understand by the general public to be used by the GIS industry to describe what we've been viewing. If you move beyond Terraserver-USA to look for free sources of raster data (many city and state governments offer free downloads), you'll need to be comfortable talking about panchromatic and multispectral imagery.

Panchromatic Imagery

You'll commonly see black-and-white photos listed as *panchromatic* images. Ironically, this is a Greek word that translates as "all colors." So, how did this little piece of misdirection find its way into common usage? The term *panchromatic* refers to the sensor on the camera instead of the resulting image. The sensor records information from across the visible spectrum but stores it as a black-and-white image. By getting data from the entire spectrum, the image is incredibly crisp. Have you ever noticed the amount of detail in a black-and-white portrait? OK, so that's the marketing answer. Another more realistic answer is that panchromatic sensors are generally cheaper than full-color sensors, and the resulting image is smaller in terms of storage requirements than its full-color counterpart. When you're trying to store coverage of the entire United States, every little pixel adds up.

Yet another reason to use the term *panchromatic* instead of *black and white* is that the images aren't technically black and white—they display a couple hundred shades of gray. (You can start humming Procol Harum's "A Whiter Shade of Pale" to yourself at this point.)

A typical grayscale image uses 1 byte (8 bits) to store 256 distinct levels of gray per pixel. If you've got a 8,000 by 8,000 pixel image, you're looking at 64,000,000 pixels of data to be stored on disk. If you use 1 byte to store the gray level per pixel, you've got a 64MB file on your hands. (Of course, we're ignoring image formats that offer compression at this point. We'll talk about that later in the chapter.)

To simplify this even further, let's consider how a true black-and-white, two-color image could be stored as a file. Since each pixel can be only one of two colors, the color information for each pixel can be stored in a single bit. (See Figure 4.7, on the following page.)

A 1-bit raster image would end up being pretty worthless to us in the real world—hardly a photograph at all—but an 8-bit image is surprisingly expressive; 256 shades of gray gives us the detailed panchromatic images that we've been looking at throughout this chapter.

Modern computer applications such as web browsers can display 8-bit imagery without a problem. However, you might stumble across 16-bit imagery available for download on the Web. These files use 2 bytes to store grayscale information per pixel. This means you can see 65,536 levels of gray instead of a mere 256.

Example of a simple 1-bit (two color) raster

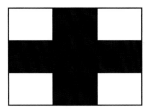

Color raster
(pixels are either
black or white)

Digital representation
(pixel values are
either 1 or 0)

Figure 4.7: STORING A TRUE BLACK-AND-WHITE IMAGE

Although this sounds like a heck of a deal (more is better, right?), if you try to pull a 16-bit image up in a typical viewer, all you'll see are black pixels. The 8-bit viewer will simply not know what to do with the additional information, so it will effectively "max out" all of the pixels at a value of 255. Think of the distribution of color values on a bell curve. For 8-bit imagery, the values will spread out somewhere from 0 to 255. Now what happens if you extend the range to 65,536? Chances are very good, statistically speaking, that nearly *all* of the color values will be greater than 255 (the maximum value that an 8-bit viewer can handle). Thus, you end up looking at mostly pure-black pixels.

On the other hand, if you pull a 16-bit image up in an image viewer that can handle 16-bit data, you'll be in good shape. Photogrammetists doing deep scientific study of the imagery can derive much subtler changes from pixel to pixel using 16-bit imagery rather than 8-bit. Most high-end GIS software can display 16-bit imagery out of the box. You can also download a free viewer called FreeLook from RSI.[5]

---

5. ftp://ftp.rsinc.com/pub/freelook_4.1/

We'll focus on 8-bit imagery for the remainder of this book. It's nice to know that 16-bit imagery is out there, if only so that you know what to do if you pull up an all-black image.

Multispectral Imagery

Up to this point we've been focused on panchromatic imagery. But what about the color stuff? By *color*, you surely mean "multispectral," don't you? Like the term *panchromatic*, *multispectral* refers to the capabilities of the sensor. Only coincidentally in this case does the name also describe the resulting image.

A multispectral camera has more than one sensor, each tuned to record data from a specific portion of the electromagnetic spectrum. The most common sensor groupings pick up data in the RGB bands. (RGB stands for Red, Green, and Blue). If you've ever done any web development or Adobe Photoshop work, you should be well acquainted with RGB color notation. (Surely you've heard the poem "Roses Are #FF0000, Violets Are #0000FF"....)

We're still dealing with 8-bit imagery at this point; only now we have 3 bytes of color information stored for every one pixel of data. With three 256 value ranges of color that can be combined, we can express an astounding 16,777,216 unique colors (8-bit RGB multispectral rasters are often called *natural color* images).

Things would be pretty straightforward if we just stopped there, but those pesky scientists are always messing things up for us simple folk. Multispectral sensors aren't limited to just taking natural color images. It's common to have sensors on board that can capture data outside of the visual spectrum. (The Landsat 7 satellite can capture—ironically—eight different bands of information, while the Terra satellite offers data across *thirty-six distinct bands*.) People doing vegetation analysis love dealing with infrared spectral information.

All the common image file formats have three slots to store color information, but there is nothing stopping us from populating the bytes with non-RGB spectral information. *False-color* images generally swap out at least one of the RGB bands for data outside the visual spectrum such as infrared. This combination makes vegetation really pop out. For example, take a look at the false-color image of Las Vegas, Nevada. (See Figure 4.8, on the next page—image courtesy of NASA.[6]) The analyst

---

6.   http://earthobservatory.nasa.gov/Newsroom/NewImages/images.php3?img_id=16318

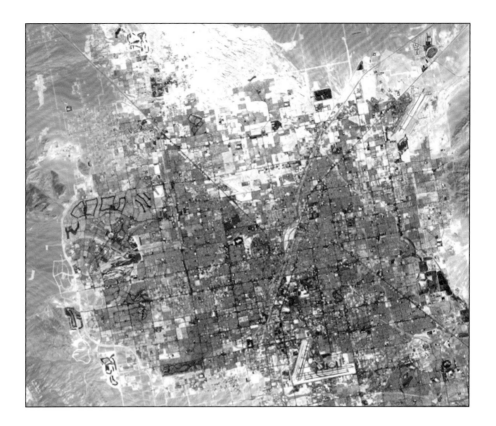

Figure 4.8: A FALSE-COLOR IMAGE OF LAS VEGAS EMPHASIZING THE VEGETATION

who put this image together swapped the red band out for the infrared band. Only in a false-color image could the grass in the medians shine brighter than the neon lights on the Strip in Vegas.

For the rest of the book, when we're dealing with multispectral imagery, we'll be looking at natural-color pictures. Again, it's just nice to know what else is out there when you stumble across oddly colored pictures.

4.6 Scale and Resolution

We're almost ready to begin downloading our own rasters, but we need to know a few more things about the imagery before we get there. We've already talked about how our pixels are colored. Now we need to figure out how big our pixels are.

Scale and Resolution in the Analog World

When dealing with paper maps, pixels aren't of much use to us as a unit of measure; the size of your map is generally measured in inches or centimeters. However, the physical size of your map is only half of the equation—you'll still want to know how much ground space the paper map represents. What you're looking for is the *scale* of the map. This is commonly expressed as a ratio: 1:1000 means that 1 unit on the map is equivalent to 1,000 of those same units on the ground.

This notion of ratios comes up again and again in cartography. For example, let's say you have a 30 cm by 30 cm (1 foot by 1 foot) paper map that shows you a 30 km by 30 km (18.6 miles by 18.6 miles) area on the ground. Our map scale is 30:3,000,000.

That looks bit odd, doesn't it? Map scales are usually reduced so that the left side of the ratio is 1. Dividing both sides of the ratio by 30 gives us a more normal-looking map scale of 1:100,000—1 cm on the map represents 100,000 cm on the ground. To further refine this ratio, 100,000 cm is really 1,000 m, which is 1 km. You might see a scale for this hypothetical map expressed as "1 centimeter on the map represents 1 kilometer on the ground," but the least ambiguous way to express the scale is to say simply it is 1:100,000 and leave the interpretation up to the reader.

Now let's say that you want to see a bigger area of the earth on your map. If you want to see twice as much ground space per side (60 km), you have two options: you could double the physical size of your map to 60 cm, or you could cram 60 km into the same 30 cm map. In the first case, you are maintaining the same scale as the earlier map. If you hold the size of your map constant, something has got to give. That something is the level of detail or the *resolution* of the map. Your effective scale is now 1:200,000 (1 cm on the map represents 2 km on the ground). You have a lower-resolution map—in other words, you can see less detail.

If you move in the opposite direction—increasing your resolution—either your map will get progressively larger or you will be able to see less total ground space on the same-sized map. Do you see how if you hold the size of your map constant, there is an inverse relationship between the resolution and the total ground space? You can see either less total earth at a higher level of detail or more total earth at a lower level of detail. (This should remind you of our imaginary basketball globe story earlier in the book.)

This magic ratio explains why statewide highway maps are so darn big. They have to be 2 to 3 feet on a side to display all of the highways at a resolution that you can see easily. But highway map resolution doesn't allow you to navigate your way through local neighborhoods; no single piece of paper could realistically hold that level of detail. If you've ever been out house hunting in your real estate agent's car, the agent probably has a thick neighborhood guide that fits ten to twelve city blocks to a standard 8.5 by 11 page.

Scale and Resolution in the Digital World

Let's now move our focus back to digital mapping. Digital images are measured in pixels (a combination of the two words *picture element*). Pixels are like degrees in that they are a relative unit of measure when it comes to distance. For example, my laptop screen optimally runs at a resolution of 1280 by 854. I have a 15-inch PowerBook G4, so we can figure out the *dots per inch* (DPI) of my monitor using some pretty simple math: 1,280 pixels divided by 15 inches gives me a DPI of about 85. (Historically, people have used 72 DPI as a benchmark for computer displays, but as you'll see in a moment that number can be changed with the click of a button.)

I use my laptop for presentations quite a bit, but I have yet to find an LCD projector that will allow me to run at native resolution. If I'm lucky, I'll get knocked down to 1024 by 800, but more often than not, I end up running at 800 by 600. Obviously, the physical size of my laptop screen doesn't change, but my resolution and corresponding DPI takes a pretty big hit. A 15-inch screen displaying 800 pixels yields a DPI of a little more than 53. Just like my paper map in the previous section, I lose total desktop space (ground space), but I can see everything else in much greater detail (resolution). When I disconnect the projector, my desktop gets much bigger, but my individual icons get much smaller.

Looking now at raster images, we still need a way to express "this much on my screen represents this much on the ground." Unfortunately, as we just learned, expressing things in inches or centimeters can be problematic. The only two absolutes we have are the dimensions of the image in pixels and the ground space that each pixel represents. Since you can't very well measure ground space in pixels, we lose the traditional notion of a scale ratio. Instead, we talk about *ground sample distance* (GSD).

For example, we know that a typical DOQQ is 8,000 pixels across in image space and 8 kilometers across in ground space. This gives us a GSD of 1 meter per pixel. Regardless of your screen resolution, your image resolution will always be 1 pixel = 1 meter. (For more information on DOQQs, see either Terraserver-USA's About page[7] or the USGS Factsheet.[8] Both are chock-full of geobabble that shouldn't scare you in the least if you've made it this far.)

Most of the DOQQs date from the mid-1990s. The USGS has been systematically updating its data set with newer, higher-resolution, multispectral imagery. The Urban Areas data set generally dates from 2000 and later. Its GSD ranges from 0.5 meters (roughly 1.5 feet) down to 0.15 meters (6 inches). As storage gets cheaper and sensors get more powerful, the USGS will update its data set accordingly. It keeps the DOQQ data set around for now because it has more complete coverage of the United States, but eventually the panchromatic country-wide mosaic will be completely replaced by the newer high-resolution imagery. (For more information, see the fact sheet about high-resolution orthoimagery.[9])

If you want to prove to yourself that the multispectral rasters on Terraserver-USA are higher resolution than the panchromatic DOQQs, go back to your view of the state capitol. Zoom in as far as you can on the Aerial data set, and then flip over to the Urban Areas tab. You should have a couple more clicks to zoom in. Did you also notice that once you zoomed into the maximum resolution on the Urban Areas tab, the Aerial tab disappeared? Zoom a couple of clicks out, and the other tab should reappear.

So, what's going on? The mapmakers wanted to make sure that you didn't exceed the native resolution of the imagery. *Downsampling* (zooming out) doesn't pose much risk—if you want to see a lower-resolution snapshot of the imagery, you can easily adjust the GSD without affecting the quality of the output. Of course, you'll see less detail, but then again that's what you asked for, isn't it? You are losing detail, but the original image has all of the data necessary to safely show you the data at the newly requested resolution.

---

7. http://terraserver-usa.com/about.aspx?n=AboutUsgsdoqs
8. http://erg.usgs.gov/isb/pubs/factsheets/fs05701.html
9. http://edc.usgs.gov/products/aerial/hiresortho.html

On the other hand, *upsampling* the data beyond the native resolution can cause serious output issues. By zooming closer than what the imagery can support, the pixels get blocky and generally icky looking. Your image gets pixelated because you're asking to see more information than the image can provide.

Both Google Maps and Terraserver-USA optimize performance by pre-downsampling the data to a series of fixed levels. This is called *pyramiding* your data set; each time you reduce the resolution but don't increase the ground space coverage, the total width and height of your image is reduced. At native 1-meter resolution, a DOQQ is 8,000 pixels by 8,000 pixels. If you downsample the image to 2-meter resolution, your image is now 4,000 by 4,000 pixels. If you downsample to 4-meter resolution, your image drops to 2,000 by 2,000 pixels. Hence, you have the pyramid effect.

Screen Resolution vs. Print Resolution

As if all of this image resizing isn't complicated enough, there is one more gotcha waiting to getcha. That gotcha shows up once you try to create a "dead-tree" (printed) edition of your raster. Earlier in this section we talked about typical screen resolutions in DPI. My laptop's native DPI is about 85 but can drop down to 55 based on what the external projector can support. If you've looked at your printer specs recently, you know that printers generally start at 300 DPI and can go up to 600 DPI or higher. This means that the physical size of your map can vary greatly between what you can see on your screen and what comes from your printer.

Our trusty DOQQ is about 94 inches wide on my screen, or close to 8 feet wide (8,000 pixels at 85 DPI)—that's a lot of scrolling. However, that same DOQQ printed out at 600 DPI is just more than 13 inches wide. The focus of this book is on digital mapmaking, but it's nice to know what will happen when your users press Ctrl+P.

4.7 Orthorectification

We have one more technical issue to discuss before we can actually download some imagery—the issue of orthorectification. You'll hear people call it many things. Some people shorten it to just *ortho*, as in, "Have you seen the high-res color orthos on Terraserver-USA?"

Others use the full name *orthographic rectification*. Regardless, ortho-rectifying your imagery is an important last step for display purposes, especially if you plan to superimpose vector data overtop of it.

The USGS hits you with the following definition of *orthorectification* in the very first paragraph of the DOQQ data sheet: "A digital orthophoto quadrangle (DOQ) is a computer-generated image of an aerial photo-graph in which image displacement caused by terrain relief and cam-era tilts has been removed. It combines the image characteristics of a photograph with the geometric qualities of a map." Whew! So what does that really mean?

Think of it this way: imagine taking a picture of your best friend. You'll most likely have them face the camera directly and have their head fill most of the frame. On the other hand, you could take a profile shot from the side. You could even lay down on the ground and shoot straight up. You could get on the top rung of a ladder and shoot straight down. Although the different exotic camera angles might add artistic flair to their portrait, most famous portraits and driver's license photos alike are taken from straight on.

We generally strive for the same effect when we are creating a map. We want a perfectly top-down view of the AOI. There are always different angles you could use. (Remember the *New Yorker* map where New York City is in the foreground and the rest of the world kind of fades off into the distance?) But most maps—road maps, atlases, even Google Maps and Terraserver-USA—give us a top-down view of the world.

This top-down view is all fine and good, but since remote sensing in-volves a camera, it will by extension also always involve a camera angle. This is called the *off-nadir* sensor angle. If your sensor is tilted at a 15-degree angle off to the left, the GSD for the pixels nearest the sensor (along the right side of the image) will be different from the GSD of the pixels farthest away from the sensor (along the left side of the image). Terrain such as mountains and hills only exacerbates the problem. Orthorectifying an image adjusts the far pixels so it looks as though they were shot from directly overhead. It changes the image to look as if it were shot at a zero-degree off-nadir angle.

Orthogonal is Greek for "right angle." That is literally what we are doing to the image: mathematically changing (correcting, or *rectifying*) the camera angle back to exactly 90 degrees over the AOI. Moreover, it makes the sensor appear to be directly overhead *each pixel in the raster*.

This is what gives it, as the poets at the USGS said, "the geometric qualities of a map."

So, what are the dangers of nonorthorectification?

- You cannot get accurate distance measurements from the image since the GSD is not constant among pixels.
- Vector overlays might not line up correctly with the image (like a vector roads layer matching up to the actual roads in the image).
- Mosaicking nonortho'd images can be difficult, causing errors like what we saw earlier in the chapter when we discussed pixel misregistration.

The Raw Ingredients of an Ortho

It is *far* beyond the scope of this book to discuss the gory details of how to actually orthographically rectify an image. That, as they say, is a job best left to the professionals. It requires specialized software and a steady hand... (OK, maybe just specialized software, but you get the point). I am a happy consumer of orthos, never having actually created one in my life. However, I do like knowing a little bit about a lot of things, so I can share with you the raw materials that go into making an orthoimage.

The first thing you'll need to know is the image metadata with regard to the sensor. You'll need to know the off-nadir angle, and you'll also need to know the *target azimuth* angle. This is where the sensor was in relation to the image. A target azimuth of 0 degrees means that the sensor was due north of the image, 90 degrees means it was due east, 180 degrees means due south, and 270 degrees means due west. Once you know where the sensor was located and how far it was tilted when the image was taken, the ortho software can effectively compensate for them.

When you have the sensor artifacts accounted for, you can then turn your focus to terrain artifacts. If the AOI is relatively flat, there will be very little horizontal displacement to worry about. On the other hand, if you are shooting an area with a bunch of hills and valleys, you'll want to know exact elevations so that the ortho software can compensate for it. Recall from Chapter 3, *Projections*, on page 33 that a digital elevation model (DEM) stores a height measurement per pixel. The higher the resolution of your DEM, the more accurate your ortho will be.

Now that you have effectively compensated for all of the noise, all you have left to do is figure out a way to tie the pixels back to their correct locations on the earth. To do this, you will need a set of *ground control points* (GCPs). These are points on the earth for which you know the exact lat/long address. (You'll also hear this referred to informally as *ground truth*.)

You could take a GPS out to the middle of a farmer's field and record your location, but it wouldn't be very useful as a GCP. What you need to do is take a measurement at a location that will be easy to spot in the image—for example, a corner of a building or the center of the intersection of two streets. If you have a couple of GCPs around the edges of your image and one or two in the center, the ortho software can then create *tie-points* (points in the image that correspond to your GCPs) and can *rubbersheet* the image so that your tie-points match up with the GCPs.

The more GCPs you have, the more accurate your ortho will be. The better your DEM, the better the ortho. You get the idea: the finished product is only as good as the materials with which you start.

4.8 Downloading Free Rasters

Well, we finally made it. It has probably been so long that you can't remember what we started out to do in the first place. (If I remember correctly, it had something to do with GIS.) We finally have mastered enough jargon to download some free imagery. If you are smart enough to ask for "8-bit natural-color multispectral high-resolution orthorectified imagery" by name, then you deserve to get some free pixels.

Let's start by downloading a *low-resolution* image of the earth. What, that doesn't sound very impressive? I know, I know—every time I hear *low-resolution* I think of 1970s-era computer graphics like Pong. Fortunately, in remote sensing terms, low res doesn't have the same negative connotations. By *low-resolution*, I mean the GSD of the image, not the quality of the image.

There are no hard and fast rules, but *high resolution* generally refers to imagery with a GSD of 2 meters or less. The DOQQ and Urban Areas scenes are considered high resolution. *Medium-resolution* imagery has a GSD of 15 m to 30 m. Rasters from the Landsat series of satellites fall into this category.

e a r t h   o b s e r v a t o r y

home • data & images • features • news • reference • missions • experiments • search

glossary   on ◉ off ○

NEWS

the **BLUE MARBLE**

true-color global imagery at 1km resolution

This spectacular "blue marble" image is the most detailed true-color image of the entire Earth to date. Using a collection of satellite-based observations, scientists and visualizers stitched together months of observations of the land surface, <u>oceans</u>, sea ice, and clouds into a seamless, true-color mosaic of every square <u>kilometer</u> (.386 square mile) of our planet. These images are freely available to educators, scientists, museums, and the public. Preview images and links to full <u>resolution</u> versions—up to 21,600 <u>pixels</u> across—are located below.

<u>Close-ups</u> at full (1km per pixel) resolution

Figure 4.9: DOWNLOAD FREE EARTH IMAGES FROM NASA'S BLUE MARBLE WEBSITE.

Low-resolution imagery is anything higher than that. It usually, but not always, refers to rasters that cover the world extent.

NASA, not surprisingly, has some gorgeous images of the earth from space. Let's visit the Blue Marble website.[10] (See Figure 4.9.) As the tag line says, "True-color global imagery at 1 km resolution."

The first image you see on the website is a mosaic of scenes captured between June 2001 and September 2001. (See Figure 4.10, on the facing page.) The pictures were taken by the Terra and Aqua satellites using a moderate-resolution imaging spectroradiometer (MODIS) sensor. The MODIS sensor captures 12-bit data across 36 bands at a GSD ranging from 250 m to 1 km depending on the band.[11]

---

10. http://earthobservatory.nasa.gov/Newsroom/BlueMarble/BlueMarble_2002.html
11. http://modarch.gsfc.nasa.gov/about/specifications.php

Figure 4.10: NASA's eponymous Blue Marble

Although the picture of the globe is pretty, let's scroll down and get some imagery that will be more useful to us as a basemap layer. The first Cartesian image you'll see is labeled Land Surface, Shallow Water, and Shaded Topography. Notice that this is a cloud-free mosaic. (See? Even a raster can be an abstract representation of the real world. This view of the earth doesn't exist outside the magic of Photoshop. Finding a cloud-free day to take a picture of a small AOI usually isn't too tough, but there is no way that you could take a picture of the entire world and expect it to be cloud-free. There are *always* clouds somewhere.)

Go ahead and download the 2,048 by 1,024 TIFF file.[12] This will be more than adequate for our mapping needs. Notice that the full-res 1 km GSD imagery is so large that it had to be broken up into two separate downloads—40,000 pixels is a *lot* of imagery.

Pop quiz: what is the GSD of the downsampled image we just downloaded? The circumference of the world at the equator is 40,074 km. The image width is 2,048 pixels. That gives us a GSD of just under 20 km per pixel.

The next thing we should do is download a desktop GIS application that can handle both raster and vector data. ESRI ArcExplorer does a great job with shapefiles, but it cannot open image files. Quantum GIS (QGIS)[13] is an open source desktop application that fits the bill nicely. Pull down the appropriate binary for your platform, and install it.

Let's open our world basemap in QGIS. Go to the Layer menu, and choose Add a Raster Layer. Navigate to where you saved the Blue Marble image. (See Figure 4.11, on the next page.)

This certainly is pretty, but unfortunately it's not geographic data at this point. How can we tell? Well, let's try to superimpose a vector layer over the top of it. (You know what's coming already, don't you? We are returning to the Valley of the Mismatched Projections....)

Pull down a world vector shapefile.[14] Choose Layer/Add a Vector Layer in QGIS. Just like the good old days of Chapter 2, *Vectors*, on page 7, your data layers don't quite line up. (See Figure 4.12, on the next page.)

At least this data misregistration is a little bit easier to catch than the errant Colorado highways that plagued us earlier. As a matter of fact,

---

12. http://earthobservatory.nasa.gov/Newsroom/BlueMarble/Images/land_shallow_topo_2048.tif

13. http://qgis.org

14. http://www.cipotato.org/DIVA/data/misc/world_adm0.zip

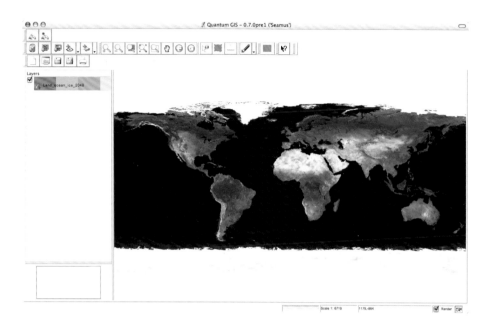

Figure 4.11: VIEWING THE BLUE MARBLE BASEMAP IMAGE IN QGIS

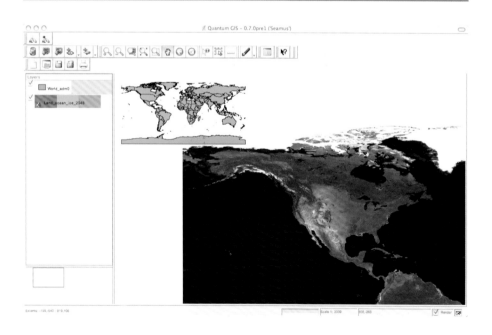

Figure 4.12: MISREGISTERED WORLD VECTOR AND RASTER LAYERS

this error almost makes sense. Move your mouse pointer around until you find the coordinates (0,0). On the vector layer, you end up at the intersection of the equator and the Prime Meridian (just off the west coast of Africa). In the raster layer it might be a bit tougher to see, but you are actually at the very topmost left pixel of the image. Since QGIS didn't know how to map the image in geographic space, it just used the pixel space coordinates and lined up the map layers as best it could.

TIFF, GeoTIFFs, and World Files

So, now the question is how do we get our pretty pixels georeferenced? *Tagged Image File Format* (TIFF) images are popular in the GIS community because of their extensible design. The binary header of the image can be used to store all kinds of information, including geographic data such as tie-points and the GSD. Without this data, we cannot correlate pixel space to ground space. Both TIFF and the *GeoTIFF* extension are well documented; see the TIFF 6.0 spec[15] and the GeoTIFF 1.0 spec.[16]

You can use the command-line tool listgeo[17] to see the geographic contents stored in the header of a GeoTIFF file. To confirm that the Blue Marble TIFF is a plain old TIFF instead of true GeoTIFF, type list-geo land_ocean_ice_2048.tif at a command prompt. Listgeo will come up empty-handed:

```
$ listgeo land_ocean_ice_2048.tif
Geotiff_Information:
   Version: 1
   Key_Revision: 1.0
   Tagged_Information:
      End_Of_Tags.
   Keyed_Information:
      End_Of_Keys.
   End_Of_Geotiff.


Corner Coordinates:
 ... unable to transform points between pixel/line and PCS space
```

Just because the geodata isn't embedded in the TIFF file doesn't mean that all hope is lost: we can create a companion *world file* that contains the required geodata. A world file is a plain ASCII text file, so it isn't too tough to whip up. But before we do that, let's pull down a real

15. http://partners.adobe.com/public/developer/tiff/index.html
16. http://www.remotesensing.org/geotiff/spec/geotiffhome.html
17. http://www.remotesensing.org/geotiff/geotiff.html

GeoTIFF[18] just to prove that they exist. Running listgeo on a true Geo-TIFF will give us a bit more information than we saw in the previous example:

```
$ listgeo 001027_0100_020904_17_6h_utm22.tif
Geotiff_Information:
   Version: 1
   Key_Revision: 1.0
   Tagged_Information:
      ModelTiepointTag (2,3):
         0                0                0
         281602           5366189          0
      ModelPixelScaleTag (1,3):
         60               60               0
      End_Of_Tags.
   Keyed_Information:
      GTModelTypeGeoKey (Short,1): ModelTypeProjected
      GTRasterTypeGeoKey (Short,1): RasterPixelIsArea
      GTCitationGeoKey (Ascii,17): "UTM     22 T E008"
      GeogAngularUnitsGeoKey (Short,1): Angular_Degree
      ProjectedCSTypeGeoKey (Short,1): PCS_NAD83_UTM_zone_22N
      ProjLinearUnitsGeoKey (Short,1): Linear_Meter
      End_Of_Keys.
   End_Of_Geotiff.

PCS = 26922 (NAD83 / UTM zone 22N)
Projection = 16022 (UTM zone 22N)
Projection Method: CT_TransverseMercator
   ProjNatOriginLatGeoKey: 0.000000 (  0d 0' 0.00"N)
   ProjNatOriginLongGeoKey: -51.000000 ( 51d 0' 0.00"W)
   ProjScaleAtNatOriginGeoKey: 0.999600
   ProjFalseEastingGeoKey: 500000.000000 m
   ProjFalseNorthingGeoKey: 0.000000 m
GCS: 4269/NAD83
Datum: 6269/North American Datum 1983
Ellipsoid: 7019/GRS 1980 (6378137.00,6356752.31)
Prime Meridian: 8901/Greenwich (0.000000/  0d 0' 0.00"E)
Projection Linear Units: 9001/metre (1.000000m)

Corner Coordinates:
Upper Left    (  281602.000, 5366189.000) ( 53d57' 5.16"W, 48d24'39.51"N)
Lower Left    (  281602.000, 5146709.000) ( 53d50'35.18"W, 46d26'18.96"N)
Upper Right   (  511582.000, 5366189.000) ( 50d50'36.14"W, 48d26'55.44"N)
Lower Right   (  511582.000, 5146709.000) ( 50d50'56.87"W, 46d28'25.87"N)
Center        (  396592.000, 5256449.000) ( 52d22'18.59"W, 47d27'11.79"N)
```

As you can see, you can stuff of whole bunch of geodata into the header of a GeoTIFF.

---

18. http://geogratis.cgdi.gc.ca/download/landsat_7/ortho/geotiff/utm/

A world file is far more primitive, but it contains at least enough information to allow the raster to line up with your vector layers. The world file format was defined by ESRI, but it is recognized by most GIS software packages. It is a six-line text file that gives the GSD of the pixels and the geographic tie-point of the upper-leftmost pixel. By convention, a world file should be named the same as your image file with a .tfw file extension. The world file for land_ocean_ice_2048.tif should be named land_ocean_ice_2048.tfw. (.tfw files are used with .tiff images. Later in this chapter, you'll see .jgw files used to georeference .jpg images.)

Create land_ocean_ice_2048.tfw using the text editor of your choice. The first and fourth lines are the X and Y GSD values. This data wasn't available for download anywhere—I created it using the values we already know.

```
0.176
0
0
-0.176
-180
90
```

Earlier we calculated the GSD of the image to be roughly 20 km per pixel. If the map units were measured in km, you'd use the value 20 for the first and fourth lines. But we're too smart to fall for that—the WGS84 projection uses degrees as map units, not meters or kilometers. (Of course, if we were looking at UTM data, meters would be entirely appropriate.) So knowing that the map covers 360 degrees west to east and that the image size is 2,048 pixels, simply divide degrees by pixels to get 0.176 degrees per pixel.

The second and third values in the world file are the rotation values for the pixels in case north isn't truly up in the image. The last two values are your tie-point—geographic X and Y coordinates for the (0,0) coordinate in pixel space. Knowing that the left border of the image is the International Date Line, -180 is used for the X coordinate. The negative number guarantees that values will increase in a positive direction as you move your cursor east, hitting zero at the Prime Meridian and eventually 180 on the far-right margin. Using 90 for the Y coordinate yields the same effect—as the mouse pointer moves south, the value will decrease, hitting zero at the equator and flipping to a negative number until the cursor hits -90 at the bottom of the image.

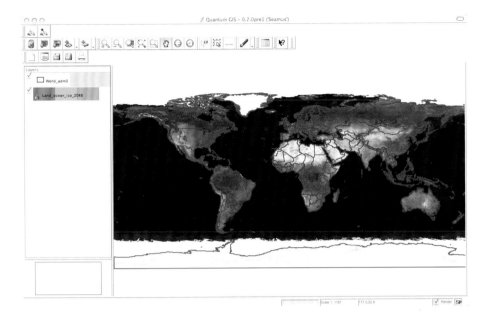

Figure 4.13: THE BLUE MARBLE, AFTER ADDING A WORLD FILE

Please be aware that I am playing pretty fast and loose with this world file. Technically, the X and Y coordinates are supposed to represent the *center* of the pixel in the upper-left corner. This world file misregisters the pixels in the image by half a GSD. Listgeo will show us the errors of my lax ways in just a moment. Also, this trick will work only with images that are unprojected. Any projected image—especially one that uses a nonequirectangular coordinate space or rotates the image in the slightest—will fail miserably using this trick. File this under "good enough for now, although not 100% accurate."

With our new world file in place, let's see whether QGIS has a better time lining up our data. Remove the Blue Marble raster by right-clicking the element in the Layers list along the left and clicking Remove. Now add it back in by choosing Layer/Add a Raster Layer. After styling the vector layer a bit and moving it to the top of this list, you should see something like Figure 4.13.

Dealing with GeoTIFFs is admittedly easier than simple TIFF files with a world file—you have one less file to worry about. Let's convert our Blue Marble image into a GeoTIFF. The libgeotiff package gives us just the command we are looking for: geotifcp. This command merges a TIFF file and a world file into a single GeoTIFF. One quick geotifcp -e land_ocean_ice_2048.tfw land_ocean_ice_2048.tif world.tif, and we have a GeoTIFF world image, with a shorter name to boot:

```
$ listgeo world.tif
Geotiff_Information:
   Version: 1
   Key_Revision: 1.0
   Tagged_Information:
      ModelTiepointTag (2,3):
         0.5                    0.5              0
        -180                    90               0
      ModelPixelScaleTag (1,3):
         0.176                  0.176            0
      End_Of_Tags.
   Keyed_Information:
      End_Of_Keys.
   End_Of_Geotiff.


Corner Coordinates:
Upper Left    (     -180.088,       90.088)
Lower Left    (     -180.088,      -90.136)
Upper Right   (      180.360,       90.088)
Lower Right   (      180.360,      -90.136)
Center        (        0.136,       -0.024)
```

Even though the image and the vector layer appear to line up visually, listgeo shows us the error in my "hack-and-slap" ways when it comes to the world file I put together earlier. Notice the upper-left corner is listed as -180.088, 90.088. The extra 0.088 (which doesn't actually exist on the face of the earth) is the 1/2 GSD error I got from naively using the upper-left coordinate of the pixel instead of calculating the center of the pixel. If you were to zoom in far enough (and the image was high enough resolution), you'd clearly see some misregistration with the vector layer.

The moral to this story is, "Friends don't let friends write their own world files." Or is it, "When is 'good enough' truly good enough?" Any high-accuracy geospatial work will require you to pay special attention to the world file or the spatial metadata stored in the GeoTIFF. Then again, any imagery used for high-accuracy geospatial work will most likely already have this information in place. The quick-and-dirty approach I used to get the imagery to line up with the vector layer was just that—quick and dirty.

Terraserver-USA and GeoJPGs

Using a world file works with high-res imagery as well as low, TIFF images, or something else. In this next example, we'll follow the same simple steps we used for the Blue Marble example:

1. Find the vector layers.
2. Find the raster layers.
3. Decide on a projection.
4. Lather, rinse, repeat.

We found some pretty nice high-res raster layers on Terraserver-USA. Go back to your Colorado State Capitol building scene. To get the biggest bang for your buck, make sure you are viewing the largest possible image size. In the upper-left corner (next to the zoom bar), you should see three progressively larger boxes labeled Size. Click the largest box.

Now let's download the image. We could right-click each tile and download it individually, but then we'd end up having to mosaic it back on our end. To save us the trouble, the developers of Terraserver-USA gave us a Download link in the upper-right corner. This does the mosaicking on the server side. You can now right-click the image and save it locally. You should end up with a file named download.ashx.jpg.

JPG, huh? Well, it makes sense—not many browsers support TIFFs natively. JPG brings some pretty good compression to the table, although it is a *lossy* compression algorithm. To reduce the size of the file, it throws away data. It's not ideal for scientific applications, but it's not bad for pretty pixel applications. And technically, pretty pixels are all that we have right now. There isn't any embedded geographic data in this JPG. Listgeo works only on GeoTIFFs, but we can use gdalinfo to query the file. gdalinfo download.ashx.jpg tells us that that we are in pixel space, not geographic space: the coordinate system is empty, and the corner coordinates are clearly the dimensions of the image.

```
$ gdalinfo download.ashx.jpg
Driver: JPEG/JPEG JFIF
Size is 1000, 800
Coordinate System is ''
Corner Coordinates:
Upper Left  (    0.0,    0.0)
Lower Left  (    0.0,  800.0)
Upper Right ( 1000.0,    0.0)
Lower Right ( 1000.0,  800.0)
Center      (  500.0,  400.0)
```

```
Band 1 Block=1000x1 Type=Byte, ColorInterp=Red
Band 2 Block=1000x1 Type=Byte, ColorInterp=Green
Band 3 Block=1000x1 Type=Byte, ColorInterp=Blue
```

For the Blue Marble world raster, I felt pretty comfortable whipping up my own world file. Knowing the world extents in decimal degrees and the image extents in pixels made it pretty straightforward. But I don't have any idea what my extents are here, either in pixels or geographic. Luckily, the last option along the upper-right corner of the Terraserver-USA page allows us to download a world file. Create a file named download.ashx.jgw, and copy the world file values into it:

```
2.000000
0.000000
0.000000
-2.000000
500000.000000
4399600.000000
```

It looks like we have a GSD of 2 meters. (Depending on your zoom level and how much you've scrolled around, your values might not match mine exactly. That's OK. You can zoom in and out and play around on your own.) My corner coordinate is now 500000.000000, 4399600.000000. I'm having a hard time believing that those values are WGS84. They look more like UTM, don't they? I guess that makes sense as well—remember that UTM is great for "squaring up" your pixels at high resolutions; 2 m is clearly high resolution, so Terraserver-USA is simply serving up the appropriate projection for the job.

The world file doesn't have a parameter for the projection, so you have to do a bit of guessing. Thankfully, Terraserver-USA can confirm our guesses when we click the Info link in the upper-right corner. (See Figure 4.14, on the next page.) It clearly shows the projection (UTM 13 N), the GSD (2 m), and the image extent (1000 by 800 pixels). The coordinates around the perimeter of the image are given in degrees/minutes/seconds, decimal degrees, and UTM. The coordinates in the upper-left corner should match up with what appears in your world file.

Now that our world file is in place, type gdalinfo download.ashx.jpg. The values are expressed in meters instead of pixels.

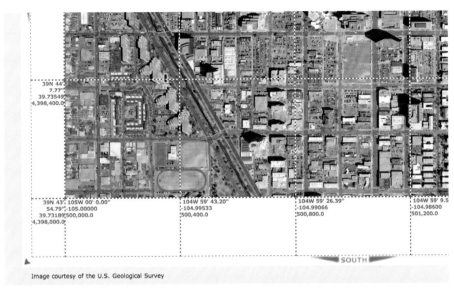

Image courtesy of the U.S. Geological Survey

Image Information:
Projection: North American Datum 1983 / UTM Zone 13N
Provider: U.S. Geological Survey
Resolution: 2.000 meters per pixel
Size: 1000 pixels wide by 800 pixels high
Type: Urban Areas High Resolution Natural Color Imagery

House and Home Demographics:
▣ Schools, Crime and Demographics for 80203
▣ Schools, Crime and Demographics for 80204

Figure 4.14: TERRASERVER-USA INFO

Our image is happily georeferenced and ready for mapping:

```
$ gdalinfo download.ashx.jpg
Driver: JPEG/JPEG JFIF
Size is 1000, 800
Coordinate System is ''
Origin = (499999.000000000000000,4399601.000000000000000)
Pixel Size = (2.000000000000000,-2.000000000000000)
Corner Coordinates:
Upper Left  (  499999.000, 4399601.000)
Lower Left  (  499999.000, 4398001.000)
Upper Right (  501999.000, 4399601.000)
Lower Right (  501999.000, 4398001.000)
Center      (  500999.000, 4398801.000)
Band 1 Block=1000x1 Type=Byte, ColorInterp=Red
Band 2 Block=1000x1 Type=Byte, ColorInterp=Green
Band 3 Block=1000x1 Type=Byte, ColorInterp=Blue
```

Let's open a new map in QGIS and give the much maligned Colorado roads shapefile another chance at redemption. There aren't any highways in our map extent, so return to the CDOT website,[19] and download the statewide "Public Roads – Local" shapefile. This gives us a vector layer of city streets. (The entire state is a 23MB download, so feel free to just download the Denver County data set instead—1.4MB is a bit quicker to pull down, and I can tell how excited you are to get this licked....) A quick look at LROADS.prj tells us that we are dealing with NAD83, UTM 13 N data.

Add the vector layer LROADS to QGIS, and then add download.ashx.jpg. Swap the layers around so that the vector layer is on top. Now zoom into the state capitol. Once again, even though we are dealing with different file types from different data providers, the data layers line up quite nicely since they are in a common projection. (See Figure 4.15, on the facing page.)

The last thing we'll do in this chapter is convert the JPG to a GeoTIFF. The gdal_translate[20] command makes short work of it. Notice that you can use gdal_translate to swap bands around, change the scale of the output image, and even reproject it. This command allows you to do all types of raster manipulation, although we'll be happy just converting our image to a GeoTIFF. One quick gdal_translate download.ashx.jpg state_capitol.tif and a second listgeo state_capitol.tif to confirm that the world file was picked up, and we are happily on our way. You could add the new image to the QGIS map to prove to yourself that the conversion went well, but I'm feeling lucky.

4.9 Conclusion

We covered a lot of ground in this chapter. We looked at the Colorado State Capitol building and Mile High Stadium to practice being photogrammetrists. We visited Google Maps and Terraserver-USA. We learned about mosaics, tessellation, and panchromatic and multispectral images. We figured out how scale and resolution are interrelated.

---

19. http://www.dot.state.co.us/App_DTD_DataAccess/GeoData/index.cfm?fuseaction=GeoDataMain\&MenuType=GeoData
20. http://www.remotesensing.org/gdal/gdal_utilities.html#gdal_translate

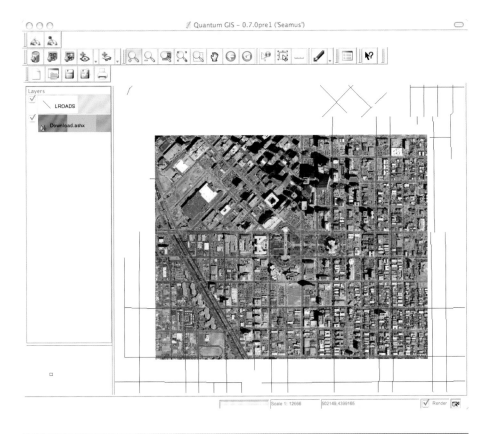

Figure 4.15: COLORADO ROADS ON THE TERRASERVER-USA HIGH-RES RASTER

We learned about orthorectification and downloading low-, medium-, and high-resolution rasters. We downloaded QGIS to view our rasters and learned how GeoTIFFs, World Files, and GDAL make working with rasters easy.

In the next chapter, we'll be back in vector land. Only this time, we'll be importing our vectors into a database and performing some spatial queries.

Chapter 5

Spatial Databases

Chances are good that at some point you are going to need to store a large volume of spatial data. The free data you download will most likely be scattered around in individual files. In this chapter, you'll learn how to import geodata into a database and perform some basic spatial queries.

5.1 Why Bother with a Spatial Database?

Over the past several chapters we downloaded a bunch of shapefiles. Although shapefiles are a decent transportation format, in production you'll most likely want to load that vector data into a database. Why? Well, you'll want to do this for the same reasons you use a database for nonspatial data:

- *Speed*: Generally speaking, you'll get better performance out of data served from a database than you will from a shapefile. Databases are optimized for serving up large volumes of repetitive data, and spatial data fits this description perfectly.
- *Multiuser support*: Spatial data tends to be reference data, and reference data is generally meant to be shared among many users. Storing the data in a database gives you the added benefit of remote access via a standard interface (JDBC, ODBC, PERL/DBI, and others). It also allows you to add security to the equation— making some data read-only for certain users and blocking others from seeing it altogether.

- *Querying*: This is by far the biggest benefit. Just as traditional databases allow you to perform traditional queries ("Show me all products where category equals *hardware*"), spatial databases allow you to perform spatial queries ("Show me all points that fall within a 20 mile radius of this point").

Finding a database that is spatially enabled is getting easier by the day. All of the major commercial databases offer spatial data types either natively or as a standard extension.

For example, modern versions of Oracle offer native spatial data types. Your table's fields can be strings and numbers or can be points, lines, and polygons. They offer native indexing for spatial data types to speed up queries. They even give you SQL extensions that allow you to query the data spatially.[1] IBM's DB2[2] has spatial capabilities, and ESRI ArcSDE[3] and MapInfo Professional[4] are commercial add-ons that allow you to store spatial data in Microsoft SQL Server.

Although the commercial vendors' capabilities are quite impressive, this book is about free and open source solutions. PostgreSQL is a strong open source database that supports most (if not all) of the features of its commercial counterparts. There is a spatial add-on for PostgreSQL that is quite robust, is well supported, and is considered one of the major pillars of the open source GIS community.

PostGIS[5] takes advantage of PostgreSQL's extensibility to provide a solid spatial database solution. PL/PgSQL is the procedural SQL language of PostgreSQL. PostGIS leverages this feature to add spatial capabilities. The end result is not unlike adding a new JAR to your Java classpath—it is tough to see where PostgreSQL ends and PostGIS begins once everything is installed and configured.

5.2 Installing PostgreSQL and PostGIS

The most recent version of PostgreSQL as of this writing is 8.2.1. The most recent version of PostGIS is 1.2.1. You can certainly download precompiled binary versions of these applications, but part of the ethos of open source is building the projects from source.

---

1. http://www.oracle.com/technology/products/spatial
2. http://www-306.ibm.com/software/data/spatial/
3. http://www.esri.com/software/arcgis/arcsde/
4. http://www.mapinfo.com/
5. http://postgis.refractions.net

What About the Rasters?

This chapter focuses solely on storing vector data in a database. Why? Well, that is your only option in the open source world.

The same, however, cannot be said for commercial offerings. Almost all of the commercial spatial databases allow you to store imagery right in your tables. The ingest function breaks the image up into chips or tiles (usually about 16k in size, although this is user configurable) and then stores them in a BLOB field. (BLOB stands for Binary Large OBject.)

Opinions are mixed as to whether storing rasters in a database table adds any real benefit. Opponents of it point out that vector data can easily be represented as text, whereas imagery data is almost always stored in a binary format. Vector data makes sense when you need to run queries such as "Please return a list of all of the points that fall within this polygon," while raster data tends to be more visual than informational in nature.

Supporters of rasters in databases like that you can store data that is identical in nature (resolution, projection, and so on) as one big coverage. Terraserver-USA* is a great real-world example of this—all of its imagery is stored in Microsoft SQL Server.

Although PostGIS doesn't support rasters as of this writing, it is a frequent topic of discussion on the mailing list. Don't be surprised if someone finally gets around to adding that feature. Remember, open source software allows you to "scratch your own itch" by adding new software features that solve your business needs or personal interests.

---

*. http://www.terraserver-usa.com

This allows you to always have access to the latest and greatest version. (Binaries tend to lag a version or two behind the most recent release, and plus you don't get to selectively enable and disable features and integration points.) Of course, part of the agony of building open source projects from source is the downward spiral of dependency hell. Thankfully, both PostgreSQL and PostGIS have pretty straightforward, garden-variety installations.

```
% ./configure
% make
% make install
```

If you are running a Unix-like OS and have a GNU GCC compiler available, I highly recommend building PostgreSQL and PostGIS from source. (For step-by-step instructions, see Appendix A, on page 235.) You can, of course, always find binary versions for Linux from the usual RPM and Apt sources. Mac folks can use the analogous Fink or MacPorts project.

If you are running Windows, you can download a precompiled version of PostgreSQL.[6] PostGIS is included in the binary distribution of PostgreSQL.

5.3 Adding Spatial Fields

In this section, we'll explore the built-in PostGIS tables and then add tables of our own.

The PostGIS documentation is quite comprehensive.[7] Featuring details on more than 150 functions, the downloadable PDF is an invaluable resource to have within arm's reach. In this chapter, we'll focus on a broad overview of some of the more common functions.

Exploring the Built-in PostGIS Tables

In Appendix A, on page 235, the installation had you create a simple table named "test." If you downloaded precompiled binaries instead of installing from source, please quickly run through the steps (ignoring the installation bits, of course), and make sure that the user and sample table is created:

```
create table test (id int, name varchar(25));
```

---

6. http://www.postgresql.org/download/
7. http://postgis.refractions.net/documentation/

Let's get back into PostgreSQL and look around. Make sure you are logged in as the PostgreSQL user (su - postgres), and get into the interactive PostgreSQL terminal (psql g4wd). Type \d to get a list of available tables:

```
g4wd=# \d
                List of relations
 Schema |        Name         |   Type   |  Owner
--------+---------------------+----------+----------
 public | geometry_columns    | table    | postgres
 public | spatial_ref_sys     | table    | postgres
 public | test                | table    | postgres
(3 rows)
```

In addition to the test table you created, there are a couple of PostGISspecific tables. The geometry_columns table contains data about every spatial column in the database. Type \d geometry_columns to see the fields:

```
g4wd=# \d geometry_columns
            Table "public.geometry_columns"
      Column       |          Type          | Modifiers
-------------------+------------------------+-----------
 f_table_catalog   | character varying(256) | not null
 f_table_schema    | character varying(256) | not null
 f_table_name      | character varying(256) | not null
 f_geometry_column | character varying(256) | not null
 coord_dimension   | integer                | not null
 srid              | integer                | not null
 type              | character varying(30)  | not null
Indexes:
    "geometry_columns_pk" PRIMARY KEY, btree
(f_table_catalog, f_table_schema, f_table_name, f_geometry_column)
```

There are four important columns. The f_table_name column contains the name of the table that is spatially enabled. f_geometry_column contains the name of the column in the table that holds the geometric data. srid contains the spatial reference ID, or the projection of the data. This is the EPSG number we discussed earlier: an integer that uniquely identifies the projection. Finally, type is the geometric data type.

Yep, we're back to points, lines, and polygons again. (There are a few fancy variations on that theme—we'll get to them in a second.)

Take a look at the other PostGIS table:

```
g4wd=# \d spatial_ref_sys
         Table "public.spatial_ref_sys"
  Column    |          Type          | Modifiers
------------+------------------------+-----------
 srid       | integer                | not null
 auth_name  | character varying(256) |
 auth_srid  | integer                |
 srtext     | character varying(2048)|
 proj4text  | character varying(2048)|
Indexes:
    "spatial_ref_sys_pkey" PRIMARY KEY, btree (srid)
```

This table lists the EPSG codes that PostGIS uses. For example, recall that the U.S. Census Bureau states the shapefile was in the 4269 projection. Let's see whether PostGIS's definition of 4269 jives with what we saw in Chapter 3, *Projections*, on page 33. Type select * from spatial_ref_sys where srid = 4269;. (Hint: if you've got wide fields in your table, type \x to turn on expanded display. It'll make your query output easier to read. To turn it off, type \x again.)

```
g4wd=# \x
Expanded display is on.
g4wd=# select * from spatial_ref_sys where srid = 4269;
-[ RECORD 1 ]---------------------------------------------
srid      | 4269
auth_name | EPSG
auth_srid | 4269
srtext    | GEOGCS["NAD83",
DATUM["North_American_Datum_1983",
SPHEROID["GRS 1980",6378137,298.257222101, AUTHORITY["EPSG","7019"]],
AUTHORITY["EPSG","6269"]],
PRIMEM["Greenwich",0,AUTHORITY["EPSG","8901"]],
UNIT["degree",0.01745329251994328,AUTHORITY["EPSG","9122"]],
AUTHORITY["EPSG","4269"]]
proj4text | +proj=longlat +ellps=GRS80 +datum=NAD83 +no_defs
```

Adding Geometric Columns by Hand

Let's add a spatial field to our test table. Geometric fields are not added using SQL Data Definition Language (DDL). Instead, we use AddGeometryColumn(). This not only adds the field to the table, but it also updates the geometry_columns table. The full syntax of AddGeometryColumn() is as follows:

```
AddGeometryColumn(<table name>, <column name>,
              <srid>, <datatype>, <num dimensions>)
```

Which Projection Should I Choose?

When creating fields in PostGIS, most times the question of which projection you should use is dictated by the other data sets you want to integrate with. Since the data we've been working with up to this point came to us in 4269 (or was reprojected into 4269 using ogr2ogr), the most obvious choice for us to use moving forward would be... (drumroll, please)...4269.

But which projection should you use if you don't really know which projection your data is in? For example, we're going to find some lat/long points on the Internet in just a bit that don't really tell us which projection they're in. You might also get the data from your GPS unit. (You *do* have a GPS unit, don't you?)

The safest bet, in the absence of any hard data, is to use EPSG 4326—plain old WGS-84. Most times, this is the projection used by GPS units. This is projection used by most websites when they expose lat/long points. It is as close as we have, as an industry, to a default or generic projection. And given that both ogr2ogr and PostGIS are built atop Proj4, both make it trivial to reproject your data into the magical correct projection if it is discovered after the fact.

The first three parameters should be pretty self-explanatory. We specify the name of the existing table, the name of the proposed new column, and the SRID we'd like to use for the projection. We can technically use -1 for the SRID (meaning "no SRID"), but this is really useful only for purely Cartesian data. If you are planning to store real geospatial data in the field, you should supply a real SRID. All of the data in your table is expected to be in the same projection. You can have many tables in the same database, all with different projections.

The fourth parameter is the data type. PostGIS follows the same spec we encountered first in Section 3.7, *Getting Your Data Layers Aligned*, on page 53: OpenGIS Simple Features Implementation Specification for SQL.[8] Not only does the spec define canonical representations of projections, it defines canonical representations of spatial data types as well. These are called the *well-known text* (WKT) representations of the basic data types.

---

8. http://portal.opengeospatial.org/files/?artifact_id=829

Here is the simplest possible subset of the WKT data types that PostGIS supports:

POINT(10 20)
> Specifies a single point.

LINESTRING(10 20,12 21,13 31)
> Specifies a single line. It must contain at least two vertices: a start point and an end point.

POLYGON((10 20,40 50,40 70,10 20))
> Specifies a single polygon. It must contain at least four vertices (the first and last being identical—this is how you close the polygon.) Note the double parentheses.

We should note a couple of things about the WKT format. First, notice that there are no commas between the coordinates. Commas are used *between* coordinate pairs instead. Second, remember almost every geometry in the world comes in the form of (lat/long)—except when they don't. (I hate that....) The WKT format expects them to be in the form of long/lat pairs.

The POINT data type is pretty straightforward, other than missing the comma in between the coordinates. You will, however, mistakenly type LINE instead of LINESTRING about two dozen times, getting progressively more frustrated each time. According to the OGC, a LINE is technically different from a LINESTRING. A LINE contains only two points; a LINESTRING contains more than two. PostGIS supports only the LINESTRING form, since a LINE can be represented by a LINESTRING.

And then there is the POLYGON. Remembering to repeat the first and last coordinate pairs is tough enough, but remembering to used double parentheses—why on earth would the OGC have subjected us to that? Well, like the LINESTRING, there is more than meets the eye when it comes to defining a POLYGON.

Technically, a POLYGON has one external ring and zero or more internal rings, or holes. The previous definition just specifies the external ring. If you had holes in your POLYGON, then you would have a comma-delimited set of rings, each surrounded by parentheses, for example, POLYGON((0 0, 0 100, 100 100, 100 0, 0 0), (50 50, 50 60, 60 60, 60 50, 50 50)).

Once you get used to looking at double parentheses, the next set of WKT geometries don't look so bad. The previous trio defined single-element

data types. You can also cluster or aggregate like elements into MULTI*
data types:

MULTIPOINT(10 20, 30 40, 50 60)
> Specifies a composite element that contains one or more points.

MULTILINESTRING((10 20,12 21,13 31), (99 89,79 69,59 49))
> Specifies a composite element that contains one or more lines.

MULTIPOLYGON(((10 20,40 50,60 70,10 20)), ((0 0,0 100, 100 100, 100 0, 0 0)))
> Specifies a composite element that contains one or more polygons.

You don't ever have to use MULTI* data types if you don't want to, but
you can do some interesting things with them if you have items that
semantically belong in a single row (or data element). We'll see a prime
example of this when we import the U.S. Census Bureau shapefile in
just a moment.

Finally, there are a couple of generic data types. GEOMETRY is the
parent data type of all geometric elements. You'll see it used a couple
of chapters from now when we access PostGIS via its JDBC driver. A
GEOMETRYCOLLECTION allows you to aggregate multiple potentially
disparate data types into a single element. It's not uncommon to get
GEOMETRYCOLLECTIONs back in the result of aggregate (GROUP BY)
queries.

The fifth and last parameter to the AddGeometryColumn() function specifies the number of dimensions the element must have. We'll be focusing on simple planar (two-dimensional) data sets in this chapter—-all
of our points will be represented by simple (X Y) coordinates. If we
needed to store points that also had elevation data (X Y X), we would
specify a dimension of 3. If we needed to track elevations that changed
over time, we could create four-dimensional points. And finally, if we
needed to store spatial data relating to Motown recording artists, we'd
use points that support the Fifth Dimension. (Sorry, I couldn't resist.)

Now that we have all of information down, let's add a spatial field to
our test table. To add a field name location that supports a simple two-
dimensional point in the WGS-84 projection, type the following:

```
select AddGeometryColumn('test', 'location', 4326, 'POINT', 2);
```

To verify that it worked, type \d test:

```
g4wd=# \d test
            Table "public.test"
  Column  |         Type         | Modifiers
----------+----------------------+-----------
 id       | integer              |
 name     | character varying(25) |
 location | geometry             |
Check constraints:
    "enforce_dims_location" CHECK (ndims("location") = 2)
    "enforce_geotype_location" CHECK (geometrytype("location") =
        'POINT'::text OR "location" IS NULL)
    "enforce_srid_location" CHECK (srid("location") = 4326)
```

See our new location field at the bottom of the list? It's interesting that it shows up as a generic GEOMETRY data type, even though we specified POINT. Don't worry, though. See the three new constraints placed on the field? Inserts on our table will fail if the field isn't a two-dimensional POINT in the WGS-84 projection. Not too shabby, eh?

We can also verify that our new location column made it into the geometry_columns table:

```
g4wd=# select * from geometry_columns;
-[ RECORD 1 ]-----+----------------------
f_table_catalog   |
f_table_schema    | public
f_table_name      | test
f_geometry_column | location
coord_dimension   | 2
srid              | 4326
type              | POINT
```

It will come as no surprise that there is a complementary function to AddGeometryColumn() that allows us to remove spatial fields from tables: DropGeometryColumn(table, column). This will do the appropriate ALTER TABLE command and remove the pointer record in geometry_columns. Rather than doing a DROP TABLE command and leaving an orphan record in geometry_columns, you can do a DropGeometryTable(table).

5.4 Inserting Spatial Data

Now that we have our spatial field in place, let's start adding some data.

We'll use a traditional INSERT statement, with one small twist. We already know what the WKT representation of a POINT looks like; for the Colorado state capitol, it is POINT(-104.98716 39.73909). Unfortunately, PostgreSQL isn't going to inspect our strings for us and "automagically" determine the difference between Plain Old Strings and Plain Old Strings That Happen To Contain Well-Known Text Geometries. So when we're inserting geodata, we need to tip off PostgreSQL using the GeomFromText(string, srid) function:

```
insert into test(id, name, location) values
    (1, 'Colorado State Capitol', GeomFromText('POINT(-104.98716 39.73909)', 4326));
```

To verify that it worked, type select * from test;:

```
g4wd=# select * from test;
-[ RECORD 1 ]-----------------------------------------------
id       | 1
name     | Colorado State Capitol
location | 0020000001000010E6C05A3F2DA122FAD74043DE9A8049667B
```

Well, um, clearly *something* got inserted into our geometry field. Since none of the constraints was violated, I guess that we can just assume that everything is OK.

5.5 Querying Spatial Data

Yeah, I didn't think you'd be satisfied with that answer. The truth is, PostGIS stores all geodata in a binary format. If the text representation of the point is called WKT, then the binary format is called—you guessed it—*well-known binary* (WKB).

GeomFromText() actually created a WKB object from the text string we provided. The flip side of GeomFromText() is AsText(). This converts the WKB back to WKT for human consumption:

```
g4wd=# select id, name, AsText(location) from test;
-[ RECORD 1 ]---------------------
id     | 1
name   | Colorado State Capitol
astext | POINT(-104.98716 39.73909)
```

Much better, eh? There's only one more thing we should do, and it's purely cosmetic. Notice that the third field is now named astext? This, too, will come back to haunt you someday. "What do you mean you can't find the location field? It is *right there*!" Adjust the query one more time to this: select id, name, AsText(location) as location from test;.

While we're playing around with query output formats, a couple of other things might come in handy. Did you notice that the SRID was missing from the location field? Interestingly, the SRID is not part of the WKT definition. If you'd like the SRID included in your output, try AsEwkt(geom) for Extended WKT. (Since all of the data in that column is presumably using the same projection, having the SRID included in the default output would be needlessly repetitive.)

Another output formula that is rapidly gaining popularity is *Scalable Vector Graphics* (SVG), which allows you to define vectors using a specific dialect of XML. Try AsSvg(geom) to get your data returned as an SVG fragment.

The appeal of SVG is that it is an open standard, created by the W3C.[9] Firefox 1.5 and Opera 8 already have native support for rendering SVG. Apple Safari should support it by the time you are reading this. If you're using a browser that doesn't support SVG natively, you can download a free plug-in from Adobe.[10]

Another XML dialect that has more mainstream support in the GIS community is Geography Markup Language (GML). It is defined by—who else?—the OGC. Try AsGml(geom) to get a well-formed snippet of GML. (For more about GML, see Chapter 7, *Using OGC Web Services*, on page 147.) For fans of the desktop application Google Earth, PostGIS offers AsKML(geom). (For more about KML, see Chapter 9, *Bringing It All Together*, on page 193.)

5.6 Introspection of Spatial Data

Let's add a few more records so that we can begin doing interesting aggregate stuff:

```
insert into test(id, name, location) values
  (2, 'Broncos Stadium', GeomFromText('POINT(-105.02101 39.74630)', 4326));

insert into test(id, name, location) values
  (3, 'foo', GeomFromText('POINT(-300 400)', 4326));
```

Does that last insert statement give you heartburn? Yeah, me too. POINT(-300 400) is clearly not a valid WGS-84 POINT. In just a bit we'll

---

9. http://www.w3.org/Graphics/SVG/
10. http://www.adobe.com/svg/main.html

add another constraint to your table that at least attempts to disallow bad input. (Although, sadly, it still lets this one slip through....)

In the meantime, let's get some metadata about our records. What is the true data type?

```
g4wd=# select GeometryType(location) from test;
-[ RECORD 1 ]+------
geometrytype | POINT
-[ RECORD 2 ]+------
geometrytype | POINT
-[ RECORD 3 ]+------
geometrytype | POINT
```

The query returns POINT for each record. That makes sense. What projection is being used?

```
g4wd=# select SRID(location) from test;
-[ RECORD 1 ]
srid | 4326
-[ RECORD 2 ]
srid | 4326
-[ RECORD 3 ]
srid | 4326
```

That looks good—4326 as expected. That's nothing we couldn't find out by nosing around the various geometry tables ourselves, but having it just a simple query away is nice. And finally, is there any bogus data lurking around?

```
g4wd=# select IsValid(location) from test;
-[ RECORD 1 ]
isvalid | t
-[ RECORD 2 ]
isvalid | t
-[ RECORD 3 ]
isvalid | t
```

D'oh! Why didn't the third record get flagged false? It boils down to that silly WKT/Projection disconnect. The coordinate pair may not be valid for a particular projection, but there is nothing physically wrong with the point. It is well-formed, if nonsensical.

Truth be told, it's really hard to create a malformed point. You could supply an X without a Y, but you'd most likely catch that visually. Creating an invalid LINESTRING is easier—recall we said that it has to have at least two points. If you create a LINESTRING with only one POINT, IsValid() will return false.

The rules get even more stringent for POLYGONs. You might have fewer than four points. You might forget to close the polygon by setting the last point to the same point as the first. You might have Inner Rings that are outside of your Exterior Ring.

So, what other types of introspection can we perform on our data? Since we are dealing with POINTs, the obvious thing we might want to do is isolate the X and Y coordinates:

```
g4wd=# select id, name, AsText(location), X(location), Y(location) from test;
-[ RECORD 1 ]---------------------
id     | 1
name   | Colorado State Capitol
astext | POINT(-104.98716 39.73909)
x      | -104.98716
y      | 39.73909
-[ RECORD 2 ]---------------------
id     | 2
name   | Broncos Stadium
astext | POINT(-105.02101 39.7463)
x      | -105.02101
y      | 39.7463
-[ RECORD 3 ]---------------------
id     | 3
name   | foo
astext | POINT(-300 400)
x      | -300
y      | 400
```

If you are querying LINESTRINGs, you have methods such as Num-Points(), StartPoint(), and EndPoint() to play with. If you are dealing with POLYGONS, you can query for ExteriorRing() and NumInteriorRings().

So now that we are experts at inserting data by hand, let's get back to one of the original premises at the start of this chapter—shapefiles are a reasonable way to distribute data, but how can we slurp the data up into PostGIS?

5.7 Importing Data

Let's take a whack at inserting the shapefile of the United States that we downloaded from the U.S. Census Bureau in Section 2.8, *The Downloadable States of America*, on page 20.[11] Recall that the shapefile is in ESPG 4269 (Geographic/NAD83).

---

11. http://www.census.gov/geo/cob/bdy/st/st00shp/st99_d00_shp.zip

One of the easiest ways to get shapefiles into a PostGIS-friendly format is to use the included shp2pgsql utility in $POSTGRES_HOME/bin/. It introspects your shapefile and creates a CREATE TABLE statement and a corresponding AddGeometryColumn. It iterates through each record in the .dbf and creates individual SQL INSERT statements.

```
shp2pgsql -s <SRID> <SHAPEFILE> <TABLENAME>
```

By default, shp2pgsql dumps its output to the screen. In order to capture it in a text file, be sure to redirect the output to a file. (Thankfully, the syntax for redirection is identical on Mac, Linux, and Windows.) To convert the U.S. shapefile, type the following:

```
shp2pgsql -s 4269 st99_d00.shp us_states > us_states.sql
```

Open us_states.sql in a text editor. (Be careful—at nearly 5MB, it isn't a small file.) As you can see, running this SQL script will create a table named us_states and insert each record. To run it, type psql -f us_states.sql -d g4wd at a command prompt.

In PostgreSQL, typing SELECT count(*) from us_states; shows us that we are back to the original 273 polygons we noticed when we first encountered this file. Recall that the record count is so inflated because the coastal states have many tiny islands, each stored as one polygon per record. It bugged me then (in Section 2.9, *Viewing Feature Attributes*, on page 24), and it bugs me now. Call me crazy, but when I'm querying the United States, I want to see 50 records—no more, no less. Earlier in the book, we couldn't merge these POLYGONs into one MULTIPOLYGON per state because we were in a simple viewer. Now that we have the power of PostGIS at our fingertips, we can finally massage the data into something more expected.

5.8   Manipulating Data

So, our goal here is to merge several POLYGONs into a single MULTIPOLYGON. The question is, what criteria should we use? Typing select name from us_states; shows us many duplicates. Typing select distinct name from us_states; gets us back down to a reasonable number. (Yeah, there are 52 records instead of 50, but I won't begrudge the District of Columbia and Puerto Rico for coming along for the ride.)

To consolidate the POLYGONs into a single MULTIPOLYGON, we need to do a couple of things. We can create a new table by doing a SELECT ... INTO <NEWTABLE>. Rather than using SELECT DISTINCT ... as we did just a minute ago (which limits output to a single unique value by discarding the duplicates), we can use SELECT ... GROUP BY name to aggregate the results. Finally, we can use GeomUnion() to merge the geometries.

Putting this all together, we end up with this:

```
select name, GeomUnion(the_geom) as location into us_50
      from us_states group by name;
```

To see whether everything worked, type the following:

```
g4wd=# select name, NumGeometries(location) from us_50 order by name;
         name          | numgeometries
-----------------------+---------------
 Alabama               |             2
 Alaska                |            81
 Arizona               |             1
 Arkansas              |             1
 California            |            11
 Colorado              |             1
 Connecticut           |             1
 Delaware              |             3
 District of Columbia  |             1
 Florida               |            14
 Georgia               |             1
 Hawaii                |            27
 ...
```

5.9 Exporting Data

Now that we've tweaked our data set, let's dump it back out as a shapefile. Not surprisingly, PostGIS offers a complementary utility to shp2pgsql—pgsql2shp. Create a directory named us_50, change to it, and type the following command:

```
pgsql2shp g4wd us_50
```

This dumps the values from the us_50 table in the g4wd database to a shapefile. If you want to override the name, type the following: pgsql2shp -f foo.shp g4wd us_50.

Just to sanity check the output, you can open the shapefile in the viewer of your choice.

Alternately, you can use ogrinfo (which came along with GDAL) to do a bit of introspection:

```
$ ogrinfo -so us_50.shp us_50
INFO: Open of 'us_50.shp'
using driver 'ESRI Shapefile' successful.

Layer name: us_50
Geometry: Polygon
Feature Count: 52
Extent: (-179.147340, 17.884813) - (179.778470, 71.352561)
Layer SRS WKT:
(unknown)
NAME: String (90.0)
```

The -so flag provides a *summary only*. If you leave that flag off, you will get a screen dump for each record in the file. The first argument (the data source) is pretty straightforward. The second argument (the data layer) might seem redundant for a shapefile—after all, a shapefile can hold only a single layer, right? Well, ogrinfo allows you to introspect a variety of data sources. Type ogrinfo --formats to get a listing of everything that ogr understands:

```
$ ogrinfo --formats
Supported Formats:
  -> "ESRI Shapefile" (read/write)
  -> "MapInfo File" (read/write)
  -> "UK .NTF" (readonly)
  -> "SDTS" (readonly)
  -> "TIGER" (read/write)
  -> "S57" (read/write)
  -> "DGN" (read/write)
  -> "VRT" (readonly)
  -> "AVCBin" (readonly)
  -> "REC" (readonly)
  -> "Memory" (read/write)
  -> "CSV" (read/write)
  -> "GML" (read/write)
  -> "KML" (read/write)
  -> "PostgreSQL" (read/write)
```

Hmmm, so you see PostgreSQL there, you say? Let's get a list of available spatially enabled tables:

```
$ogrinfo PG:dbname=g4wd
INFO: Open of 'PG:dbname=g4wd'
using driver 'PostgreSQL' successful.
1: test (Point)
2: us_states (Multi Polygon)
```

Want to see what ogrinfo has to say about our original us_states layer?

```
$ ogrinfo -so PG:dbname=g4wd us_states
INFO: Open of 'PG:dbname=g4wd'
      using driver 'PostgreSQL' successful.

Layer name: us_states
Geometry: Multi Polygon
Feature Count: 273
Extent: (-179.147354, 17.884811) - (179.778473, 71.352562)
Layer SRS WKT:
GEOGCS["NAD83",
    DATUM["North_American_Datum_1983",
        SPHEROID["GRS 1980",6378137,298.257222101,
            AUTHORITY["EPSG","7019"]],
        AUTHORITY["EPSG","6269"]],
    PRIMEM["Greenwich",0,
        AUTHORITY["EPSG","8901"]],
    UNIT["degree",0.01745329251994328,
        AUTHORITY["EPSG","9122"]],
    AUTHORITY["EPSG","4269"]]
Geometry Column = the_geom
area: Integer (0.0)
division: String (1.0)
gid: Integer (0.0)
lsad: String (2.0)
lsad_trans: String (50.0)
name: String (90.0)
perimeter: Integer (0.0)
region: String (1.0)
st99_d00_: Integer (0.0)
st99_d00_i: Integer (0.0)
state: String (2.0)
```

Where ogr gets really interesting is when you're trying to nose around a remote database. Since we're looking at a local database, we use the simple syntax. You can, however, stuff a bunch of parameters into the PG: string:

```
ogrinfo PG:'host=remotehost user=bubba  password=smith dbname=g4wd'
```

Yeah, the syntax might look a bit weird, but the capabilities of the ogr suite of command-line utilities far outweigh any aesthetic misdemeanors.

So now wait a second. How come our newly created us_50 table doesn't exist according to ogrinfo? Yep—no entry in geometry_columns. (You *have* been paying attention—nice catch.)

One quick insert and ogrinfo PG:dbname=g4wd will have what it needs to interact with our new table:

```
insert into geometry_columns
(f_table_catalog, f_table_schema, f_table_name, f_geometry_column,
coord_dimension, srid, type) values ('', 'public', 'us_50',
'location', 2, 4269, 'MULTIPOLYGON');
```

Why bother? you might ask. Clearly pgsql2shp didn't need it. Well, ogrinfo does. As does ogr2ogr. Remember in Chapter 3, *Projections*, on page 33 that we used ogr2ogr to reproject our errant Colorado highways shapefile? Well, we can also use it to transform data from one format to another. Let's use it to rip the data from PostGIS into a shapefile:

```
ogr2ogr us_50_again.shp PG:dbname=g4wd us_50
```

If you do a directory listing, notice what else came along for the ride? You're right—we get projection information in the form of a us_50_again.prj file. ogrinfo -so us_50_again.shp us_50_again confirms that this data is projected in EPSG 4269.

Although getting projection information is cool, you can't really appreciate the ogr/PostGIS connection until you do something like this:

```
ogr2ogr hawaii.shp PG:dbname=g4wd
    -sql "select name, the_geom from us_states where name='Hawaii'"
```

Using ogr2ogr to rip arbitrary records out of your table using ad hoc SQL brings your PostGIS kung fu to a whole new level.

So, we've managed to go full round-trip with our spatial data—from shapefile to PostGIS to shapefile again. But PostGIS is more than just a glorified geodata bucket. You can perform some sophisticated data analysis. But before we get to the fun stuff like calculating distances and areas, you need to make sure that your spatial data is indexed.

5.10 Indexing Data

PostGIS is just like any other database: if you have a large table, indexing it will greatly increase query performance. You traditionally create indexes on fields that you query often. Indexing the name field, for example, creates a index not unlike the index in the back of this book. A book index is organized by keyword, showing you which pages a keyword appears on.

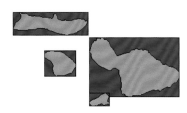

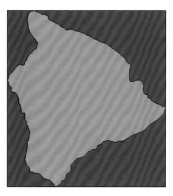

Figure 5.1: Complex polygons and their bounding boxes

A database index refers to record numbers instead of pages, but conceptually it does the same thing—it allows the query optimizer to short-circuit your search. Rather than having to do a sequential scan of each record in a table, it just refers to the index. Make sense?

For spatial queries, we want to be able to do the same type of thing; however, instead of words, we're going to create an index on the *bounding box* of the geometry. Sometimes called a *minimum bounding rectangle* (MBR), it is a simple box that can be used as a placeholder for the actual geometry (which in reality might be a complicated polygon with tens or hundreds of vertices). For an example of bounding boxes, see Figure 5.1.

Type \d us_states. You should see an index listed for the primary key, gid. shp2pgsql created this index for us. If it hadn't, you could easily create the same thing by typing this:

```
create unique index us_states_pk_index on us_states (gid);
```

That syntax will work for any nonspatial field. But to create a spatial index, the command you need to type is slightly different:

```
create index us_states_bbox_index on us_states
  using gist (the_geom);
```

Typing \d us_states shows that we now have two indexes on our table.

Once your index is created, you should do a vacuum verbose analyze us_states(the_geom);. Doing this periodically ensures that your index is optimized and up-to-date. For volatile tables (ones to which you are constantly adding or deleting information), the PostgreSQL manual suggests doing this command at least once a day. For reference data like us_states, doing it once in its lifetime is probably sufficient.

In the next section, you'll see && show up frequently in the SQL. This is telling the query to utilize the bbox index first. Oftentimes, you'll see a dramatic increase in query performance by doing a gross query first ("Hey, am I even in the ballpark?") and then doing the expensive fine-grained analysis on the reduced result set.

5.11 Spatial Queries

We've been using PostGIS to move data around. Let's spend a bit of time doing some spatial analysis.

Netstate.com lists some statistics for the state of Colorado.[12] Rather than blindly accepting the values, let's do some fact checking. For instance, the site lists the center point of the state at longitude 105° 38.5'W, latitude 38° 59.9'N. To convert these to decimal degrees, take a quick trip to http://jeeep.com/details/coord/. Type the values in the Minute Decimal box in the lower-right corner of the page, and click Submit. The resulting decimal degrees are (-105.641666, 38.998333).

What does PostGIS have to say about this? To find the center point, use the Centroid() function:

```
select name, asText(Centroid(the_geom))
     from us_states where name='Colorado';
```

The result is POINT(-105.547819910911 38.9985492904857). That's pretty close. (In the examples in this section, we're never going to get an exact match. What we're looking for is *close enough*.)

---

12. http://www.netstate.com/states/geography/co_geography.htm

Now let's fact check the bounding box. The website says Longitude: 102 W to 109 W Latitude: 37 N to 41 N. PostGIS gives us a couple of functions to verify this: Envelope() and Extent(). Envelope() returns a valid POLYGON. It is suitable for inserting into a new table. But it is also a bit verbose. If you are trying to describe a rectangle that has 90-degree corners, oftentimes geographers find it sufficient to provide only the lower-left and upper-right corners. (You will see this used quite a bit in Chapter 7, *Using OGC Web Services*, on page 147.) Extent() returns this shortcut notation:

```
select name, asText(Envelope(the_geom)) from us_states where
name='Colorado'; select name, extent(the_geom) from us_states where
name='Colorado' group by name;
```

In the second query, there was no need to use the AsText() function, because extent() returns text by default. Also note that we had to use group by name since Colorado could have had multiple POLYGONs in the table.

Getting back to our fact checking, extent() returns BOX(-109.060256958008 36.9924240112305,-102.041519165039 41.0034446716309). That jives with the website. Things are looking good.

Now let's look at the length and width of the state. The website says Colorado is 380 miles long and 280 miles wide. Let's see what PostGIS has to say about it.

Using the values from Envelope(), we can measure the bounding box horizontally and vertically using the Distance() function:

```
select distance(
GeomFromText('Point(-109.060256958008 36.9924240112305)'),
GeomFromText('Point(-109.060256958008 41.0034446716309)')
);
```

The result is 4.0110206604004. Huh? If you look real closely, you'll see that 4 is simply the arithmetic difference between the two latitude points. The distance is 4 degrees. Hrmph. That doesn't do us much good. Let's try another approach. We can reproject the points from degrees into meters using our trusty UTM 13 N projection. Recall that the SRID for UTM 13 N is 26915:

```
select distance(
transform(GeomFromText('Point(-109.060256958008 36.9924240112305)',
        4269), 26915),
transform(GeomFromText('Point(-109.060256958008 41.0034446716309)',
        4269), 26915)
);
```

The result is distance | 455802.861403081. OK, now we're getting somewhere. Let's use Google to convert those meters into miles. Type 455802.861403081 meters in miles into the Google search box. The results page says 455,802.861403081 meters = 283.222767 miles. Netstate.com said that Colorado was 280 miles wide. Looks good.

Now let's measure the other direction:

```
select distance(
transform(GeomFromText('Point(-109.060256958008 41.0034446716309)',
        4269), 26915),
transform(GeomFromText('Point(-102.041519165039 41.0034446716309)',
        4269), 26915)
);
```

The result is 598433.344979358. Google says 598,433.344979358 meters = 371.849241 miles. The website says 380 miles. That's close enough for me.

PostGIS offers a convenience function called distance_sphere(). It allows you to perform quick distance calculations on decimal degrees:

```
select distance_sphere(
GeomFromText('Point(-109.060256958008 41.0034446716309)', 4269),
GeomFromText('Point(-102.041519165039 41.0034446716309)', 4269)
);
```

The result is distance_sphere | 588820.960114999. Google says 588,820.960114999 meters = 365.876382 miles. This is a slightly more accurate measurement, but don't forget that we started with an abstraction—we're measuring the bounding box. In our case, we're not measuring the distance between two real-world points. Fifteen miles off doesn't mean too much to me when we're talking about nearly 400 miles. If, however, I was trying to calculate door-to-door driving directions, being 15 miles off would put me in a heap of trouble.

How is the website calculating the distance? We can't really tell. Maybe it's the widest point in the state. Maybe the site rounded up. We may never know, and again, it's close enough for me.

You're still not satisfied? OK, for the most accurate measurement, PostGIS offers distance_spheroid(). This function, as the name implies, allows you to specify an actual spheroid. We are using SRID 4269. What spheroid does that SRID use?

```
select * from spatial_ref_sys where srid=4269;
```

If we look hard enough at the srtext field, we can find SPHEROID["GRS 1980",6378137,298.257222101]. With that little nugget of information in hand, we can perform the following query:

```
select distance_spheroid(
GeomFromText('Point(-109.060256958008 41.0034446716309)', 4269),
GeomFromText('Point(-102.041519165039 41.0034446716309)', 4269),
'SPHEROID["GRS 1980",6378137,298.257222101]'
);
```

The result is distance_spheroid | 590332.999050949. Google says 590,332.999050949 meters = 366.815919 miles. So distance(), distance_sphere(), and distance_spheroid() all gave slightly different answers, but all were well within the ballpark.

And speaking of "within the ballpark," we can use PostGIS to find things like points within a polygon. Recall that the long/lat for the Colorado State Capitol building is (-104.98716, 39.73909):

```
select name from us_states where
  GeomFromText('Point(-104.98716 39.73909)', 4269)
  && the_geom;
```

The result confirms what we already know—that the state capitol is within the state. More accurately, it's within the bounding box of the state. && uses the spatial index to simply see whether we are in the ballpark.

For more accurate assessments, we can ask questions like Intersects, Touches, Crosses, Within, Overlaps, and Contains. (These are all defined in the same OGC, *Simple Features for Specification for SQL*, that defines the geometry types.)

```
select name from us_states where
  within(GeomFromText('Point(-104.98716 39.73909)', 4269), the_geom);
```

This query still goes fairly quickly, even though it skips the spatial index entirely and does a sequential scan on the table. For optimal performance, you should really use this:

```
select name from us_states where
  GeomFromText('Point(-104.98716 39.73909)', 4269)
  && the_geom AND
  within(GeomFromText('Point(-104.98716 39.73909)', 4269), the_geom);
```

Yes, it's long and tedious to type in by hand. But if you are trying to eke out every bit of performance, the long duplicitous syntax is well worth it.

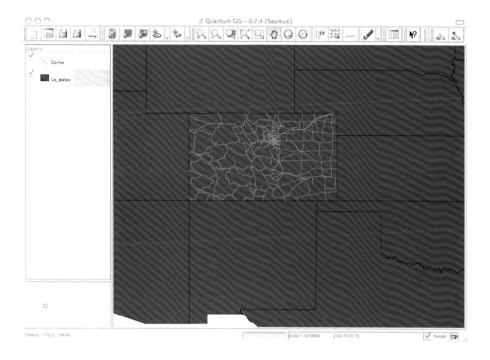

Figure 5.2: VIEWING A POSTGIS TABLE AND A SHAPEFILE USING QGIS

5.12 Visualizing Data

In the next chapter, we'll talk about OGC web services like WMS that allow you to visualize this data in a web browser. But you can also do this from standard desktop apps. Remember our good friend QGIS? Not only does it allow us to view shapefiles and rasters, it also allows us to sneak a peak at PostGIS tables. In the Layer menu, you should see an option for adding a PostGIS layer. Provide the connection information to PostgreSQL, and you will be presented with a list of tables. These tables can be mixed freely with shapefiles and rasters on disk, provided that they all share the same projection.

For example, you can view the us_states table and the co_highways shapefile simultaneously, as shown in Figure 5.2.

There is one minor gotcha with the production version of QGIS as of this writing (0.8). The 8.x PostgreSQL releases don't create a special hidden field that previous versions did: the object ID (OID). QGIS seems to prefer tables with an OID.

If you have trouble viewing PostGIS tables in QGIS, try typing the following command:

```
set default_with_oids to true;
```

Once you've issued that command, drop and re-create your tables. This database setting will be active only for the current psql session, so you'll have to remember to do it each time. Changes such as the lack of an OID can have a ripple effect throughout the community when applications are expecting it to be present. Over time, this will become less of an issue. I just mention it here as a short-term patch.

5.13 Conclusion

I hope at this point you feel more comfortable slinging your geodata around in a database. We installed PostgreSQL and spatially enabled it with PostGIS. We nosed around the built-in tables such as geometry_columns and spatial_ref_sys. We created spatial fields by hand and imported shapefiles using shp2pgsql. We queried, manipulated, and exported our data. We indexed our data for performance and visualized it using a desktop viewer.

So now that we have our data in a database, let's see how we can share this information over the Web. In the next few chapters, we'll look at ways to both visualize the data in a web browser (using WMS) and share it as a standards-compliant OGC web service (using WFS).

Creating OGC Web Services

This chapter introduces the OGC's merry band of web services. These services allow you to download raw vector data (Web Feature Service) and finished maps suitable for viewing in a web browser (Web Map Service). We'll download and install GeoServer, a Java-based OGC stack implemented as simple servlets. Our goal for this chapter is to get the services set up. In the next chapter, we'll look more closely at the details of the services and how to use them in an application.

6.1 Sharing the Wealth

We've spent the entire book gathering geodata from across the Web, scrubbing it, and getting it ready for prime time. Now we need to get it in the hands of our constituents. In some cases, this means presenting a finished map. In others, it means getting raw data to power users with a minimum of effort. Given the ubiquity of the Web, it should come as no surprise that it's where we're going to turn.

You probably remember the trouble we went through gathering the data. There wasn't a common file format. There wasn't a common projection. Simply finding the data wasn't standardized by any stretch. Rather than contributing to the forces of chaos, we should present our data in a standardized format that alleviates much of the grief that we were forced to suffer. (This flies in the face of the conventional wisdom of many cranky old programmers: "If it was tough to program, it should be tough to use as well....")

The OGC services we are about to set up are discoverable across servers and implementations. There is a consistent way to query the server, asking it what data layers it has to offer. Then you can introspect each layer, making sure you know exactly what you are going to get. Finally, you can fine-tune the output. We're going to provide services that allow you to reproject the data on the fly. You can request the output file format from a list of choices. You can set both the bounding box and the resolution to whatever you'd like, even if it distorts the output. As you can see, we're moving from being a simple data provider to a more sophisticated service provider.

6.2 OGC SOA for GIS

Service-oriented architecture (SOA) has become a popular buzzword in recent years. Creating a service-oriented architecture means that rather than creating stove-pipe solutions that solve a single problem, you focus on creating generic services that can be reused across many applications. However, one important clarification in the definition of SOA must be made up front. Some vendors have tried to co-opt the term to mean strictly *SOAP*-based services.[1] Although SOAP is one specific implementation of an SOA, it is not the only solution available. The OGC created its services long before SOAP was created. The OGC's services embody a simpler set of standards that are popularly called RESTful web services.

The term *REST*—short for Representational State Transfer—was coined by Dr. Roy Fielding in his 2000 doctoral dissertation.[2] But don't let that scare you away. The principles behind REST are pretty simple. In our case, it means that all of our queries are going to be simple HTTP GET requests. In other words, we're going to be able to hit our services by using an URL with a querystring (name/value pairs). This makes it incredibly easy to create queries and test them in your web browser.

And speaking of the Web, our SOA solution provides the easiest access to the data to the widest audience of users. A true SOA strives to provide its services in a language-, vendor-, and platform-neutral way. The OGC services abstract away the implementation details of how the data is actually stored. The consumers of our data don't need to have a shapefile viewer or a PostgreSQL driver loaded on their systems.

---

1. http://www.w3.org/TR/soap/
2. http://www.ics.uci.edu/~fielding/pubs/dissertation/top.htm

The Many Definitions of REST

SOAP is a specification. The statement "my service is SOAP 1.1 compliant" should be pretty unambiguous—at least in theory. In practice, one library might implement the specification in an incomplete way. Another one might add proprietary features. The spec is supposed to guard against this sort of thing, but it is no panacea.

REST, on the other hand, is a set of architectural principles. There is no such thing as "REST 1.1." As a result, different people have different interpretations of what it means to be truly RESTful. The popular meaning of REST is anything that uses an HTTP GET request with name/value pairs in the querystring. Dr. Fielding's meaning of REST is slightly more sophisticated, involving the use of other HTTP verbs in addition to GET such as POST, PUT, and DELETE. This disconnect in "popular" vs. "pure" interpretations of REST is the source of many bitter debates.

Before any true RESTafarians get upset, my use of the word REST throughout this book refers to the popular interpretation. Some folks call these services GETful to differentiate them from truly RESTful services. Others use more politically loaded terms such as "Low REST" and "High REST."

To be absolutely clear, the OGC specifications are GETful in the strictest sense of the word. Lumping them in with more pure-RESTful specifications such as Atom[*] is not meant to be an insult. It simply reflects the current usage of the word, ambiguity and all.

Yahoo calls its services RESTful, although deep in its FAQ[†] it acknowledges that its services technically "use REST-like RPC-style operations over HTTP GET or POST requests with parameters URL encoded into the request." Google has taken a more pure approach to REST, dropping its SOAP-based web services in favor of an Atom implementation it calls GData.[‡] Although the implementations have clear differences, both can probably safely be called RESTful in polite company.

---

[*]. http://www.ietf.org/rfc/rfc4287
[†]. http://developer.yahoo.com/faq/#rest
[‡]. http://code.google.com/apis/gdata/

Other OGC Servers

MapServer* is a mature, open source OGC server. It is a CGI application you can deploy directly in Apache. It has strong PHP development tools. Several good books are on the market that talk about MapServer, including *Web Mapping Illustrated* by Tyler Mitchell (O'Reilly).

Deegree[†] is a servlet-based OGC server like GeoServer. It, too, is open source and has an active community behind it.

Many commercial OGC solutions exist as well. I've had good experience with Ionic RedSpider,[‡] but it is by no means the only commercial solution available.

For an extensive list of software and services that are OGC compliant, see http://www.opengeospatial.org/resource/products. The installation and configuration are different for each, of course. Ease of use, features, and your preferred programming language all are factors to be considered when choosing a solution. But the beauty of the OGC standard is that they are all fully interoperable. Commercial or open source, each provides the same interface to the rest of the world.

---

*. http://mapserver.gis.umn.edu/
†. http://www.deegree.org/
‡. http://www.ionicsoft.com

They don't need a login to our database or an understanding of the particular spatial SQL dialect PostGIS uses. They get free, anonymous, standardized access to our data. The dialect they use is the same that NASA uses, that the USGS uses, and that the Canadian government uses. The power of this commonality cannot be overemphasized.

6.3 Installing GeoServer

GeoServer[3] is the quickest way to get a full-featured OGC server up and running. It is implemented in Java, but it doesn't require you to know the programming language. If you don't already have Java installed on your system, download the platform-specific installer from Sun.[4]

---

3. http://geoserver.org
4. http://java.sun.com

Figure 6.1: GEOSERVER

Two versions of GeoServer 1.4 are available for download. If you already have Tomcat or another servlet container installed, download the WAR file and deploy it as you would any other standard JEE application. If you don't have anything already installed, don't worry about it. You can download the BIN distribution. It includes the Jetty servlet container. Unzip it, change to the bin directory, and type startup.sh or startup.bat. It will start up on port 8080. Visit http://localhost:8080/geoserver to see it in action. (See Figure 6.1.) If you already have something running on port 8080, you can change the port easily by editing the file geoserver/etc/jetty.xml.

GeoServer comes preloaded with some sample data. Click the link to the Mapbuilder client to explore. These maps are autogenerated for every data set each time the server is started. Click the link to topp:states to get a feel for the map. (See Figure 6.2, on the following page.) Notice the four buttons along the top. The first two allow you to lasso an area to zoom in or zoom out. The third button allows you to drag the map to pan. The fourth returns you to the initial view.

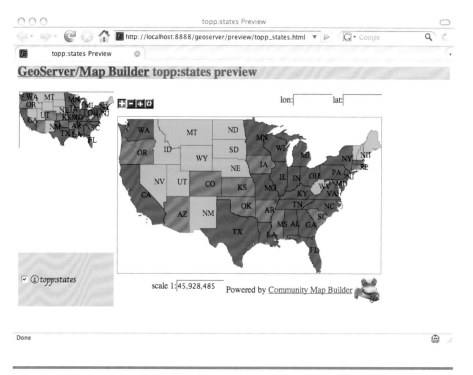

Figure 6.2: THE STATES SHAPEFILE, PRELOADED IN GEOSERVER

6.4 Adding Shapefiles Using the GUI

Let's add our own data layer. Even though there is already a US States layer in place, we'll add our old friend the U.S. Census Bureau state boundaries just to get a feel for the process.

In GeoServer, all the data is stored in geoserver/data_dir. Create a directory underneath that named us_states. Copy the U.S. Census Bureau shapefiles[5] into the directory (and don't forget to copy all three: .shp, .shx, and .dbf).

st99_d00 is now ready to be added to the GeoServer catalog. You can use the built-in GUI Admin console to do this, or you can manually edit a couple of XML files. We'll do both in the coming sections.

For our first new data layer, let's use the Admin console. On the home page, click the Config link. If you aren't logged in, you'll get redirected

---

5.   http://www.census.gov/geo/cob/bdy/st/st00shp/st99_d00_shp.zip

Late-Breaking GeoServer News

Just as this book was going to press, the 1.5 version of GeoServer hit the streets.* The examples as they stand here are nearly identical to what you'll see in 1.5. The configuration screens are largely the same, although you might find a new field here and there.

The biggest new feature you'll find in 1.5 is the ability to serve up rasters as well as vectors. You'll see a third service—WCS—show up alongside the more familiar WMS and WFS. This makes GeoServer a well-rounded offering for serving up all types of geospatial data.

*. http://blog.geoserver.org/2007/04/18/geoserver-150-released/

to the Login page. The default username is admin, and the password is geoserver. It probably goes without saying that you should change the default password, especially if this is going to be a public-facing sever. To do so, click Config > Server > Password.

Creating a new data set requires three steps. We will create a new namespace, then a data store, and finally a FeatureType.

Namespaces

Namespaces are a way to logically group your data sets. You could group them by provider (Census, USGS). You might choose to do it by country, state, or region. You could even group them according to the project with which they are associated. Of course, nothing is stopping you from just using an existing namespace as well.

For our purposes, let's create a new one named G4WD. Click Config > Data > Namespace > New. Enter G4WD in the text box, and click New. The next screen asks you for a URI. If you've ever dealt with namespaces in XML documents, this should feel familiar to you. The URI tradition-ally looks like a regular web address, although there doesn't have to be a web page or even a web server listening at that address. All this is meant to be is a unique identifier. Enter http://www.mapmap.org/g4wd, and click Submit.

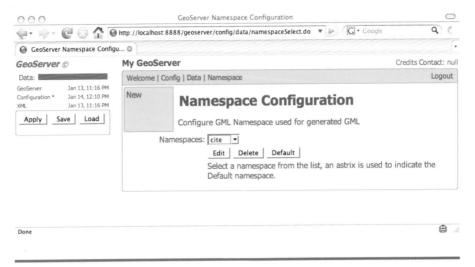

Figure 6.3: Understanding Apply, Save, and Load

At this point, the changes have been saved, but the server isn't using them. Notice the buttons in the upper-left corner? (See Figure 6.3.) Apply refreshes the server's configuration in memory. In theory, this allows to you to test your changes in the running server. In practice, I always forget to save them and lose my changes when I reboot the server. Save writes them to the config file (geoserver/data_dir/catalog.xml; we'll edit it by hand in the next section). Don't click Load—it will revert the server to the last config file. If you don't like the applied set of changes, this allows you to unapply them.

The asterisks next to the various lines give you a hint as to where things stand. An asterisk next to Configuration tells you that changes have been made but the server doesn't know about them. Clicking Apply moves the asterisk to GeoServer, telling you that the changes have been applied but not saved. Clicking Save flushes the changes to disk, removing the asterisk next to GeoServer. Click Apply and Save so that we can add a new data store using our new namespace. (No asterisks should be showing at the end of all of your button clicking.)

Data Stores

A *data store* can host many FeatureTypes. In the case of hosting shapefiles, you'll need to create a new data store for each one. Yes, this is redundant and tedious. Perhaps that is to motivate you to store your information in a true spatial database. As you'll see in a moment, we'll create a single data store for our PostGIS instance and be able to use multiple tables from the same one.

Click Config > Data > Stores > New. From the combo box, choose Shapefile. Enter us_states for the data store ID. Click New for the next screen.

On the Datastore Editor screen, choose G4WD from the Namespace combo box. For the description, type US Census Bureau US States. For the URL, type file:us_states/st99_d00.shp. Click Submit, and then click Apply and Save in the upper-left corner.

FeatureTypes

We are now ready to create a *FeatureType*. These are the individual map layers. Click Config > Data > FeatureType > New. In the combo box, you should see the data store you typed in and any data layers associated with it. In our case, the entry you are looking for is us_states:::st99_d00. (For shapefiles, the name of the .shp file is the name of the data layer. You might want to give your shapefiles friendly names for the sake of how they appear here.) Click us_states:::st99_d00, and click New. The resulting FeatureType Editor page is the most complex we've seen up to this point. (See Figure 6.4, on the following page.)

First, choose polygon from the Style combo box. These styles are defined in the OGC standard file format *Styled Layer Descriptor* (SLD). We talk more about SLDs later in this chapter.

Next, enter 4326 for the SRS. Clicking SRS List brings up a help screen with every EPSG code that GeoServer knows about. Recall that 4326 is short for plain lat/long coordinates in WGS-84. The title can be a friendly name such as "US States." This will show up onscreen as the name of your data layer.

Once you give GeoServer a proper EPSG number, you can have it generate the bounding box for the layer. (Jot down the max/min lat/long values for use in just a bit.) That new WKT should look familiar from the discussions in previous chapters. This would be a good time to update the Keywords and Abstract fields. When you are done, click Submit, and then click Apply and Save in the upper-left corner.

Viewing the Newly Added Shapefile

To verify that the shapefile got loaded correctly, let's take a look at it using the default Mapbuilder client. Go back to the main page, and

Figure 6.4: CREATING A NEW FEATURETYPE

click the Mapbuilder Client link. You should see us_states:st99_d00. Click the link to see the fruits of your labors.

It looks terrible, doesn't it? (See Figure 6.5, on the next page.) Don't worry about that for now. The dimensions of our FeatureType don't jive well with the default dimensions of the map that Mapbuilder provides (courtesy of those few Alaskan islands that cross the International Date Line). We'll fix that later in the chapter. The important thing is that you have pixels showing, albeit ugly ones. You have successfully added your first new data layer to GeoServer, and you didn't even break a sweat.

6.5 Adding Shapefiles Manually

Although adding FeatureTypes through the GUI is convenient, know-ing how to tweak the underlying configuration files is an invaluable

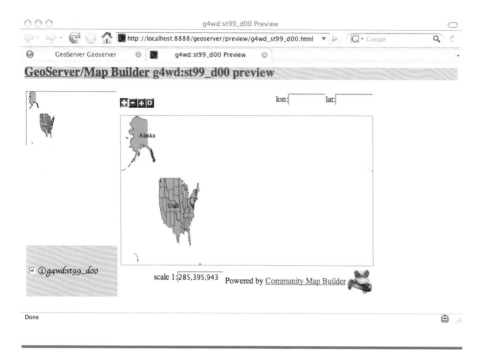

Figure 6.5: THE DISTORTED, DEFAULT MAPBUILDER VIEW

troubleshooting skill. Luckily, there aren't many moving parts when it comes to adding new FeatureTypes to GeoServer by hand.

The main file to start with is catalog.xml, found in geoserver/data_dir. It stores pointers to our namespaces, data stores, and styles:

```
<?config.xml version="1.0" encoding="UTF-8"?>
<catalog>

<!--
a datastore configuration element serves as a common data source connection
parameters repository for all featuretypes it holds.
-->
<datastores>
  <datastore namespace="g4wd" enabled="true" id="us_states" >
    <connectionParams>
      <parameter value="g4wd" name="namespace"  />
      <parameter value="file:us_states/st99_d00.shp" name="url"  />
    </connectionParams>
  </datastore>

  <datastore>
  ...
  </datastore>
</datastores>
```

```
<!--
Defines namespaces to be used by the datastores.
-->
<namespaces>
  <namespace uri="http://mapmap.org/g4wd" prefix="g4wd"  />
  <namespace uri="http://www.openplans.org/topp"
                prefix="topp" default = "true"  />
  <namespace uri="http://www.census.gov" prefix="tiger"  />
  <namespace uri="http://www.opengeospatial.net/cite" prefix="cite"  />
</namespaces>

<!--
Defines the style ids and file name to be used by the wms.
-->
<styles>
  <style filename="default_line.sld" id="line"  />
  <style filename="default_polygon.sld" id="polygon"  />
  ...
</styles>
</catalog>
```

Notice that data stores can be selectively enabled and disabled. Flip Enabled to False for the DS_poi data store. Save the file. To get Geo-Server to reflect this change, click Config in your web browser and then Load. The green bar (the health meter of GeoServer, really) is now tipped with gray. (See Figure 6.6, on the facing page.) If you misconfigure a data store or a FeatureType, this bar will have a red tip. To get things back to their original state, flip DS_poi back to enabled, save the file, and click Load once more.

For our next FeatureType, let's add the Canadian provinces.[6] Create a ca directory under geoserver/data_dir. Copy prov_ab_p_geo83_e.* to this directory. Open geoserver/data_dir/catalog.xml in a text editor. Copy one of the existing data stores, and edit the values accordingly:

```
<datastore namespace="g4wd" enabled="true" id="ca" >
  <connectionParams>
    <parameter value="g4wd" name="namespace" />
    <parameter value="file:ca/prov_ab_p_geo83_e.shp" name="url" />
  </connectionParams>
</datastore>
```

Go back to the browser window, and click Config. Click Load. To verify that everything is OK so far, click Config > Data > Stores. Choose ca from the combo box, and click Edit. Everything should match up between catalog.xml and the HTML form.

---

6. http://www.geobase.ca/geobase/en/data/cgb1.html

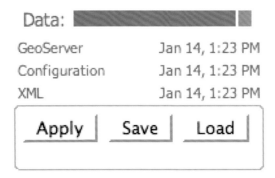

Figure 6.6: GEOSERVER WITH A DISABLED DATA STORE

We're halfway there. Let's create the FeatureType. The directory geoserver/data_dir/featureTypes contains one directory per FeatureType. Take a look in us_states_st99_d00. (Notice that the directories follow the naming convention [data store]_[featureType].) Inside that directory is an info.xml file.

```xml
<featureType datastore = "us_states" >
  <name>st99_d00</name>
  <!--
  native EPGS code for the FeatureTypeInfoDTO
  -->
  <SRS>4326</SRS>
  <title>US States</title>
  <abstract>Generated from us_states</abstract>
  <wmspath>/</wmspath>
  <numDecimals value = "8" />
  <keywords>st99_d00 us_states</keywords>
  <latLonBoundingBox dynamic = "false"
                    miny = "17.884813"
                    maxy = "71.35256064399981"
                    maxx = "179.77847000000006"
                    minx = "-179.14734"  />
  <!--
  the default style this FeatureTypeInfoDTO can be represented by.
  at least must contain the "default" attribute
  -->
  <styles default = "polygon"  />
  <cacheinfo enabled = "false" maxage = ""  />
</featureType>
```

Create the directory ca_prov_ab_p_geo83_e. (Don't you wish that we would've renamed that shapefile to something easier to type?) Copy info.xml from us_states_st99_d00 to ca_prov_ab_p_geo83_e.

Changing the data store and name to match the data store and shapefile names isn't tough. The EPSG remains 4326. (We graciously ignore typos in comments since misspelled comments are better than none.) Changing the title, abstract, and keywords is similarly not an issue.

And then there is the little issue of latLonBoundingBox. The GUI sure did a nice job of autogenerating that for us. You aren't worried about getting that data, are you? Have you forgotten our little friend ogrinfo from earlier chapters? Type

ogrinfo -so prov_ab_p_geo83_e.shp prov_ab_p_geo83_e.

See anything useful there?

```
$ ogrinfo -so prov_ab_p_geo83_e.shp prov_ab_p_geo83_e
INFO: Open of 'prov_ab_p_geo83_e.shp'
      using driver 'ESRI Shapefile' successful.

Layer name: prov_ab_p_geo83_e
Geometry: Polygon
Feature Count: 503
Extent: (-141.002750, 41.676556) - (-52.638016, 83.336213)
Layer SRS WKT:
GEOGCS["GCS_North_American_1983",
    DATUM["North_American_Datum_1983",
        SPHEROID["GRS_1980",6378137.0,298.257222101]],
    PRIMEM["Greenwich",0.0],
    UNIT["Degree",0.0174532925199433]]
UUID: String (36.0)
TYPE_E: String (10.0)
NAME: String (50.0)
SRC_AGENCY: String (10.0)
L_UPD_DATE: Date (10.0)
L_UPD_TYPE: String (2.0)
P_UPD_DATE: Date (10.0)
```

Use the information from the Extent field to complete the info.xml file. Be sure to save it once you are done changing all of the values.

```
<featureType datastore = "ca" >
  <name>prov_ab_p_geo83_e</name>
  <!--
  native EPGS code for the FeatureTypeInfoDTO
  -->
  <SRS>4326</SRS>
  <title>Canadian Provinces</title>
  <abstract>Generated from prov_ab_p_geo83_e</abstract>
  <wmspath>/</wmspath>
  <numDecimals value = "8" />
  <keywords>prov_ab_p_geo83_e ca</keywords>
  <latLonBoundingBox dynamic = "false"
                     miny = "41.676556"
                     maxy = "83.336213"
                     maxx = "-52.638016"
                     minx = "-141.002750"  />
  <!--
  the default style this FeatureTypeInfoDTO can be represented by.
  at least must contain the "default" attribute
  -->
  <styles default = "polygon"  />
  <cacheinfo enabled = "false" maxage = ""  />
</featureType>
```

Let's go back to the Config screen on more time and click Load. If no
errors show up here, then go back to the Mapbuilder client screen, and
take a look at your newly added Canadian FeatureType. (See Figure 6.7,
on the next page.) If you're not careful, you're going to get good at this.

6.6 Adding PostGIS Layers

Now that we are comfortable with shapefiles, let's turn our focus to
PostGIS.

The first step we need to take is to create the data store. Click Config >
Data > Stores > New. Select PostGIS from the combo box. Give it an ID
of local_postgis. Click New to move to the next screen. Fill in the values
required to connect to the server. (See Figure 6.8, on page 139.) Once
everything is filled in, click Submit, and then click Apply and Save.

Adding a new FeatureType is just as straightforward. Click Config >
Data > FeatureType > New. All of the spatial tables from the G4WD
database should be visible from the combo box. When you click New,
everything should be filled out and waiting for you with the exception
of the bounding box. Click Generate. You can tweak the values such as

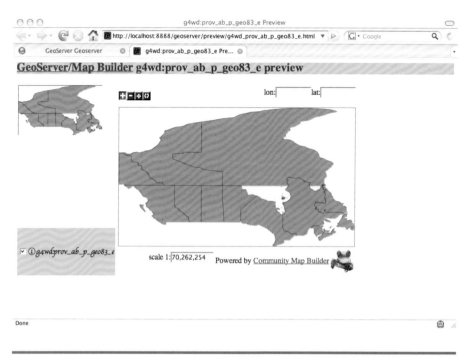

Figure 6.7: OUR MANUALLY ADDED CANADIAN PROVINCES

the style, the title, the keywords, and the abstract if you'd like. Click Submit, and then click Apply and Save.

The entry in catalog.xml is a bit more detailed than the shapefile entries we saw earlier:

```
<datastore namespace = "g4wd" enabled = "true" id = "local_postgis" >
  <abstract>Local PostGIS server</abstract>
  <connectionParams>
    <parameter value = "g4wd" name = "namespace"  />
    <parameter value = "true" name = "loose bbox"  />
    <parameter value = "postgres" name = "user"  />
    <parameter value = "password" name = "passwd"  />
    <parameter value = "true" name = "wkb enabled"  />
    <parameter value = "localhost" name = "host"  />
    <parameter value = "public" name = "schema"  />
    <parameter value = "5432" name = "port"  />
    <parameter value = "g4wd" name = "database"  />
    <parameter value = "postgis" name = "dbtype"  />
  </connectionParams>
</datastore>
```

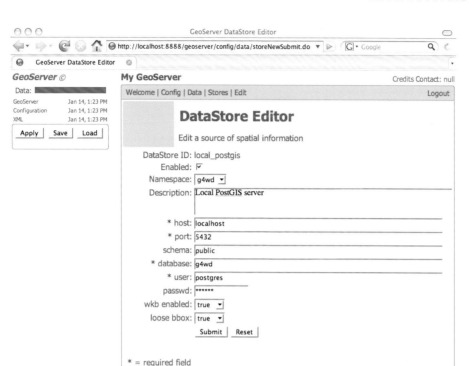

Figure 6.8: CONFIGURING A POSTGIS CONNECTION IN GEOSERVER

The info.xml file, on the other hand, looks identical to that of a shapefile:

```
<featureType datastore = "local_postgis" >
  <name>us_50</name>
  <!--
  native EPGS code for the FeatureTypeInfoDTO
  -->
  <SRS>4269</SRS>
  <title>us_50_Type</title>
  <abstract>Generated from local_postgis</abstract>
  <wmspath>/</wmspath>
  <numDecimals value = "8" />
  <keywords>local_postgis us_50</keywords>
  <latLonBoundingBox dynamic = "false"
                     miny = "17.884811400815106"
                     maxy = "71.35256195011284"
                     maxx = "179.778472900391"
                     minx = "-179.147354125977"  />
```

```
<!--
the default style this FeatureTypeInfoDTO can be represented by.
at least must contain the "default" attribute
-->
<styles default = "polygon"  />
<cacheinfo enabled = "false" maxage = ""  />
</featureType>
```

GeoServer, like QGIS, prefers PostgreSQL tables with an OID field. Follow the instructions at the end of Chapter 5, *Spatial Databases*, on page 97 to ensure your tables have the necessary OID field. For more information about GeoServer and PostGIS, see the online documentation.[7]

6.7 Styling with SLD

Now that we've solved the mechanics of getting the data displayed via GeoServer, let's focus on more aesthetic issues. Some would argue that the look and feel of the map is the most important part of this exercise.

As mentioned earlier in the chapter, all styling is done via an OGC-compliant SLD file. The SLD file format is standardized across all OGC implementations so that you can move your styles between servers as easily as you can your data. The best source of information on SLD is the specification.[8]

Recall that the styles are stored in geoserver/data_dir/catalog.xml:

```
<!--
Defines the style ids and file name to be used by the wms.
-->
<styles>
        <style filename = "giant_polygon.sld" id = "giant_polygon"  />
        <style filename = "capitals.sld" id = "capitals"  />
        <style filename = "tiger_roads.sld" id = "tiger_roads"  />
        <style filename = "poly_landmarks.sld" id = "poly_landmarks"  />
        <style filename = "green.sld" id = "green"  />
        <style filename = "simpleRoads.sld" id = "simple_roads"  />
        <style filename = "popshade.sld" id = "population"  />
        <style filename = "default_line.sld" id = "line"  />
        <style filename = "default_polygon.sld" id = "polygon"  />
        <style filename = "default_point.sld" id = "point"  />
        <style filename = "poi.sld" id = "poi"  />
        <style filename = "Lakes.sld" id = "cite_lakes"  />
</styles>
```

---

7. http://docs.codehaus.org/display/GEOSDOC/PostGIS+DataStore
8. http://www.opengeospatial.org/standards/sld

Each named style is a pointer to an SLD file stored in geoserver/data_dir/ styles. Let's pull up default_polygon.sld to see what we've been using for our U.S. states and Canadian provinces up to this point:

```xml
<?xml version="1.0" encoding="ISO-8859-1"?>
<StyledLayerDescriptor version="1.0.0"
    xsi:schemaLocation="http://www.opengis.net/sld StyledLayerDescriptor.xsd"
    xmlns="http://www.opengis.net/sld"
    xmlns:ogc="http://www.opengis.net/ogc"
    xmlns:xlink="http://www.w3.org/1999/xlink"
    xmlns:xsi="http://www.w3.org/2001/XMLSchema-instance">

  <NamedLayer>
    <Name>Default Polygon</Name>
    <UserStyle>
      <Title>A boring default style</Title>
      <Abstract>A sample style...</Abstract>
      <FeatureTypeStyle>
        <Rule>
          <Name>Rule 1</Name>
          <Title>RedFill RedOutline</Title>
          <Abstract>50% transparent red...</Abstract>
          <PolygonSymbolizer>
            <Fill>
              <CssParameter name="fill">#FF0000</CssParameter>
              <CssParameter name="fill-opacity">0.5</CssParameter>
            </Fill>
            <Stroke>
              <CssParameter name="stroke">#FF0000</CssParameter>
              <CssParameter name="stroke-width">1</CssParameter>
            </Stroke>
          </PolygonSymbolizer>
        </Rule>
      </FeatureTypeStyle>
    </UserStyle>
  </NamedLayer>
</StyledLayerDescriptor>
```

Let's make some sense of this. We have a NamedLayer that has a User-Style. (UserStyle essentially means custom style.) The UserStyle contains a FeatureTypeStyle. The FeatureTypeStyle has a rule that isn't doing much here but can be used to do conditional styling, as we'll see in the next example. The rule has a PolygonSymbolizer, which in turn describes the fill and stroke used on the polygons. The fill is the color that appears inside the polygon. The stroke is the color of the line surrounding it.

Notice that SLD uses CSS for its styling rules. Interestingly, CSS isn't XML, so SLD has to wrap each CSS styling rule in an XML element. Anything that can be expressed in CSS 2 is valid in an SLD document.

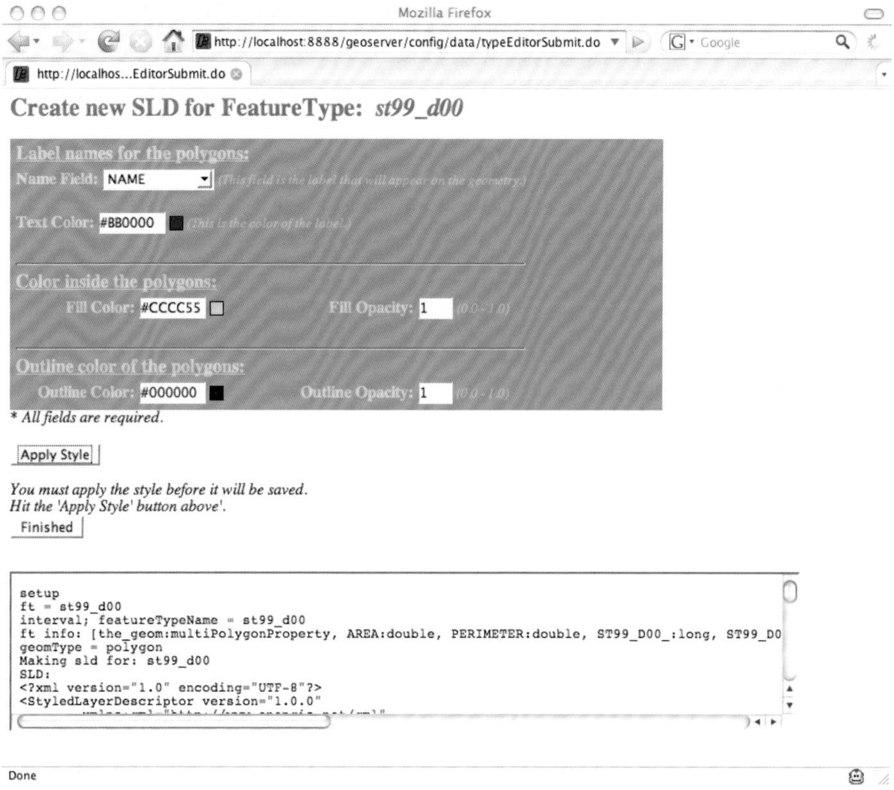

Figure 6.9: SLD EDITING

Let's make a quick change to the styling while we're here. Change the fill of the polygon to blue (#0000FF) and the stroke to black (#000000). Save the file. Back in the browser window, click Config and then Load. View the Canadian Feature in Mapbuilder to verify that your changes took place.

GeoServer offers a nice (albeit rudimentary) SLD editor. Let's create a new style for our PostGIS FeatureType. Click Config > Data > Feature-Type. Choose us_states_st99_d00 from the combo box, and click Edit. Notice that next to the Style combo box there is a Create New SLD button. Click it. (See Figure 6.9.) In addition to color widgets for the fill and stroke, you can also have SLD label your map elements. In this case, choose Name from the list of nonspatial fields. Click Apply Style and then Finished.

Look in geoserver/data_dir/styles for your newly created style. In st99_d00_style.sld, there is a new TextSymbolizer alongside your PolygonSymbolizer. (SLD also offers PointSymbolizers, LineSymbolizers, and RasterSymbolizers.)

```
<TextSymbolizer>
  <Label>
    <ogc:PropertyName>NAME</ogc:PropertyName>
  </Label>
  <Font>
    <CssParameter name="font-family">Times New Roman</CssParameter>
    <CssParameter name="font-style">Normal</CssParameter>
    <CssParameter name="font-size">12</CssParameter>
  </Font>
  <Fill>
    <CssParameter name="fill">#BB0000</CssParameter>
    <CssParameter name="fill-opacity">1</CssParameter>
  </Fill>
</TextSymbolizer>
```

Here we see, in addition to some more CSS styling, our first conditional rule. If any FeatureType has a field named NAME (case-sensitive), these styles will be applied. Otherwise, they will be ignored.

To see a more involved set of conditional rules, let's take a look at the topp:states FeatureType once again. (See Figure 6.2, on page 128.) The SLD styling creates a *choropleth*[9] map—the states are different colors based on their population. popshade.sld shows us how to accomplish this.

```
<FeatureTypeStyle>
  <Rule>
    <ogc:Filter xmlns:gml="http://www.opengis.net/gml">
      <ogc:PropertyIsBetween>
        <ogc:PropertyName>PERSONS</ogc:PropertyName>
        <ogc:LowerBoundary>
          <ogc:Literal>2000000</ogc:Literal>
        </ogc:LowerBoundary>
        <ogc:UpperBoundary>
          <ogc:Literal>4000000</ogc:Literal>
        </ogc:UpperBoundary>
      </ogc:PropertyIsBetween>
    </ogc:Filter>

    <PolygonSymbolizer>...</PolygonSymbolizer>
    <TextSymbolizer>...</TextSymbolizer>
  </Rule>
```

---

9. http://en.wikipedia.org/wiki/Choropleth

```
<Rule>
  <ogc:Filter xmlns:gml="http://www.opengis.net/gml">
    <ogc:PropertyIsLessThan>
      <ogc:PropertyName>PERSONS</ogc:PropertyName>
      <ogc:Literal>2000000</ogc:Literal>
    </ogc:PropertyIsLessThan>
  </ogc:Filter>

  <PolygonSymbolizer>...</PolygonSymbolizer>
  <TextSymbolizer>...</TextSymbolizer>
</Rule>

<Rule>
  <ogc:Filter xmlns:gml="http://www.opengis.net/gml">
    <ogc:PropertyIsGreaterThan>
      <ogc:PropertyName>PERSONS</ogc:PropertyName>
      <ogc:Literal>4000000</ogc:Literal>
    </ogc:PropertyIsGreaterThan>
  </ogc:Filter>

  <PolygonSymbolizer>...</PolygonSymbolizer>
  <TextSymbolizer>...</TextSymbolizer>
</Rule>
</FeatureTypeStyle>
```

As you can see, styling your data layers can be as simple or as involved as you would like. You can have many different styles for the same data layer. This is the embodiment of the *Model-View-Controller* (MVC) design pattern. The model (the geodata) is stored independently of any styling instructions. Similarly, the view (in this case, our SLD files) is independent of the model. The controller is the software component that combines the model and view for us. Having a clean separation of concerns for each of the three is a hallmark of a robust, reusable SOA.

The GeoServer website has many articles that talk about styling your layers in great detail.[10] Having your labels appear correctly[11] can be particularly tricky—you generally want them to appear without excessive overlap when your features get bunched together closely or superimposed over many data layers. And finally, one of the GeoServer power users has created a Google Maps SLD[12] that can give your FeatureType a familiar look and feel.

---

10. http://docs.codehaus.org/display/GEOSDOC/1.3+Style+Your+Map
11. http://docs.codehaus.org/display/GEOSDOC/LabelingOptions
12. http://docs.codehaus.org/display/GEOSDOC/Google+Maps+SLD

A friend of mine once described the ancient game of Go as something that takes an hour to learn and a lifetime to master. That description applies equally well to SLD and styling your maps. For now, you should have enough to get you started.

6.8 Conclusion

At this point, we have a functional OGC server up and running. We've installed GeoServer. We've added both shapefiles and PostGIS Feature-Types through both the GUI and the various XML configuration files. Finally, we wrapped up with OGC SLD files that describe the look and feel of our FeatureTypes. With that, all of our server-side artifacts are in place.

Now that our server is configured, let's start using it. In the next chapter, we'll have some fun making raw WMS and WFS calls. The RESTful nature of the OGC web requests make it easy to play around in your web browser and even the command line.

Using OGC Web Services

OK, getting GeoServer up and running was half the battle. Now let's start using the data layers. The nice part about focusing on standards-based interfaces is that GeoServer is nothing more than an implementation detail at this point. The previous chapter could've walked you through setting up MapServer, Deegree, Ionic RedSpider, or any other OGC-compliant server, commercial or open source. The step-by-step instructions would've varied widely, but the end result would be the same. We'd still end up right where we are at this moment.

And where we are at this moment is kicking off our deeper exploration of WMS and WFS services. We'll start by examining the low-level interfaces. We'll figure out which data layers are available to us and what fields they contain, and then we'll pull the data down. The only difference is whether we'd prefer a rendered map (WMS) or the raw bits (WFS) so that we can do the rendering ourselves on the client side.

7.1 Understanding WMS

Web Map Service (WMS) is the OGC standard[1] that you just saw in action when you were looking at the preview screens in GeoServer. (It's not surprising that GeoServer eats its own dog food—if you were serving up WMS services, what else would you use to sanity check your own services?) Since WMS is open and nonproprietary, it has become the lingua franca of the international mapping community.

---

1. http://www.opengeospatial.org/standards/wms

The first WMS version (1.0) was released in April 2000. Version 1.1 followed shortly thereafter in June 2001. Version 1.1.1 is the most widely supported version, released in January 2002. The 1.3 spec was released in December 2004, but not many servers support it at this point, including GeoServer. Version 1.1.1 is the sweet spot, and that is squarely where GeoServer lives.

The common feature of all of the specs is what makes WMS servers so easy to work with. All services are discoverable through a standard request. Once you find a data layer that looks interesting, you request it in a standard way as well. The fact that these requests are RESTful makes it a breeze to play around with by hand. Let's dig in. Even though we already know which data layers our local GeoServer instance has to offer, let's play along and ask it the WMS way.

7.2 WMS GetCapabilities

The way you find out what an OGC server has to offer is by requesting its GetCapabilities document. The welcome page of GeoServer provides hyperlinks to both WMS and WFS capabilities documents:

```
http://localhost:8888/geoserver/wms?service=WMS&
                                version=1.1.1&
                                request=GetCapabilities
```

Everything before the question mark is obviously the web address of the server. The querystring contains a couple of standard parameters. service=WMS specifies the service we're interested in. As you'll see later in the chapter, WFS is another valid service that GeoServer offers. version=1.1.1 specifies the version of the service you'd like to know about. request=GetCapabilities asks for the capabilities document.

If the server doesn't like the request, it will return an XML document explaining the problem. For example, if you leave off the version parameter, you will get an XML document back like this:

```
<?xml version='1.0' encoding="ISO-8859-1" standalone="no" ?>
<!DOCTYPE ServiceExceptionReport SYSTEM
 "http://schemas.opengeospatial.net/wms/1.1.1/exception_1_1_1.dtd">
<ServiceExceptionReport version="1.1.1">
  <ServiceException>
    msWMSDispatch(): WMS server error. Incomplete WMS request:
    VERSION parameter missing
  </ServiceException>
</ServiceExceptionReport>
```

Assuming that the GetCapabilities request is well-formed, you get a long XML document back that, in excruciating detail, describes each data layer the server has to offer. Here is the view from 20,000 feet:

```xml
<WMT_MS_Capabilities version="1.1.1">
  <Service>...</Service>
  <Capability>
    <Request>...</Request>
    <Exception>...</Exception>
    <UserDefinedSymbolization>...</UserDefinedSymbolization>
    <Layer>...</Layer>
  </Capability>
</WMT_MS_Capabilities>
```

Service contains information about the, umm, service. Capabilities tells you about the, uh, capabilities of the server. (I told you that this was easy.) The Service section contains basic metadata about the service: its name, a brief description, and who to contact if you have questions:

```xml
<Service>
  <Name>OGC:WMS</Name>
  <Title>My GeoServer WMS</Title>
  <Abstract>This is a description of your Web Map Server.</Abstract>
  <KeywordList>
    <Keyword>WFS</Keyword>
    <Keyword>WMS</Keyword>
    <Keyword>GEOSERVER</Keyword>
  </KeywordList>
  <OnlineResource xlink:type="simple"
   xlink:href="http://geoserver.sourceforge.net/html/index.php"/>
  <ContactInformation>
    <ContactPersonPrimary>
      <ContactPerson>null</ContactPerson>
      <ContactOrganization>null</ContactOrganization>
    </ContactPersonPrimary>
    <ContactPosition>null</ContactPosition>
    <ContactAddress>
      <AddressType>null</AddressType>
      <Address>null</Address>
      <City>null</City>
      <StateOrProvince>null</StateOrProvince>
      <PostCode>null</PostCode>
       <Country>null</Country>
    </ContactAddress>
    <ContactVoiceTelephone>null</ContactVoiceTelephone>
    <ContactFacsimileTelephone>null</ContactFacsimileTelephone>
    <ContactElectronicMailAddress>null</ContactElectronicMailAddress>
  </ContactInformation>
  <Fees>NONE</Fees>
  <AccessConstraints>NONE</AccessConstraints>
</Service>
```

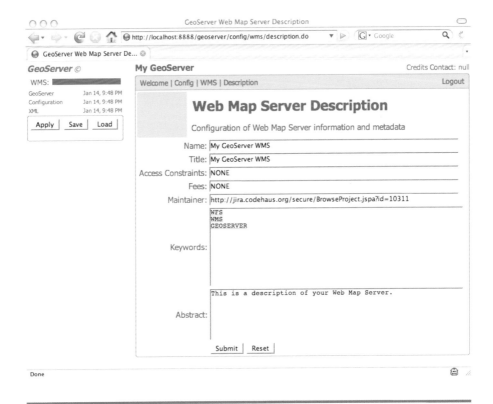

Figure 7.1: EDITING WMS SERVICE INFORMATION

Our service is pretty tight-lipped, isn't it? You can change these values by going to Config > WMS > Description. (See Figure 7.1.) You could also hand-edit /geoserver/webapps/geoserver/conf/services.xml.

Once you have that filled in, you can fill in the contact information at Config > Server. (See Figure 7.2, on the next page.)

Make the GetCapabilities request again to ensure that your changes were saved. You can do this in your browser, or you can use any command-line utility that can make a valid HTTP GET request. For example, I use wget on Mac/Unix systems:

```
wget -O wms.xml 'http://localhost:8888/geoserver/wms?service=WMS&
                 version=1.1.1&request=GetCapabilities'
```

Now that we understand the Service section, let's focus on Capabilities. It has four subsections: Request, Exception, UserDefinedSymbolization, and Layers.

Figure 7.2: EDITING WMS SERVICE CONTACT INFORMATION

Request lists the valid requests. These are the method calls that the server supports. We'll focus on the two main ones: GetCapabilities and GetMap:

```
<Request>
        <GetCapabilities>...</GetCapabilities>
        <GetMap>...</GetMap>
        <GetFeatureInfo>...</GetFeatureInfo>
        <DescribeLayer>...</DescribeLayer>
        <GetLegendGraphic>...</GetLegendGraphic>
</Request>
```

Looking into the GetCapabilities block, we see the format (technically, MIME type) of the response document and the supported HTTP methods. We'll stick to making GET requests, but the server will respond to POSTs as well.

```
<GetCapabilities>
  <Format>application/vnd.ogc.wms_xml</Format>
  <DCPType>
   <HTTP>
    <Get>
     <OnlineResource xmlns:xlink="http://www.w3.org/1999/xlink"
      xlink:type="simple"
      xlink:href="http://localhost:8888/geoserver/wms?SERVICE=WMS&"/>
    </Get>

    <Post>
     <OnlineResource xmlns:xlink="http://www.w3.org/1999/xlink"
      xlink:type="simple"
      xlink:href="http://localhost:8888/geoserver/wms?SERVICE=WMS&"/>
    </Post>
   </HTTP>
  </DCPType>
</GetCapabilities>
```

GetMap shows a similar set of information. It shows you which image formats are supported. Unlike GetCapabilities, this request must be made using HTTP GET.

```
<GetMap>
  <Format>application/pdf</Format>
  <Format>image/png</Format>
  <Format>image/jpeg</Format>
  <Format>application/vnd.google-earth.kmz</Format>
  <Format>image/svg+xml</Format>
  <Format>image/gif</Format>
  <Format>application/vnd.google-earth.kml+xml</Format>
  <DCPType>
   <HTTP>
    <Get>
     <OnlineResource xmlns:xlink="http://www.w3.org/1999/xlink"
      xlink:type="simple"
      xlink:href="http://localhost:8888/geoserver/wms?SERVICE=WMS&"/>
    </Get>
   </HTTP>
  </DCPType>
</GetMap>
```

If you're familiar with SOAP web services, this document should seem strangely familiar. It isn't truly a WSDL document, but it serves the same function, doesn't it? It's easy to create clients that automatically consume these services since the document explicitly defines all of the particulars.

The Exception and UserDefinedSymbolization sections are pretty straightforward. If the server throws an error back at you, you now

know what the MIME type will be. We already knew that our server
supports SLD, but here it is stated explicitly:

```
<Exception>
  <Format>application/vnd.ogc.se_xml</Format>
</Exception>
<UserDefinedSymbolization SupportSLD="1"
                          UserLayer="1"
                          UserStyle="1"
                          RemoteWFS="0"/>
```

Finally, we get to the real reason we care about this document at all—
the Layer section. The first thing listed in the Layer section after the
Title and Abstract (repeated here from the Service section, for those of
you paying attention) is the enumeration of all of the SRSs the server
supports. Yes, that is *every* EPSG code. GeoServer can convert among
them with ease, so it lists them all. Other servers in the wild might
support only a handful of projections.

After the supported SRSs, you are presented with a list of each FeatureType that GeoServer has configured. Dig through the list until you
find the st99_d00 layer:

```
<Layer queryable="1">
  <Name>g4wd:st99_d00</Name>
  <Title>US States</Title>
  <Abstract>Generated from us_states</Abstract>
  <KeywordList>
    <Keyword>st99_d00 us_states</Keyword>
  </KeywordList>
  <SRS>EPSG:4326</SRS>
  <LatLonBoundingBox minx="-179.14734"
                     miny="17.884813"
                     maxx="179.77847000000006"
                     maxy="71.35256064399981"/>
  <Style>
    <Name>polygon</Name>
    <Title>A boring default style</Title>
    <Abstract>A sample style...</Abstract>
    <LegendURL width="20" height="20">
      <Format>image/png</Format>
      <OnlineResource xmlns:xlink="http://www.w3.org/1999/xlink"
           xlink:type="simple"
           xlink:href="http://localhost:8888/geoserver/wms/GetLegendGraphic?
        VERSION=1.0.0&FORMAT=image/png&WIDTH=20&
        HEIGHT=20&LAYER=g4wd:st99_d00"/>
    </LegendURL>
  </Style>
</Layer>
```

No surprises here, eh? We configured all of these details when we set up the service, so seeing them presented back to us might seem a bit anticlimactic. But what if you want to work with a remote server that you don't have administrative privileges on? Take a moment to look through two capabilities documents that we'll be using later in this chapter. The first is from Iowa State. The school offers live weather feeds that we'll superimpose over our basemap layers. The second is from NASA, which offers Blue Marble raster layers.

```
http://mesonet.agron.iastate.edu/cgi-bin/wms/nexrad/n0r.cgi?
    service=wms&version=1.1.1&request=GetCapabilities
```

```
http://wms.jpl.nasa.gov/wms.cgi?
    service=wms&version=1.1.1&request=GetCapabilities
```

Doing all of this by hand might seem a bit tedious right now, but it'll give you some insight into what every OGC-enabled client does on your behalf. Neither Iowa State nor NASA uses GeoServer, but the resulting documents should look no different from what we are serving up locally.

7.3 WMS GetMap

Once you know which layers are available via GetCapabilities, you can request a rendered map using GetMap. Make this HTTP GET request from your web browser:

```
http://localhost:8888/geoserver/wms?
version=1.1.1&
request=GetMap&
srs=EPSG:4326&
bbox=-124.731422,24.955967,-66.969849,49.371735&
width=500&
height=285&
layers=g4wd:st99_d00&
styles=polygon&
format=image/png
```

You should see that darn US States data layer again. (Why won't it leave us alone?) Now add the Canadian layer. Both layers and styles accept a comma-separated list of values:

```
http://localhost:8888/geoserver/wms?
version=1.1.1&
request=GetMap&
srs=EPSG:4326&
bbox=-124.731422,24.955967,-66.969849,49.371735&
width=500&
height=285&
```

```
layers=g4wd:st99_d00,g4wd:prov_ab_p_geo83_e&
styles=polygon,polygon&
format=image/png
```

Now let's ask NASA for a raster version of the states. Unfortunately, we can't add layers from multiple servers in a single WMS request. (Stay tuned: we'll do that in just a moment using an OGC Context document.) Copy and paste your GeoServer request. All we have to change is the server address, the layer, and the style. Since the image is a raster, there really isn't a need for an SLD style to handle the coloring. The NASA GetCapabilities document doesn't list any styles, so we'll simply leave the parameter empty.

```
http://wms.jpl.nasa.gov/wms.cgi?
version=1.1.1&
request=GetMap&
srs=EPSG:4326&
bbox=-124.731422,24.955967,-66.969849,49.371735&
width=500&
height=285&
layers=BMNG&
styles=&
format=image/png
```

Being able to create GetMap requests like this by hand opens the door for all sorts of possibilities. Testing and troubleshooting become a breeze.

Now let's shift our focus to WFS services. WFS will seem incredibly familiar after all of this.

7.4 Understanding WFS

WMS's strength is that all of the rendering takes place on the server side. The output of the request is ready for display. For a browser-based client, this is convenient. However, there is a downside. Once the image is rendered, the look and feel cannot be modified. This can be limiting for a rich desktop client (such as uDig, which we'll play with later in this chapter) that has the power to do the same sophisticated rendering as a WMS server.

WMS output can be problematic in a more subtle way as well. The input is clearly geographic, but the output is a flat image file with no embedded georeferencing. GeoServer doesn't output GeoTIFFs, much less images with world files. Even if it did, modern web browsers would not do anything useful with the additional spatial information.

As a presentation tier delivery mechanism, WMS does fine work. But if you are looking to convey model data instead of view data, it falls short. Enter the companion *Web Feature Service* (WFS).[2]

WFS is designed to return pure geodata without any hints as to how the data should be portrayed. It falls into the same category as shapefiles and PostGIS; however, WFS is a web service as opposed to a file format or database dialect.

Web Coverage Service (WCS)[3] does the same for rasters as WFS does for vectors: it returns the raw data instead of the portrayed data. Since WCS is in the domain of the Uber Raster Geek, open source support for it is spotty but growing. GeoServer offers experimental support for WCS.

Version 1.0.0 of WFS was released in May 2002. Version 1.1.0 was released three years later in May 2005. Similar to the latest WMS spec, support for the latest WFS spec lags considerably behind the more prevalent WFS 1.0.0. GeoServer offers 1.0.0 support.

7.5 WFS GetCapabilities

Let's do the same GetCapabilities request for GeoServer's WFS that we did for WMS:

```
http://localhost:8888/geoserver/wfs?service=WFS&
version=1.0.0&request=GetCapabilities
```

The format of a WFS GetCapabilities document is slightly different from WMS's, but the concepts are the same:

```
<WFS_Capabilities version="1.0.0"
 xsi:schemaLocation="http://www.opengis.net/wfs
 http://localhost:8888/geoserver/schemas/wfs/1.0.0/WFS-capabilities.xsd">
  <Service>...</Service>
  <Capability>...</Capability>
  <FeatureTypeList>...</FeatureTypeList>
  <ogc:FilterCapabilities>...</ogc:FilterCapabilities>
</WFS_Capabilities>
```

---

2. http://www.opengeospatial.org/standards/wfs
3. http://www.opengeospatial.org/standards/wcs

WFS Service contains the same metadata that WMS Service does. Capability lists the available service calls:

```
<Capability>
  <Request>
    <GetCapabilities>
      <DCPType>
        <HTTP>
          <Get onlineResource="http://localhost:8888/geoserver/wfs?"/>
        </HTTP>
      </DCPType>
      <DCPType>
        <HTTP>
          <Post onlineResource="http://localhost:8888/geoserver/wfs?"/>
        </HTTP>
      </DCPType>
    </GetCapabilities>
    <DescribeFeatureType>...</DescribeFeatureType>
    <GetFeature>...</GetFeature>
    <Transaction>...</Transaction>
    <LockFeature>...</LockFeature>
    <GetFeatureWithLock>...</GetFeatureWithLock>
  </Request>
</Capability>
```

We'll focus on the three most popular: GetCapabilities, DescribeFeatureType, and GetFeature. These are used to read geodata from the service. GeoServer is notable in that it supports *Transactional WFS* (WFS-T)[4] as well. Transaction, LockFeature, and GetFeatureWithLock allow you to write data back to the service. We'll limit ourselves to consuming WFS data, but being able to write data back via a standardized open interface opens the door to interesting uses such as devices sending real-time location information back to the server. Implementing something like that is, as they say, an exercise for the reader.

The FeatureTypeList corresponds to the Layers list in WMS. It starts with a list of Operations (Query is for WFS; the others are for WFS-T). After that, it presents a list of available FeatureTypes.

```
<FeatureTypeList>
  <Operations>
    <Query/>
    <Insert/>
    <Update/>
    <Delete/>
    <Lock/>
  </Operations>
```

---

4. http://www.opengeospatial.org/standards/wfs

```
<FeatureType>
  <Name>g4wd:st99_d00</Name>
  <Title>US States</Title>
  <Abstract>Generated from us_states</Abstract>
  <Keywords>st99_d00 us_states</Keywords>
  <SRS>EPSG:4326</SRS>
  <LatLongBoundingBox minx="-179.14734"
                      miny="17.884813"
                      maxx="179.77847000000006"
                      maxy="71.35256064399981"/>
</FeatureType>

<FeatureType>...</FeatureType>
<FeatureType>...</FeatureType>
...
</FeatureTypeList>
```

The last list of items in the WFS GetCapabilities document is
Filter_Capabilities. You'll see these in action when we begin doing Get-
Feature requests. They allow you to limit the amount of data that comes
back to you based on the criteria you pass in. Think of it as SQL for
WFS.

```
<ogc:Filter_Capabilities>
  <ogc:Spatial_Capabilities>
    <ogc:Spatial_Operators>
      <ogc:Disjoint/>
      <ogc:Equals/>
      <ogc:DWithin/>
      <ogc:Beyond/>
      <ogc:Intersect/>
      <ogc:Touches/>
      <ogc:Crosses/>
      <ogc:Within/>
      <ogc:Contains/>
      <ogc:Overlaps/>
      <ogc:BBOX/>
    </ogc:Spatial_Operators>
  </ogc:Spatial_Capabilities>
  <ogc:Scalar_Capabilities>
    <ogc:Logical_Operators/>
    <ogc:Comparison_Operators>...</ogc:Comparison_Operators>
    <ogc:Arithmetic_Operators>
      <ogc:Simple_Arithmetic/>
      <ogc:Functions>...</ogc:Functions>
    </ogc:Arithmetic_Operators>
  </ogc:Scalar_Capabilities>
</ogc:Filter_Capabilities>
```

7.6 WFS DescribeFeatureType

OK, so we know that there is a FeatureType named g4wd:st99_d00 based on the FeatureTypeList in the GetCapabilities document. What else can our WFS tell us about this little nugget? I'm so glad you asked. Let's do a DescribeFeatureType request:

```
http://localhost:8888/geoserver/wfs?service=WFS&
version=1.0.0&
request=DescribeFeatureType&
typeName=g4wd:st99_d00
```

DescribeFeatureType returns an XML schema document describing the structure of the data set. The schema document lists each field and its data type:

```
<xs:schema  targetNamespace="http://mapmap.org/g4wd"
        xmlns:g4wd="http://mapmap.org/g4wd"
        xmlns:gml="http://www.opengis.net/gml"
        xmlns:xs="http://www.w3.org/2001/XMLSchema"
        elementFormDefault="qualified"
        attributeFormDefault="unqualified"
        version="1.0">
  <xs:import namespace="http://www.opengis.net/gml"
   schemaLocation="http://localhost:8888/geoserver/schemas/gml/2.1.2/feature.xsd"/>
  <xs:complexType xmlns:xs="http://www.w3.org/2001/XMLSchema"
        name="st99_d00_Type">
    <xs:complexContent>
      <xs:extension base="gml:AbstractFeatureType">
        <xs:sequence>
          <xs:element name="the_geom"
              minOccurs="0"
           nillable="true"
           type="gml:MultiPolygonPropertyType"/>
          <xs:element name="AREA" minOccurs="0" nillable="true"
                  type="xs:double"/>
          <xs:element name="PERIMETER" minOccurs="0" nillable="true"
                  type="xs:double"/>
          <xs:element name="ST99_D00_" minOccurs="0" nillable="true"
                  type="xs:long"/>
          <xs:element name="ST99_D00_I" minOccurs="0" nillable="true"
                  type="xs:long"/>
          <xs:element name="STATE" minOccurs="0" nillable="true">
    ...
```

So, now we know that the g4wd:st99_d00 layer is a multipolygon. We also know about the nonspatial attributes that will be coming along for the ride. We're ready—show us the data.

7.7 WFS GetFeature

To get the actual data, do a GetFeature request. (Recall that in WMS it was a GetMap request.)

```
  http://localhost:8888/geoserver/wfs?service=WFS&
version=1.0.0&
request=GetFeature&
typeName=g4wd:st99_d00
```

This returns the entire FeatureType as a well-formed Geographic Markup Language (GML)[5] document. The good news is GML is an open standard. The bad news is it is incredibly verbose. Thankfully, you can append outputFormat=GML2-GZIP to the end of your GetFeature request to have the server gzip the output on the fly. (outputFormat=GML2 is the default output type.)

```
<wfs:FeatureCollection xmlns:wfs="http://www.opengis.net/wfs"
 xmlns:g4wd="http://mapmap.org/g4wd"
 xmlns:gml="http://www.opengis.net/gml"
 xmlns:xsi="http://www.w3.org/2001/XMLSchema-instance"
 xsi:schemaLocation="http://www.opengis.net/wfs
  http://localhost:8888/geoserver/schemas/wfs/1.0.0/WFS-basic.xsd
  http://mapmap.org/g4wd
  http://localhost:8888/geoserver/wfs/DescribeFeatureType?typeName=g4wd:st99_d00">
<gml:boundedBy>
 <gml:Box srsName="http://www.opengis.net/gml/srs/epsg.xml#4326">
  <gml:coordinates xmlns:gml="http://www.opengis.net/gml"
            decimal="." cs="," ts=" ">
    -179.14734,17.884813 179.77847,71.35256064
  </gml:coordinates>
 </gml:Box>
</gml:boundedBy>
<gml:featureMember>
 <g4wd:st99_d00 fid="st99_d00.1">
   <g4wd:the_geom>
     <gml:MultiPolygon
             srsName="http://www.opengis.net/gml/srs/epsg.xml#4326">
      <gml:polygonMember>
       <gml:Polygon>
         <gml:outerBoundaryIs>
           <gml:LinearRing>
             <gml:coordinates xmlns:gml="http://www.opengis.net/gml"
                      decimal="." cs="," ts=" ">
               -147.78711088,70.24536349 -147.765104,70.219806 ...
             </gml:coordinates>
           </gml:LinearRing>
         </gml:outerBoundaryIs>
       </gml:Polygon>
```

---

5. http://www.opengeospatial.org/standards/gml

```
        </gml:polygonMember>
      </gml:MultiPolygon>
    </g4wd:the_geom>
    <g4wd:AREA>271.254383622068</g4wd:AREA>
    <g4wd:PERIMETER>227.171421517178</g4wd:PERIMETER>
    <g4wd:ST99_D00_>2</g4wd:ST99_D00_>
    <g4wd:ST99_D00_I>1</g4wd:ST99_D00_I>
    <g4wd:STATE>02</g4wd:STATE>
    <g4wd:NAME>Alaska</g4wd:NAME>
    <g4wd:LSAD>01</g4wd:LSAD>
    <g4wd:REGION>4</g4wd:REGION>
    <g4wd:DIVISION>9</g4wd:DIVISION>
    <g4wd:LSAD_TRANS></g4wd:LSAD_TRANS>
  </g4wd:st99_d00>
 </gml:featureMember>


 <gml:featureMember>...</gml:featureMember>
 <gml:featureMember>...</gml:featureMember>
 ...
</wfs:FeatureCollection>
```

It reads like Shakespeare, doesn't it? This is the abridged version, no
less, since what I am showing you here is only one of the 273 records.
Oh, and I also truncated the avalanche of lat/long pairs in the
gml:coordinates element. Old Will wouldn't be too pleased if he ever
found about the liberties I took with his GML, would he?

Pushing large amounts of data across the wire, even if it is on a local
LAN, can present logistical challenges. Binary file formats take up a
fraction of the GML footprint, but they don't offer the transparency of
plain text. It is admittedly a trade-off—size and speed for simplicity.
Let's look at ways that we can trim this GML output into more bite-
sized pieces.

7.8   Filtering WFS GetFeature Requests

Remember the SLD for the choropleth map? (See Section 6.7, *Styling
with SLD*, on page 140.) It used criteria to color the states differently
based on the value of the population field. We didn't dwell on it at the
time, but these Filters are a well-defined OGC specification as well.[6]
PropertyIsBetween, PropertyIsLessThan, and PropertyIsGreaterThan
are all examples of OGC Filters. Looking back at the WFS GetCapabilities document, the Filter_Capabilities section gives you a nice overview
of the Filter syntax.

---

6.   http://www.opengeospatial.org/standards/filter

We can use Filters in a slightly different context here. This time, we'll combine Filters with GetFeature requests to limit the amount of GML that gets sent down the wire to us. For example, let's say that we wanted to see only the Colorado state polygon. Here is the Filter syntax:

```
<ogc:Filter xmlns:ogc="http://www.opengis.net/ogc">
  <ogc:PropertyIsEqualTo>
    <ogc:PropertyName>NAME</ogc:PropertyName>
    <ogc:Literal>Colorado</ogc:Literal>
  </ogc:PropertyIsEqualTo>
</ogc:Filter>
```

You already know what the GetFeature request looks like. If you glob that Filter onto the end of the GetFeature request using a filter= parameter, the GML you get back should be limited to a single Colorado polygon:

```
http://localhost:8888/geoserver/wfs?service=WFS&
version=1.0.0&
request=GetFeature&
typeName=g4wd:st99_d00&
filter=<ogc:Filter xmlns:ogc="http://www.opengis.net/ogc">
<ogc:PropertyIsEqualTo><ogc:PropertyName>NAME</ogc:PropertyName>
<ogc:Literal>Colorado</ogc:Literal></ogc:PropertyIsEqualTo></ogc:Filter>
```

OK, let me be the first to point out that stuffing XML into an QueryString is a crime against humanity. To make matters worse, technically the filter string should be URL encoded (%3Cogc:Filter%3E), which renders it a total abomination. Did you just hear that? That was the sound of the HTTP GET request being stretched beyond its capabilities. Industry best practices suggest that you limit the length of your GET requests to 255 characters or less. Does that mean that we are out of luck? Put on your web developer hat for a moment—is there another HTTP method that is generally used for longer, more complex submissions to a web server?

Looking back at the WFS GetCapabilities document in the Capabilities section, you should see that GetFeature supports both HTTP GET and POST. I use GETs for simple requests, but sometimes POSTing your request to a WFS server is the only way to go. Thankfully, GeoServer makes POSTing sample requests almost as easy as just pasting GET requests into your browser's address line. To see what I'm talking about, go to Welcome > Demo, and click the Sample Requests link. (See Figure 7.3, on the next page.)

The request combo box gives you a bunch of interesting samples. The entries that end with .url are HTTP GETs. The ones that end with .xml

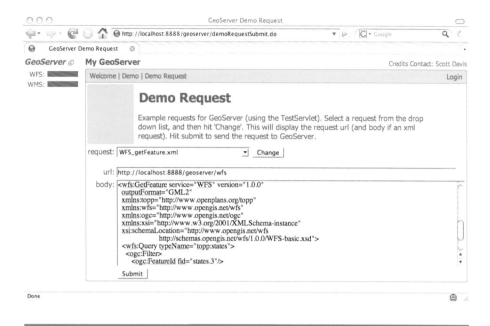

Figure 7.3: GEOSERVER TESTING TOOL FOR EXPERIMENTING WITH HTTP POSTS

are HTTP POSTs. Choose WMS_getCapabilities.url, and click Change. The URL line will be updated accordingly. Click Submit, and you'll see a familiar document returned.

Now choose WFS_getCapabilities.xml, and click Change. You not only get a new URL, but the body is filled in as well. Click Submit once more to perform the request.

```
<GetCapabilities
  service="WFS"
  xmlns="http://www.opengis.net/wfs"
  xmlns:xsi="http://www.w3.org/2001/XMLSchema-instance"
  xsi:schemaLocation="http://www.opengis.net/wfs
    http://schemas.opengis.net/wfs/1.0.0/WFS-basic.xsd"/>
```

OK, I admit that this makes me long for the simple elegance of an HTTP GET. All of that nasty schema stuff makes this request more complicated than it needs to be. Since we're not using any elements from those namespaces, we can shorten it a bit:

```
<GetCapabilities service="WFS"/>
```

Ah, that's better. But those pesky namespace declarations will come back later with a vengeance. This was only a temporary reprieve.

While we're still in the early stages of playing around with POSTs, it's worth mentioning a command-line tool that you'll want to get familiar with: cURL. cURL comes standard on Mac and Linux boxes. You can go to the cURL website[7] to download Windows binaries.

The XML for WFS requests is going to get complicated in a hurry. You should get in the habit of saving the XML to a text file and using cURL to submit the POST. For example, save the GetCapabilities XML to the filename getcapabilities.xml. Type the following at a command prompt in the same directory as the file you just created. (Ignore the line breaks—all of this must be on the same line for it to work.)

```
curl --request POST
    --header "Content-Type: text/xml"
    --data @getcapabilities.xml
    http://localhost:8888/geoserver/wfs
```

The GetCapabilities document should flash by in the console. If you want to save the results to a file, add --output somefile.txt to the command.

OK, let's return to the task at hand. We want to filter our GetRequest. Here's what a plain GetRequest looks like in XML:

```
<wfs:GetFeature xmlns:wfs="http://www.opengis.net/wfs"
                service="WFS"
                version="1.0.0"
                outputFormat="GML2">
  <wfs:Query typeName="g4wd:st99_d00" />
</wfs:GetFeature>
```

Not bad. I can match this XML to the QueryString in my mind. Since we're about to begin filtering the output, I like to think about it in terms of SQL as well. The query we just performed would be written in SQL as select * from st99_d00;.

The first filtering we'll do is limiting the number of fields returned in the GML. In SQL I'd write select NAME, AREA, PERIMETER from st99_d00;.

---

7. http://curl.haxx.se/

Using Filter XML, it looks like this:

```
<wfs:GetFeature xmlns:wfs="http://www.opengis.net/wfs"
                xmlns:ogc="http://www.opengis.net/ogc"
                service="WFS"
                version="1.0.0"
                outputFormat="GML2">
  <wfs:Query typeName="g4wd:st99_d00">
    <ogc:PropertyName>NAME</ogc:PropertyName>
    <ogc:PropertyName>AREA</ogc:PropertyName>
    <ogc:PropertyName>PERIMETER</ogc:PropertyName>
  </wfs:Query>
</wfs:GetFeature>
```

Notice that we had to add the OGC namespace in order to use the PropertyName elements. Paste this XML block into the body text area on the Demo Request screen, and click Submit. (Make sure that the URL field is pointing to the WFS service.) Or use cURL. Either way, the resulting GML should contain only those three named elements. Stripping out that massive geometry field (the_geom) might not make much sense from a mapping perspective, but it sure makes our query results more manageable, doesn't it?

Now that we've limited the fields, let's limit the number of records returned as well. To do a select NAME, AREA, PERIMETER from st99_d00 where NAME = 'Colorado';, try this:

```
<wfs:GetFeature xmlns:wfs="http://www.opengis.net/wfs"
                xmlns:ogc="http://www.opengis.net/ogc"
                service="WFS"
                version="1.0.0"
                outputFormat="GML2">
  <wfs:Query typeName="g4wd:st99_d00">
    <ogc:PropertyName>NAME</ogc:PropertyName>
    <ogc:PropertyName>AREA</ogc:PropertyName>
    <ogc:PropertyName>PERIMETER</ogc:PropertyName>
    <ogc:Filter>
      <ogc:PropertyIsEqualTo>
        <ogc:PropertyName>NAME</ogc:PropertyName>
        <ogc:Literal>Colorado</ogc:Literal>
      </ogc:PropertyIsEqualTo>
    </ogc:Filter>
  </wfs:Query>
</wfs:GetFeature>
```

That GML is getting smaller all the time, isn't it? If you are doing this in Firefox, the XML renderer does a nice job of indenting everything for display purposes. But if you do a View > Source, you'll probably be pretty disappointed. The XML is returned as a single string with no line breaks. (Those of you using cURL probably already noticed this.) Another Unix standard tool, Tidy,[8] will help make the output fit for human consumption. If you saved your output to a file named co.xml, try the following:

```
tidy -xml co.xml
```

Not bad, eh? This time, type tidy -xml -i co.xml to indent the output as well:

```
$ tidy -xml -i co.xml
No warnings or errors were found.
```

```
<?xml version="1.0" encoding="utf-8"?>
<wfs:FeatureCollection xmlns:wfs="http://www.opengis.net/wfs"
xmlns:g4wd="http://mapmap.org/g4wd"
xmlns:gml="http://www.opengis.net/gml"
xmlns:xsi="http://www.w3.org/2001/XMLSchema-instance"
xsi:schemaLocation="http://www.opengis.net/wfs
http://localhost:8888/geoserver/schemas/wfs/1.0.0/WFS-basic.xsd
http://mapmap.org/g4wd
http://localhost:8888/geoserver/wfs/DescribeFeatureType?typeName=g4wd:st99_d00">

  <gml:boundedBy>
    <gml:null>unknown</gml:null>
  </gml:boundedBy>
  <gml:featureMember>
    <g4wd:st99_d00 fid="st99_d00.166">
      <g4wd:AREA>28.03919812051</g4wd:AREA>
      <g4wd:PERIMETER>22.0191923313779</g4wd:PERIMETER>
      <g4wd:NAME>Colorado</g4wd:NAME>
    </g4wd:st99_d00>
  </gml:featureMember>
</wfs:FeatureCollection>
```

To complete your Unix kung fu, you could always pipe the cURL results directly into Tidy:

```
curl --request POST
     --header "Content-Type: text/xml"
     --data @gf-criteria.xml
     http://localhost:8888/geoserver/wfs
     | tidy -xml -i
```

OK, back to filtering. In our final example, we'll perform a spatial query. Oftentimes you just want results back from an arbitrary bounding box.

---

8. http://tidy.sourceforge.net/

(What, you've forgotten your WMS queries already?) To limit our results to a specific BBOX, try this:

```
<wfs:GetFeature xmlns:wfs="http://www.opengis.net/wfs"
                xmlns:ogc="http://www.opengis.net/ogc"
                xmlns:gml="http://www.opengis.net/gml"
                service="WFS"
                version="1.0.0"
                outputFormat="GML2">
  <wfs:Query typeName="g4wd:st99_d00">
    <ogc:PropertyName>NAME</ogc:PropertyName>
    <ogc:PropertyName>AREA</ogc:PropertyName>
    <ogc:PropertyName>PERIMETER</ogc:PropertyName>
    <ogc:Filter>
      <ogc:BBOX>
        <ogc:PropertyName>the_geom</ogc:PropertyName>
          <gml:Box srsName="http://www.opengis.net/gml/srs/epsg.xml">
            <gml:coordinates>-109.31,36.72 -101.87,41.03</gml:coordinates>
          </gml:Box>
      </ogc:BBOX>
    </ogc:Filter>
  </wfs:Query>
</wfs:GetFeature>
```

Notice the third namespace, gml? We need it to define a simple box. Just in case you're curious, the output is all of the states that touch Colorado. The bounding box used for the criteria is slightly wider than the minimum bounding rectangle (MBR) of Colorado.

OK, filtering completes our spelunking tour of the internals of WMS and WFS. We've by no means demonstrated every possible example of what you can do with these different standards, but you should know enough to at least feel comfortable.

7.9 Conclusion

OGC interfaces are great to work with; the RESTful interface is easy to use. Knowing that all OGC servers provide capabilities documents means that you'll never have to guess which data layers are available, what your styling options are, or what file formats and EPSG codes are allowed. A WMS GetMap request allows you to specify every last detail of the finished map. If the raw data is what you're looking for, WFS DescribeFeatureType and GetFeature are more your speed. And knowing that GML can potentially be pretty verbose, having OGC Filters in your toolkit means that you can be sure that you'll get only as much information as you ask for.

Now let's move back up the stack. The next chapter looks at three high-level applications that all grok the OGC standards. Mapbuilder is an OGC Ajax web framework. OpenLayers is another Ajax web framework with a twist: it not only speaks OGC fluently, but it also speaks proprietary mapping dialects such as the Google Maps API as well. uDig is a GUI desktop application that has wonderful OGC support.

Chapter 8

OGC Clients

Here in our third (and final) OGC chapter, we look at applications and web frameworks that consume OGC services. We start with Mapbuilder, an Ajax framework that ships with GeoServer. Next, we look at another Ajax framework named OpenLayers. This toolkit was inspired by the architecture of Google Maps. We finish the chapter with uDig, a desktop viewer that allows you to mix OGC data sets with local shapefiles and PostGIS data sets.

8.1 Mapbuilder

Mapbuilder is the Ajax toolkit that powers the map previews in Geo-Server. We're going to take a look at it in greater detail because you get it for free—why wouldn't you use it? Additionally, it gives us an excuse to look at another OGC standard, the Web Map Context file.

Recall that the preview maps are autogenerated each time GeoServer starts. (See Section 6.3, *Installing GeoServer*, on page 126.) That makes them a great learning tool. No matter how badly things get screwed up, you are always just a restart away from starting over with a clean slate. Of course, this can also be a hindrance. If you're not careful, all of your changes to the files can get blown away in a single reboot. Later in this section we'll copy a map out of harm's way so that our changes will be permanent.

Let's go hunting for those default maps. Take a look at geoserver/webapps/geoserver/preview. You should see three files per preview map. These files take the form [namespace]_[layername]. g4wd_st99_d00.html is the map. g4wd _st99_d00.xml is the OGC Context file. Finally, g4wd_st99_d00Config.xml is the Mapbuilder configuration file. Let's take a closer look at each one.

The HTML Map

Open g4wd_st99_d00.html in a text editor:

```html
<html>
<head>
  <title>g4wd:st99_d00 Preview</title>
  <link rel="stylesheet" href="../../style.css" type="text/css">
  <link rel="stylesheet" href="../mb/lib/skin/default/html.css"
      type="text/css">
  <script type="text/javascript">
    var mbConfigUrl='g4wd_st99_d00Config.xml';
  </script>
  <script type="text/javascript" src="../mb/lib/Mapbuilder.js"></script>
</head>
```

In the head section, a couple of CSS files are linked in. The core Map-builder.js file is included as well. But most important, a pointer back to the Mapbuilder config file is created.

```html
<body onload="mbDoLoad()">
<table border="0">
  <tr>
    <td valign="top" id="locatorMap"
        style="background-color: white;" />
    <td rowspan="2" valign="top">
      <table border="0">
        <tr>
          <td align="left" id="mainButtonBar"/>
          <td align="right" id="cursorTrack" />
        </tr>
        <tr>
          <td colspan="2" id="mainMapPane"
              style="background-color: white;" />
        </tr>
        <tr align="right">
          <td colspan="2">
            <table>
              <tr>
                <td align="left" id="mapScaleText"/>
                <td align="right">
                  Powered by
                  <a href="http://mapbuilder.sourceforge.net">
                    Community Map Builder
                  </a>
                </td>
                <td>
                  <img src="../mb/lib/skin/default/images/Icon.gif" alt="" />
                </td>
              </tr>
            </table>
          </td>
```

```
        </tr>
      </table>
    </td>
  </tr>
  <tr><td id="legend" /></tr>
  <tr><td colspan="3" id="featureList" /></tr>
  <tr><td colspan="3" id="transactionResponse" /></tr>
  <tr><td colspan="3"><div id="eventLog" /></td></tr>
</table>
</body>
</html>
```

Ignoring the cardinal sin of using HTML tables for page layout (hey, this is free code—you get what you pay for), what should leap out at you is the copious use of id attributes. These ids are placeholders for the various map widgets. The most important one of the bunch is mainMapPane—that is where the data layer appears. Everything else is reasonably well named. Widgets such as locatorMap, cursorTrack, and mapScaleText should leave little to the imagination in terms of what they do.

If you strip away everything else on the page, here is a bare-bones Mapbuilder map:

```
<html>
<head>
  <title>g4wd:st99_d00 Preview</title>
  <link rel="stylesheet" href="../../style.css" type="text/css">
  <link rel="stylesheet" href="../mb/lib/skin/default/html.css"
        type="text/css">
  <script type="text/javascript">
    var mbConfigUrl='g4wd_st99_d00Config.xml';
  </script>
  <script type="text/javascript" src="../mb/lib/Mapbuilder.js"></script>
</head>

<body onload="mbDoLoad()">
  <div id="mainMapPane" style="background-color: white;" />
</body>
</html>
```

Before we can try this bare-bones HTML, we need to "skinny" down the Mapbuilder config file as well. Right now it is expecting many more ids to be available on the page. It'll fail silently until we get those two files back in sync again. (OK, technically it will throw errors into the JavaScript console. But who looks there, right?)

The Config File

The Mapbuilder config file contains the instructions used to fill in the id placeholders with working widgets. Open g4wd_st99_d00Config.xml in a text editor. There's a lot going on, isn't there? The following is a greatly thinned-out config file. It won't actually run, but it will help us see the basic elements without getting bogged down in all the details.

```
<MapbuilderConfig>
  <models>
    <Context id="mainMap">
      <defaultModelUrl>g4wd_st99_d00.xml</defaultModelUrl>
      <widgets>
        <MapPane id="mainMapWidget">...</MapPane>
      </widgets>
    </Context>

    <Context id="locator">
      <defaultModelUrl>g4wd_st99_d00.xml</defaultModelUrl>
      <widgets>
        <MapPane id="locatorWidget">...</MapPane>
      </widgets>
    </Context>
  </models>

  <widgets>
    <ZoomIn id="zoomIn">
      <buttonBar>mainButtonBar</buttonBar>
      <targetModel>mainMap</targetModel>
      ...
    </ZoomIn>
    <ZoomOut id="zoomOut">
      <buttonBar>mainButtonBar</buttonBar>
      <targetModel>mainMap</targetModel>
      ...
    </ZoomOut>
    <DragPan id="dragPan">
      <buttonBar>mainButtonBar</buttonBar>
      <targetModel>mainMap</targetModel>
      ...
    </DragPan>
    <Reset id="reset">
      <buttonBar>mainButtonBar</buttonBar>
      <targetModel>mainMap</targetModel>
      ...
    </Reset>
  </widgets>

</MapbuilderConfig>
```

Notice that the model element has two Contexts. The preview map has two maps—the main one in the center and the little map up in the left corner. Each Context has a pointer back to a OGC Context file. This, as you'll see in just a moment, is where you define the data layers to be displayed. Notice the clean separation of MVC concerns? Here, we're simply defining a map widget, which doesn't much care what data it displays. Defining the map layers and the styling is someone else's job.

Each Context has a list of widgets. I'm displaying only the important one here—the map widget. Notice that there are widgets defined outside of a context as well. These are the zoom buttons. They are tied back to a specific Context through the targetModel element.

Removing all of the extraneous stuff, here is a bare-bones Mapbuilder config file to go with our stripped-down HTML file:

```
<?xml version="1.0" encoding="utf-8" standalone="no"?>
<MapbuilderConfig version="0.2.1"
    id="referenceTemplate"
    xmlns="http://mapbuilder.sourceforge.net/mapbuilder"
    xmlns:xsi="http://www.w3.org/2001/XMLSchema-instance"
    xsi:schemaLocation="http://mapbuilder.sourceforge.net/mapbuilder
       ../../mapbuilder/lib/schemas/config.xsd">
  <models>
    <Context id="mainMap">
      <defaultModelUrl>g4wd_st99_d00.xml</defaultModelUrl>
      <widgets>
        <MapPane id="mainMapPane">
          <mapContainerId>mainMapContainer</mapContainerId>
        </MapPane>
      </widgets>
    </Context>
  </models>
  <skinDir>../mb/lib/skin/default</skinDir>
</MapbuilderConfig>
```

Save this file, and click the Refresh button in your browser. (See Figure 8.1, on the next page.) Notice that we don't have to update Geo-Server when we make changes to these files. The server infrastructure is in place; we're just playing around in the web tier. All of the normal web development life cycles apply.

The OGC Web Map Context File

Let's take a look at the last file of the three. Open g4wd_st99_d00.xml in a text editor:

The Context file is short, sweet, and to the point. It defines the viewable nonspatial attributes of the map such as the size and the title. It also identifies the data layer(s) that should be included on the map. (You'll learn more about multiple layers in just a moment.)

Figure 8.1: A SIMPLE MAPBUILDER MAP

```
<ViewContext>
  <General>
    <Window width="500" height="285"/>
    <BoundingBox SRS="EPSG:4326"
                 minx="-179.14734"
                 miny="17.884813"
                 maxx="179.77847000000006"
                 maxy="71.35256064399981"/>
    <Title>g4wd:st99_d00 Map</Title>
    <KeywordList>
      <Keyword>g4wd:st99_d00</Keyword>
    </KeywordList>
    <Abstract></Abstract>
  </General>
  <LayerList>
    <Layer queryable="1" hidden="0">
      <Server service="OGC:WMS" version="1.1.1"
              title="g4wd:st99_d00 Preview">
        <OnlineResource xlink:type="simple" xlink:href="../wms"/>
      </Server>
      <Name>g4wd:st99_d00</Name>
      <Title>g4wd:st99_d00</Title>
      <SRS>EPSG:4326</SRS>
      <FormatList><Format current="1">image/png</Format></FormatList>
    </Layer>
  </LayerList>
</ViewContext>
```

Figure 8.2: THE U.S. MAP WITH BETTER DIMENSIONS

Like the SLD file, the Context file is an OGC standard[1] that can be shared across server implementations. Write this file once, and it is reusable from one server to the next.

This file finally allows us to do something about our poor, misshapen U.S. map. The culprits are right there in plain sight: the Window and BoundingBox elements. The Window is the same size for all of the preview maps. The aspect ratio is roughly 2:1 (width:height); 500 pixels wide by 285 pixels high is a reasonable default if we assume a minimum screen resolution of 800 by 600 for our web visitors.

The problem is the dimensions of the BoundingBox. They don't come close to matching the ratio of the Window, giving us the dreaded "Silly Putty" effect once again. Let's naively pretend that EPSG 4326 is a planar projection to keep the concepts simple. We'll figure out in raw degrees what our map dimension should be and use them unchanged as pixel coordinates.

First, let's tackle the longitude. Notice that the min and max are both basically 180 degrees. That means the width of the map runs the full 360 degrees. (Recall that there are a couple of Alaskan islands that cross the International Date Line, making for a pretty wide map.) If we let 1 pixel equal 1 degree, then our Window should have a width of 360.

Looking at the latitude, the height should be roughly 71–17, or 54 pixels tall. That's not very tall, so let's double both values to give us a map 720 pixels wide by 108 pixels tall.

---

1. http://www.opengeospatial.org/standards/wmc

Figure 8.3: ADJUSTING THE BBOX TO THE MAP ASPECT RATIO

Save the file, and hit Refresh in your browser. (See Figure 8.2, on the preceding page.) The map dimensions might be kind of funny, but the data layer is visibly less distorted than it was before.

The other thing we can do is adjust the BBOX to something that fits the aspect ratio of the map. Open topp_states.xml in a text editor. Notice the BBOX it is using to frame just the lower 48 states:

```
<Window width="500" height="285"/>
<BoundingBox SRS="EPSG:4326"
             minx="-124.731422"
             miny="24.955967"
             maxx="-66.969849"
             maxy="49.371735"/>
```

Flip our BBOX and Window settings to match these values, and click Refresh in your browser. (See Figure 8.3.)

If we wanted to tweak the aspect ratio of the map using our naive algorithm, the dimensions are 58 by 32. Multiplying each by eight yields 464 by 256—pretty close to the existing 500 by 285.

Building a Permanent Map

OK, we've had our fun. Restart GeoServer to get the default map in place. Visit the preview map for st99_d00 one more time to make sure that it has all of the widgets back in place.

Now let's move it out of harm's way. Create a directory named g4wd in geoserver/webapps/geoserver/. Copy st99_d00*.* from preview to the new directory. We're unashamedly taking the easy way out here—remember all of those relative references to CSS and JavaScript files? By creating our own directory at the same depth as preview, we're ensuring that none of the paths will break.

To make sure that there is no aspect ratio distortion, set the BBOX to be the maximum possible and the Window to a perfect 2:1 ratio to match. Pull it up in a browser so that you can see your changes as you go.

```
<Window width="500" height="250"/>
<BoundingBox SRS="EPSG:4326"
             minx="-180"
             miny="-90"
             maxx="180"
             maxy="90"/>
```

As the name LayerList implies, a Context document supports multiple layers. What happens if you add the Canadian Provinces layer? Copy it from the Canadian Context document. While we're at it, let's change the titles to something a bit more user-friendly. The legend should reflect these changes. (See Figure 8.4, on the following page.)

```
<LayerList>
  <Layer queryable="1" hidden="0">
    <Server service="OGC:WMS" version="1.1.1"
            title="g4wd:st99_d00 Preview">
      <OnlineResource xlink:type="simple" xlink:href="../wms"/>
    </Server>
    <Name>g4wd:st99_d00</Name>
    <Title>US</Title>
    <SRS>EPSG:4326</SRS>
    <FormatList><Format current="1">image/png</Format></FormatList>
  </Layer>
  <Layer queryable="1" hidden="0">
    <Server service="OGC:WMS" version="1.1.1"
            title="g4wd:prov_ab_p_geo83_e Preview">
      <OnlineResource xlink:type="simple" xlink:href="../wms"/>
    </Server>
    <Name>g4wd:prov_ab_p_geo83_e</Name>
    <Title>Canada</Title>
    <SRS>EPSG:4326</SRS>
    <FormatList><Format current="1">image/png</Format></FormatList>
  </Layer>
</LayerList>
```

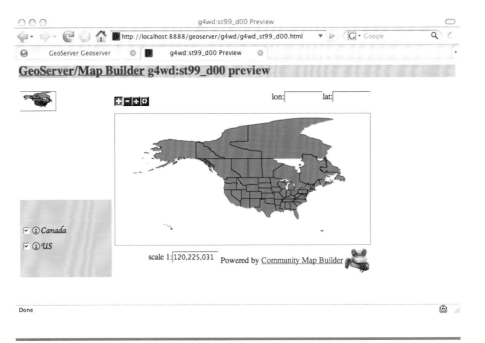

Figure 8.4: MAPBUILDER DISPLAYING TWO LAYERS

Notice that you can use the checkboxes in the legend to turn the layers on and off. Pretty cool, eh? We aren't limited to local data layers either. Let's add a live radar weather layer. Iowa State University offers this data up in an OGC feed:

```
<Layer queryable="1" hidden="0">
  <Server service="OGC:WMS" version="1.1.1" title="weather">
   <OnlineResource xlink:type="simple"
    xlink:href="http://mesonet.agron.iastate.edu/cgi-bin/wms/nexrad/n0r.cgi"/>
  </Server>
  <Name>nexrad-n0r-m45m</Name>
  <Title>Weather</Title>
  <SRS>EPSG:4326</SRS>
  <FormatList><Format current="1">image/png</Format></FormatList>
</Layer>
```

If you copy one of the existing layers, you need to adjust four values. The server Title attribute needs to be something unique. The OnlineResource HREF can point either to a local server or to a remote one. (Technically, it needs to point to that server's GetCapabilities document. Surprised? You shouldn't be.) You should change the Name element to the name of the data layer. Finally, change the Title element to what you'd like to appear in the legend.

The way this weather data gets to us is interesting. The National Oceanic and Atmospheric Administration (NOAA) offers a free weather web service,[2] but unfortunately it is SOAP-based. We can get the data, but not in a format that can be easily mapped. The Iowa State University Department of Agronomy offers the same data, but as a WMS service.[3] Are you beginning to see the power of a standards-based solution?

Remember our old friend the Blue Marble raster set? NASA offers it up as an WMS service.[4] Let's add it our map. Put it at the end of the LayerList.

```
<Layer queryable="1" hidden="0">
  <Server service="OGC:WMS" version="1.1.1" title="blue marble">
    <OnlineResource xlink:type="simple"
      xlink:href="http://wms.jpl.nasa.gov/wms.cgi?"/>
  </Server>
  <Name>BMNG</Name>
  <Title>Blue Marble</Title>
  <SRS>EPSG:4326</SRS>
  <FormatList><Format current="1">image/png</Format></FormatList>
</Layer>
```

Hmmm. Did your vector layers disappear? Opacity issues, right? Move the Blue Marble layer to the top of the list, and refresh your browser. Better? Good. (See Figure 8.5, on the next page.)

Now that we have several layers interacting, we might want to go back and play with the SLDs a bit more. Maybe you'd like to turn off the fill color in the U.S. and Canadian data layers. Maybe you want to tweak the borders to bright yellow so that they stand out against the dark Blue Marble background. The possibilities are endless.

Unfortunately, finding WMS servers on the Web is as hit or miss as finding the raw data. The upside is that once you've found a server, integrating it is a breeze (as we just demonstrated). And asking whether a website supports WMS is a pretty unambiguous question. Either it does or it doesn't. For example, you can pull data from TerraServer-USA via WMS.[5]

A couple of good directories of WMS services are available. Refractions Research[6] (the folks behind PostGIS) uses the Google Web API to har-

---

2. http://www.weather.gov/xml/
3. http://mesonet.agron.iastate.edu/ogc/
4. http://onearth.jpl.nasa.gov/
5. http://terraserver.microsoft.com/WebServices.aspx
6. http://www.refractions.net/white_papers/ogcsurvey/index.php

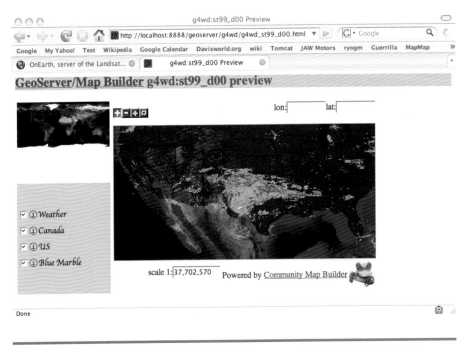

Figure 8.5: PULLING IN DATA LAYERS FROM REMOTE SERVERS

vest servers from the across the Web. ExploreOurPla.net[7] offers a big generated listing of WMS servers as well.

Take this opportunity to poke around these listings and find some other interesting data layers. Knowing that you are just a copy and paste away from a new data set makes the power of OGC interfaces manifest.

8.2 OpenLayers

Why introduce another Ajax mapping framework? Nothing is intrinsically wrong with Mapbuilder. There are, however, a couple of reasons why I find OpenLayers[8] an attractive alternative:

- I can create a map in significantly fewer lines of code using a single file instead of three.

---

7. http://exploreourpla.net/gis/wms-servers/

8. http://openlayers.org/

- OpenLayers, as the name implies, supports multiple data providers. In addition to OGC services, it allows us to mix in data from Google Maps, Yahoo Maps, and so on.
- OpenLayers provides better support for tessellated map layers.

Let's start by creating a simple OpenLayers map. Since you've already created a g4wd directory under geoserver/webapps/geoserver, let's add our new HTML files there. Create a file named ol.html:

```
<html xmlns="http://www.w3.org/1999/xhtml">
  <head>
    <style type="text/css">
      #map {
        width: 500px;
        height: 250px;
        border: 1px solid black;
      }
    </style>
    <script src="http://www.openlayers.org/api/OpenLayers.js"></script>
    <script type="text/javascript">
      //NOTE: geographic center of the US
      var lon = -98.583333;
      var lat = 39.833333;
      var zoom = 3;
      var map, us;

      function init(){
        map = new OpenLayers.Map( $('map') );
        us = new OpenLayers.Layer.WMS( "US",
                  "http://localhost:8888/geoserver/wms?",
                  {layers: 'g4wd:st99_d00'} );
        map.addLayer(us);
        map.setCenter(new OpenLayers.LonLat(lon, lat), zoom);
        map.addControl( new OpenLayers.Control.LayerSwitcher() );
      }
    </script>
  </head>
  <body onload="init()">
    <div id="map"></div>
  </body>
</html>
```

If you've ever worked with the Google Maps API,[9] this code should look very familiar. (If you haven't ever worked with the Google Maps API, I wrote a book[10] that can get you up and running in a hurry.)

---

9. http://www.google.com/apis/maps/
10. http://www.pragmaticprogrammer.com/titles/sdgmapi/

In both Google Maps and OpenLayers, notice that you include the library with a single script element. This pulls in the library from across the Internet. I like doing this because it frees me from keeping up with bug fixes and feature enhancements. I always have the latest version of the API with each page view. Of course, you can also download the OpenMaps library to your local server. You might choose to do that to improve performance, to minimize bandwidth consumption over an expensive WAN link, or to simply lock in the feature set of a specific version of the library.

Like Google Maps and Mapbuilder, you tie map widgets to HTML elements through their id attributes. Unlike Mapbuilder, you define your map in JavaScript instead of an OGC Context document.

An OpenLayers.Layer.WMS object accepts four parameters in the constructor:

- The first argument is the name of the layer. This shows up in the legend.
- The second argument is the URL to the WMS server. You don't need to include any of the GetCapabilities parameters, but you do need to make sure you include the trailing question mark.
- The third argument specifies the layer(s). As you'll see in a bit, this is where you pass in any name/value pairs that you'd like appended to the QueryString.
- The fourth argument (not shown here) is a set of OpenLayers-specific arguments. Again, you will see this in action in just a moment.

After the newly minted WMS layer is added to the map, we center the map and specify a zoom level. These zoom levels are like the fixed zoom levels in Google Maps; 0 is zoomed out to the world level, and 16 is zoomed into street level. Finally, we add a little plus sign in the upper-right corner of the map that allows us to turn data layers on and off. Since there's only one layer in place right now, this control is kind of boring. Don't worry, we'll put it to use shortly. If everything got typed in correctly, you should see your US States layer once again. (See Figure 8.6, on the facing page.)

So, in 30 lines of HTML we have a fully functional map that rivals the capabilities of its Mapbuilder counterpart. OpenLayers does the same thing as Mapbuilder, but it comes in at a higher level of abstraction. You just point it at a GetCapabilities document and let it handle the

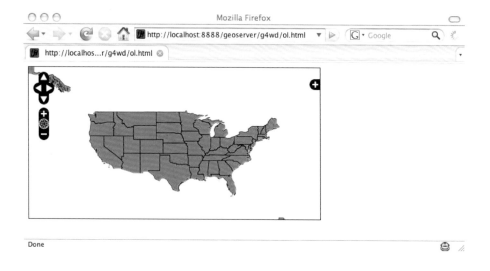

Figure 8.6: A SIMPLE OPENLAYERS MAP

minutia for you. Notice that we didn't have to worry about setting both the map dimensions and the BBOX? Avoiding the "Silly Putty" effect is baked into the OpenLayers framework.

Adding a second layer to the map is simple. Just add a comma and the layer name:

```
us = new OpenLayers.Layer.WMS( "US",
    "http://localhost:8888/geoserver/wms?",
    {layers: 'g4wd:st99_d00,g4wd:prov_ab_p_geo83_e'} );
```

But to really see what OpenLayers can do, let's add the Blue Marble layer once again:

```
<html xmlns="http://www.w3.org/1999/xhtml">
  <head>
    <style type="text/css">
      #map {
        width: 500px;
        height: 250px;
        border: 1px solid black;
      }
    </style>
    <script src="http://www.openlayers.org/api/OpenLayers.js"></script>
    <script type="text/javascript">
      //NOTE: geographic center of the US
      var lon = -98.583333;
      var lat = 39.833333;
```

```
      var zoom = 3;
      var map, us, canada, blueMarble;

      function init(){
        map = new OpenLayers.Map( $('map') );
        blueMarble = new OpenLayers.Layer.WMS( "Blue Marble",
                        "http://wms.jpl.nasa.gov/wms.cgi?",
                        {layers: 'BMNG', format: 'image/png'},
                        {isBaseLayer:true});
        map.addLayer(blueMarble);

        us = new OpenLayers.Layer.WMS( "US",
             "http://localhost:8888/geoserver/wms?",
             {layers: 'g4wd:st99_d00',
              format: 'image/png', transparent: true},
             {isBaseLayer:false, opacity:0.5} );
        map.addLayer(us);

        canada = new OpenLayers.Layer.WMS( "Canada",
             "http://localhost:8888/geoserver/wms?",
             {layers: 'g4wd:prov_ab_p_geo83_e',
              format: 'image/png', transparent: true},
             {isBaseLayer:false, opacity:1.0} );
        map.addLayer(canada);

        map.setCenter(new OpenLayers.LonLat(lon, lat), zoom);
        map.addControl( new OpenLayers.Control.LayerSwitcher() );
      }
    </script>
  </head>
  <body onload="init()">
    <div id="map"></div>
  </body>
</html>
```

We define three separate map layers this time: blueMarble, us, and canada. blueMarble has to be a separate layer since it is coming from a separate WMS server. I separated us and canada so that they could be turned on and off independently.

Notice that we're passing in additional arguments for the GetMap request. In blueMarble, we specify both the layer and the format. If you don't tell it otherwise, OpenLayers defaults to JPEG for the image format.

Since we want to be able to adjust the opacity of the image (and JPEG doesn't support alpha transparency), we request PNG instead. The online documentation[11] shows you what the default values are for the GetMap request:

```
DEFAULT_PARAMS: {
  SERVICE: "WMS",
  VERSION: "1.1.1",
  REQUEST: "GetMap",
  STYLES: "",
  EXCEPTIONS: "application/vnd.ogc.se_inimage",
  FORMAT: "image/jpeg"
}
```

In blueMarble, we also see the fourth constructor argument come into play. {isBaseLayer:true} tells OpenLayers to treat this as a BaseLayer instead of an overlay.[12] BaseLayers are essentially mutually exclusive. The LayerSwitcher in the upper-right corner presents all BaseLayers as radio buttons. You can flip among them easily, but they cannot be displayed simultaneously. Overlays, on the other hand, can be displayed simultaneously. The LayerSwitcher presents the user with checkboxes instead of radio buttons.

If you are going to treat your map layers as overlays, you should pay attention to a few other tricks. In both us and canada, we pass in the standard but optional transparent argument with the GetMap request. The image format must be PNG or GIF to support transparency. This tells the WMS server to send the areas that aren't features back as transparent pixels instead of a solid color. In the fourth argument, we tell OpenLayers that these layers aren't basemaps, so treat them as overlays instead. And finally, we tell OpenLayers to adjust the opacity level of the entire feature. You can always set the opacity in the server-side SLD, but being able to tweak it here gives you much finer control of the display of the overlays. Opacity must be a float ranging from 0.0 (fully transparent) to 1.0 (fully opaque). Play around with this map, flipping the overlays on and off, tweaking the opacity levels, and so on. (See Figure 8.7, on the next page.)

OpenLayers Tips 'n' Tricks

OpenLayers is a young framework. It is advancing at light speed. Rather than present you with more code that is sure to be obsolete by the time you read this, I'll leave you with a couple of pointers.

---

11. http://trac.openlayers.org/wiki/Layer/WMS
12. http://trac.openlayers.org/wiki/BaseLayersAndOverlays

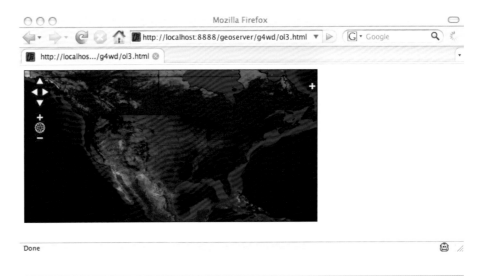

Figure 8.7: OPENLAYERS WITH MAP LAYERS FROM DIFFERENT SERVERS

Support for data providers other than WMS is where much of the growth in the framework is happening. For an example of using Google Maps, Yahoo Maps, Microsoft's Windows Live Local, and others, see the sample application in the gallery.[13]

Be sure to choose View > Source on all of the examples; they are good sources for additional public WMS servers.

For example, the nice world vector layer you see on the OpenLayers home page is this:

```
var wms = new OpenLayers.Layer.WMS( "OpenLayers WMS",
    "http://labs.metacarta.com/wms/vmap0",
    {layers: 'basic'} );
```

Even if you don't use the OpenLayers framework, the data is exposed as a WMS layer that can be used in uDig, Mapbuilder, or anything else that is fluent in OGC. Browse the GetCapabilities document to see what other layers are available.

---

13. http://www.openlayers.org/gallery/multiple.html

As you scavenge around the more recent OpenLayer examples, you'll see data coming from a slightly different URL:

```
var ol_wms = new OpenLayers.Layer.WMS( "World Map",
  "http://labs.metacarta.com/wms-c/Basic.py?",
  {layers: 'basic', format: 'image/png' } );
var jpl_wms = new OpenLayers.Layer.WMS( "Satellite",
  "http://labs.metacarta.com/wms-c/Basic.py?",
  {layers: 'satellite', format: 'image/png' } );
```

These data layers are being served up using the experimental WMS-C[14] format. This data is tessellated instead of being served up as one big image. MetaCarta[15] is doing quite a bit of experimentation with tessellated data and sharing its results with the open source community. OpenLayers is just one example of this.

So, what is the big deal with tiled images? Go back and look at one of the preview maps from GeoServer. Notice that you can drag the image with your mouse, but does it behave like Google Maps? Nope. The image is exactly the size of the onscreen map. When you drag it, you see white pixels. When you stop dragging, Mapbuilder sends in a new request for a new image.

Contrast that behavior with Google Maps. When you drag a map from them, you almost never see white pixels. How do they do that? Simple. Google Maps uses 256 by 256 pixel tiles. A typical map might be a grid of five or more *visible* tiles per row and column, along with a couple of extra tiles preloaded outside the viewable map boundaries. On a fast connection, you might never see the individual tiles. But pay attention the next time you start Google Maps cold. Or try dragging from one corner of the map to the opposite corner quickly. You might be able to outrun your browser cache and see the individual tiles downloading.

The Google Maps model scales incredibly well. Each tile has a fixed name and dimensions. This means that it can be cached everywhere from the local browser, up through a corporate proxy server, to the ISP, and finally Google itself. Because the details of the maps are not customizable by the end user, Google is able to achieve great economies of scale—everyone gets the same pixels.

---

14. http://wiki.osgeo.org/index.php/WMS_Tiling_Client_Recommendation
15. http://www.metacarta.com

Deconstructing Google Maps

If you'd like a deeper explanation of the mechanics of Google Maps, go to http://www.mapmap.org/ryogm. There you'll find a slide show and working code examples of how to roll your own Google Maps. Step through the pages in order, 1.html through 12.html. Be sure to choose View > Source and read the comments for pointers to the important bits each step of the way. In less than 200 lines of client-side JavaScript and *no* server-side code, you can have your very own slippy map interface.

In contrast, WMS imagery is generated on demand. Since every WMS request is unique (because of the map size, the bbox, the zoom level, the included layers, the styling—you get the idea), caching is virtually impossible. OpenLayers tries to get around this by making multiple WMS requests, simulating a tiled image. In practice, this will most likely end up having a negative effect on performance if the server is not prepared to handle the additional load. WMS servers that are expecting a few large, coarse-grained map requests will now be inundated with many more than the expected number of requests. What was once a single 1,000 by 1,000 pixel image could now be upward of thirty-six distinct 256 by 256 pixel images by the time you take into account the offscreen tiles needed to enable the smooth panning effect. Having to render thirty-five more images than originally expected, multiplied by each user of the system, could severely impact performance if the server is already at capacity.

To help mitigate this on the server side, MetaCarta introduced Tile-Cache.[16] TileCache is a facade that sits between the WMS client and the actual WMS server. It accepts standard WMS requests from the client and requests tiles of a predefined size from the back-end server. It then caches the tiles for future requests. The code is relatively new, but it is a novel solution to the problem of optimizing WMS performance. Tile-Cache and GeoServer make a pretty compelling one-two punch. Check out the documentation[17] for step-by-step instructions on getting the two up and running.

---

16. http://labs.metacarta.com/wms-c/
17. http://docs.codehaus.org/display/GEOSDOC/TileCache+Tutorial

Even though these OGC maps are served up from a web server, you aren't limited to simple browser-based clients. Let's leave the web tier and revisit the desktop again.

8.3 uDig

To take our newfound OGC knowledge out for a spin on the desktop, there is no better vehicle than uDig.[18] Short for User-friendly Desktop Internet GIS, uDig lives up to the promise of its moniker. As you can tell by the URL, it is sponsored by Refractions Research, the same folks who brought us PostGIS, GEOS, and others. With solid support for shapefiles and PostGIS, uDig allows you to seamlessly integrate those local resources with OGC web services.

After you install uDig, start it. If you are a Java developer, this screen might seem strangely familiar. uDig was built using the Rich Client Platform (RCP),[19] an offshoot of the Eclipse IDE project.

The first thing we'll want to do is add our WMS to the Catalog area at the bottom of the screen:

- Right-click the bottom pane, and choose Import.
- On the next screen, you could cheat and just import a Context document to get an instant map, but what fun would that be? Let's add our WMS server by clicking Data.
- Choose Web Map Server.
- Enter the URL to our server's GetCapabilities document:
  http://localhost:8888/geoserver/wms?service=wms&version=1.1.1&request=GetCapabilities.

If all goes well, you should see a new icon for our WMS. Expanding the list shows all the data layers. Right-click US States, and choose Add to Current Map. (See Figure 8.8, on the following page.)

Now let's try a WFS request. Right-click the Catalog area, and choose Import again. Walk through the same steps you did before, only this time choose Web Feature Service, and point it to: http://localhost:8888/geoserver/wfs?service=wfs&version=1.0.0&request=GetCapabilities. Add the Canadian Provinces layer to the current map.

---

18. http://udig.refractions.net/
19. http://wiki.eclipse.org/index.php/Rich_Client_Platform

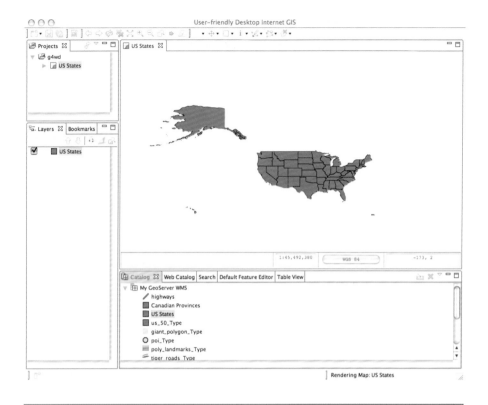

Figure 8.8: UDIG DISPLAYING WMS DATA

You might notice a bit of a lag adding this new layer compared to adding the last one. The difference, of course, is the amount of data being sent down to uDig from the server. A WMS request sends down an image that is a couple hundred kilobytes. A WFS request could be many megabytes. No additional rendering is necessary for the WMS image. Of course, no additional styling is possible, either. Right-click the US States layer in the list along the left part of the screen. Choosing Change Style reveals a limited list—only the SLDs you defined on the server. That makes sense, doesn't it? Now choose Change Style for the Canadian Provinces layer. You are presented with a screen that looks similar to the SLD editor provided by GeoServer. In fact, clicking the XML option shows you that you are, indeed, creating an SLD document. The only difference is that the data is being rendered on the client side instead of the server side.

Let's save this map. Right-click the Layers list, and choose Export. Choose OWS Context, give it a filename, and click Finish. If you open the resulting document side by side with the Context document we created in GeoServer, you'll notice a difference right away. The GeoServer document is a Web Map Context document. The uDig document is a *OWS Context* document.[20] Yup, yet *another* OGC standard. Old-school Context documents are limited to WMS layers. The newer OWS Context documents support WFS and WCS layers as well as WMS layers.

We won't take the time here to do it, but please experiment on your own with adding in local shapefiles. Create a new connection to your PostGIS database, and add some more data layers. Open some of the rasters you have. Pull in the weather data from the Iowa State WMS server. A good desktop viewer will allow you to pull in data from a variety of sources.

Now fire up QGIS. Notice that it, too, offers OGC support, as well as shapefiles, rasters, PostGIS, and so on. But if neither of these applications strikes your fancy, maybe OpenJUMP[21] will. Yet another option is OSSIM.[22] The list goes on and on.

8.4 Conclusion

Do you see what has happened here? Without realizing it, you now have a full set of resources at your fingertips. You're moving among vector and raster data sets with ease. Local files? No problem. Database access? Got it. Web services? Of course. Need a web client? You know two. Desktop client? You have nearly half a dozen installed and ready to go. Command-line utilities? You betcha!

You, my friend, are officially "in the club." If there was an official neo-geography card, you'd be carrying it.

In the next, final chapter of the book, we'll work through a real-world challenge. We'll take a set of data that has nothing but some street addresses and spatially enable it. We'll mix it in with our existing base-map data. We'll serve it up over the Web and call it a day. Ready for graduation?

---

20. http://www.opengeospatial.org/projects/initiatives/contextie
21. http://openjump.org/wiki/show/HomePage
22. http://www.eogeo.org/Projects/projects_wiki/OSSIM

Chapter 9

Bringing It All Together

Here we are—the last chapter of the book. Let's see whether we can bring all of the concepts we've learned up to this point together into one tidy bundle. We'll find a data set that is *nearly* ready to be plotted on a map. We'll geocode it, mix it in with some existing basemap data, stuff it into a spatial database, front it with some OGC web services, and present the users with a browser-based slippy map. Ready?

9.1 From CSV to SQL

As you dig through the data you have in your application, you'll find that some of it is *nearly* mappable. By that I mean that it has address/city/state/ZIP information, but it probably lacks the lat/long points necessary to plot it on a map. We saw geocoders in action in Section 4.4, *Temporal Analysis*, on page 66, so we know that it is possible to translate a human-readable street address into a lat/long coordinate pair. Before, Google and Terraserver-USA were geocoding for us under the covers. Let's take a nearly mappable data set and geocode it ourselves.

For our example here, we'll download a list of colleges and universities from the National Center for Educational Statistics.[1] Feel free to substitute your customer database, your personal address book, or anything else that has addresses but no lat/long points.

---

1. http://nces.ed.gov/

The NCES offers all sorts of finished reports, but we want to get our hands on the raw data. I'd give you a direct URL, but it is hidden behind a usage agreement screen, so you'll have to follow along step by step. Don't worry, it's not too bad:

1. Go to http://nces.ed.gov/ipedspas/dct.

2. You'll be greeted by an intimidating screen informing you that your login has expired. Don't worry—click Login.

3. On the next screen, click Guest Level.

4. A NCES data usage agreement will pop up. Once you have read it thoroughly, click I Agree to the Terms Above.

5. On the next screen (don't worry, we're almost there), click the Dataset Cutting Tool (DCT).

6. Click Download Data Files.

7. Pick the year 2005 and the "Institutional Characteristics and Student Charges" survey.

8. Download the first data file in the list, HD2005. (The file in the last column, Dictionary, contains a detailed description of each field. While you're pulling things down, you might as well grab this file as well.)

For all of your troubles, you are rewarded with a 700KB ZIP file. Unzip it to reveal a 2.2MB CSV file. Yup, comma-separated values. If you are on a Unix machine, you can type wc -l hd2005.csv to see that we have more than 7,000 rows of data. (Windows users will just have to trust me.) Unix folks can type head hd2005.csv to see what our raw materials are: 55 fields of potential map data. (Windows users are wondering why their OS won't let them do cool things like that.) We'll limit ourselves to the first six fields:

unitid: Unit ID

instnm: Institution name

addr: Address

city: City

stabbr: State

zip: ZIP code

There is plenty more interesting information hidden in there: phone numbers and web addresses, the name of the "chief administrator," the highest degree offered (two year, four year, graduate, PhD), the size of the staff, and even the enrollment totals. To keep things simple (you're probably already exhausted after finding the data to download), we'll just pop the schools onto a map and call it a day.

Choosing a Programming Language

I've tried to avoid showing bias toward any particular programming language up to this point. You might have guessed that I'm a Java guy from some of the desktop apps we used (ESRI ArcExplorer, uDig) or my choice of OGC servers (GeoServer). Yes, these are all implemented in Java, but I hope you'll agree that you didn't need to know a lick of Java in order to take full advantage of them.

At this point, however, we're going to need to write some code to transform the colleges CSV file into a format that can be inserted into Post-GIS. We're also going to need to do some geocoding to get the much needed lat/long points in place. To do this, I'm going to reach for my current programming language of choice: Groovy.[2] It offers the concise power of Ruby but runs on the Java Virtual Machine, thereby allowing me to leverage the rich Java ecosystem of open source libraries and utilities. I'm certainly not suggesting that Groovy is the only way we could get this task done. If Groovy isn't your language of choice, I hope the syntax is expressive enough to allow you to translate it to your mother tongue. If this is your first exposure to Groovy, it won't be a half-bad language tutorial either. (For step-by-step instructions for installing Groovy, see Appendix B, on page 241.)

Transforming the Data

We first need to transform our CSV file into SQL. Remember in Section 5.7, *Importing Data*, on page 110 how shp2pgsql transformed a shapefile into a text file filled with valid SQL INSERT statements? Our script, csv2pgsql, is modeled after the same tool. Now might be a good time to pull up one of those .sql files into the text editor of your choice to refresh your memory.

---

2. http://groovy.codehaus.org/

Red Dot Fever

Mapping Hacks (O'Reilly) author Schuyler Erle coined the phrase *red dot fever** to describe what we're doing here—sticking pushpins on a map. This is, admittedly, the most primitive thing we could possibly do in terms of cartography. If there was a Maslow's Hierarchy of Mapping Needs,† this would be on the very bottom tier of the pyramid.

Assessing the current crop of web mapping APIs offered by the "Big 3" (Google, Yahoo, and Microsoft), Schulyer laments, "At present, all that these map APIs offer is ultimately a way to put points on a map—what we've for years half-jokingly referred to as *red dot fever*.... Where is the broader palette for telling new and different stories on the Web with maps? Where is the bidirectionality, the interactivity, the wiki nature?" He wrote this in April 2006, but it is still an apt assessment of state-of-the-art mapping today. Which of those providers does more than offer you point-to-point driving directions? Not to take away from their considerable achievements, but they've only just scratched the surface of what can be done with web-based mapping.

Consider the broader palette that our colleges map could offer. We could create a choropleth separating out two-year from four-year institutions. How about showing large institutions vs. small? There are fields that identify a university as "historically black" or "tribal." There are fields that pertain to financial aid, as well as whether the school is public or private. Interested in a medical degree? How about institutions that have hospitals on-site? There is even a field that shows "degree of urbanization"—is the college located in a rural town or in the middle of a busy city?

Who is using the map? If you are the target audience, then who are you? Are you a high-school junior researching colleges? Do you want one that is far away from your home town, one that has a specific degree program, or one that has a major football program? Are you a parent looking for institutions that fit within your child's college fund budget? Are you a working professional looking to get a master's degree? Are you a professor

(Continued...)

---

*.   http://mappinghacks.com/2006/04/07/web-map-api-roundup/

†.   http://en.wikipedia.org/wiki/Maslow's_hierarchy_of_needs

---

Red Dot Fever (cont.)

looking for an institution to do post-graduate work? Are you the head of an institution wondering how you match up to others in your area? Are you a government official researching the institutions in your district for funding reasons?

Is this meant to be a read-only map, or do you want to solicit input from your users? Can they rate the colleges like they would books on Amazon? Can they update incorrect information? Can they add missing institutions?

All of those questions (and more) could be answered using this data set. We could move beyond simple "red dot fever" toward a map that conveys real information—a map that tells a story. We could make a dozen or more maps from this one data source that don't show a single dot. Keep that in mind as you put together your own maps.

But don't forget Maslow's pyramid either. You need to have red dots on a map before you can move up the Hierarchy of Mapping Needs and do any of that much cooler stuff. Schuyler won't yell at you if you are creating new maps where there were none. I promise. More maps are always a good thing. Just don't be fooled into thinking that your job is done once you have your first map up with red dots on it. Your work has just begun....

The file starts a SQL transaction with BEGIN, creates the table, inserts the data record by record, and then commits the transaction with END. Here is a truncated version of what we want to end up with:

```
BEGIN;
CREATE TABLE college (
"id" numeric PRIMARY KEY,
"name" varchar(255),
"address" varchar(255),
"city" varchar(255),
"state" varchar(255),
"zip" varchar(255)
);

insert into college ("id", "name", ...) values(...);
insert into college ("id", "name", ...) values(...);
insert into college ("id", "name", ...) values(...);
...
END;
```

Creating the Table

Let's start with creating the SQL to create the table. Create a file named csv2pgsql.groovy, and type the following:

```
outputFile = new File("college.sql")
if(outputFile.exists()){ outputFile.delete() }
ddl = """
BEGIN;
CREATE TABLE college (
"id" numeric PRIMARY KEY,
"name" varchar(255),
"address" varchar(255),
"city" varchar(255),
"state" varchar(255),
"zip" varchar(255)
);
"""

outputFile.append(ddl)
outputFile.append("END;")
```

We create a new file named college.sql and delete it if it already exists (we're going to be running this script over...and over...and over...). Next, we store the entire string to create the college table in the ddl variable. Groovy's triple quotes allow you to place anything inside of them without worrying about new lines or escaping internal quotes. Finally, we append the ddl variable to the output file and end the transaction.

Groovy code doesn't require compilation, so type groovy csv2pgsql to run it. Look at the contents of the resulting college.sql file. Does everything seem OK? Then let's hand it to PostgreSQL to test it:

```
psql -U postgres -d g4wd -f college.sql
```

Next, log into our database—psql -U postgres -d g4wd. \d should reveal our new table. \d college should confirm that all of the fields are in order. Type drop table college; to make sure that we are ready for the next run. If you try to create a table that already exists, you'll see the following error message:

```
BEGIN
psql:college.sql:10: ERROR:  relation "college" already exists
ROLLBACK
```

It doesn't do any permanent damage. It's just annoying. You'll see it plenty of times in this chapter. You'll get used to it.

Inserting Records

Now let's tackle getting those row values converted to SQL INSERT statements. The irony is both are comma-delimited strings, but each is *just* different enough to require a bit of massaging.

Before we write the code, let's create a smaller sample data set. Copy the first six lines out of hd2007.csv into a file named sample.csv. Once we're confident that our parsing algorithm works on six rows, we'll turn it loose on all 7,000. Now, let's add some new code to csv2pgsql.groovy:

```
outputFile = new File("college.sql")
if(outputFile.exists()){ outputFile.delete() }
ddl = """
BEGIN;
CREATE TABLE college (
"id" numeric PRIMARY KEY,
"name" varchar(255),
"address" varchar(255),
"city" varchar(255),
"state" varchar(255),
"zip" varchar(255)
);
"""

outputFile.append(ddl)
// new code
//
insertStart = """insert into college ("id", "name", "address",
                                "city", "state", "zip") values("""
insertEnd = ");"

counter = 0
inputFile = new File("sample.csv")
inputFile.splitEachLine(","){ tokens ->
  if(counter == 0) {
    /* skip the headers */
    counter++
  }
  else{
    println "${counter++} ${tokens[1]}" //show what is going on
    insertMiddle = ""
    for(i in 0..5){
      insertMiddle += "${tokens[i]},"
    }
    insertMiddle = insertMiddle[0..-2] //strip off trailing comma
    outputFile.append("${insertStart}${insertMiddle}${insertEnd}\n")
  }
} // end new code

outputFile.append("END;")
```

We start by creating insertStart and insertEnd variables. Note that Groovy's triple quotes come to the rescue once again in insertStart—no escaping internal quotes for us, thank you very much. Next, we open sample.csv and walk through it line by line. splitEachLine tokenizes the line on the comma character and puts the results in an array named tokens. The remainder of the code creates the data for the values part of the INSERT statement, sandwiches it between the boilerplate start and finish, and writes it to our output file.

Yes, it pains me that we start with a comma-delimited string, tokenize the string, and then turn it back into a comma-delimited string. Since we are interested in only the first six fields, there is really no other way do this, as redundant as it might seem.

Don't forget that until recently programmers were evaluated by the number of lines of code (LOC) they produced. Old habits die hard, I guess.

Run groovy csv2groovy, and look at the resulting college.sql file. Look good? Let's see what PostgreSQL thinks about it:

```
$ psql -U postgres -d g4wd -f college.sql
BEGIN
psql:college.sql:10: NOTICE:  CREATE TABLE / PRIMARY KEY will
create implicit index "college_pkey" for table "college"
CREATE TABLE
psql:college.sql:11: ERROR:  column "Community College of the
Air Force" does not exist
LINE 1: ..., "address", "city", "state", "zip") values(00636,"Community...
                                                               ^
psql:college.sql:12: ERROR:  current transaction is aborted,
commands ignored until end of transaction block
psql:college.sql:13: ERROR:  current transaction is aborted,
commands ignored until end of transaction block
psql:college.sql:14: ERROR:  current transaction is aborted,
commands ignored until end of transaction block
psql:college.sql:15: ERROR:  current transaction is aborted,
commands ignored until end of transaction block
ROLLBACK
```

D'oh! What happened? I'll wait here while you copy the error messages into a search engine and research the problem.

What's that you say? PostgreSQL expects table and field names to be surrounded by double quotes but string values to be surrounded by single quotes? Excellent work.

Let's see whether we can fix that:

```
inputFile = new File("sample.csv")
use(Fixer){
  inputFile.splitEachLine(","){ tokens ->
    if(counter == 0) {
      /* skip the headers */
      counter++
    }
    else{
      println "${counter++} ${tokens[1].fixQuote()}" //show what is going on
      insertMiddle = ""
      for(i in 0..5){
        insertMiddle += "${tokens[i].fixQuote()},"
      }
      insertMiddle = insertMiddle[0..-2] //strip off trailing comma
      outputFile.append("${insertStart}${insertMiddle}${insertEnd}\n")
    }
  }
}
outputFile.append("END;")

class Fixer{
  static String fixQuote(String self){
    if(self.startsWith("\"")){
      return "'" + self[1..-2] + "'"
    }
    else{
      return self
    }
  }
}
```

class Fixer defines a method fixQuote that will flip a double quote into a single quote. Strings in Groovy can be treated like an array of characters. self[0] returns the first character of the string—in this case, the offending double quote. So self[1] is the next character after the double quote. If the first element in an array is [0], what would you expect [-1] to be? In Groovy, array element notation "wraps around," so [-1] is actually the last character in the array—the other offending double quote. self[-2] is one character in from the last character, again skipping the poor, misunderstood double quote.

Yes, RegEx gurus could've done the same thing in one mass of unpronounceable characters. They are also usually fluent in Klingon. Neither bodes well for the readability of their code or their prospects for a date this Friday night. Any other questions? I didn't think so....

Surrounding the chunk of code with a use(Fixer) block bolts the fixQuote method onto every object inside of it. In our case, we use it on the Strings returned from the token array. What you are witnessing here is Groovy's version of metaprogramming. It is far less elegant than the metaprogramming capabilities of Ruby or JavaScript but light years ahead of what native Java has to offer. At the end of the day, it seems like a reasonable compromise to me.

Let's rerun this code and see whether it meets PostgreSQL's standards of excellence:

```
$ psql -U postgres -d g4wd -f college.sql
BEGIN
psql:college.sql:10: NOTICE:  CREATE TABLE / PRIMARY KEY
will create implicit index "college_pkey" for table "college"
CREATE TABLE
INSERT 0 1
INSERT 0 1
INSERT 0 1
INSERT 0 1
INSERT 0 1
COMMIT
```

All right, it passed the test on the sample set. Let's see how it does on the full data set. Change the line inputFile = new File("sample.csv") to read inputFile = new File("hd2005.csv"), and rerun it:

```
$ groovy csv2pgsql
...
6593 'Illinois Welding School'
6594 'Institute of Network Technology'
6595 'Instituto Pre-Vocacional e Indust de Puerto Rico'
6596 'Instituto Tecnologico Empresarial'
Caught: java.lang.reflect.InvocationTargetException
        at c4$_run_closure1_closure2.doCall(c4.groovy:32)
        at c4$_run_closure1.doCall(c4.groovy:23)
        at c4$_run_closure1.doCall(c4.groovy)
        at c4.run(c4.groovy:22)
        at c4.main(c4.groovy)
```

Wow. Every time I catch a java.lang.reflect.InvocationTargetException, the first thing I do is open up my source data file and look at line 6596:

```
443119,
"Instituto Tecnologico Empresarial",
"Munoz Rivera St #22,",
"Trujillo Alto",
"PR",
"00976"
```

Do you see it? java.lang.reflect.InvocationTargetException translates to "Dude, you forgot to take into account embedded commas in your double-quoted fields. Check out that trailing comma after 'Munoz Rivera St #22'—it is really harshing my mellow." (I always imagine that the JVM talks like the turtle in *Finding Nemo*. It keeps me from throwing my computer out of the window when it spews indecipherable nonsense like java.lang.reflect.InvocationTargetException.)

So, my naive reliance on splitEachLine caught up with me less than 500 lines from the end of the data file. Of course, realistically this bug messed up plenty of other earlier records—it was only the bizarre occurrence of a malformed field with a comma that probably shouldn't be there in the first place that tipped us off at all.

Let's trap for embedded commas in quoted fields by replacing the stock splitEachLine with a slightly more intelligent custom function:

```
inputFile = new File("hd2005.csv")
use(Fixer){
  inputFile.eachLine{ line ->
    String[] tokens = line.getNext(6)
    if(counter == 0) {
      /* skip the headers */
      counter++
    }
    else{
      println "${counter++} ${tokens[1].fixQuote()}" //show what's going on
      insertMiddle = ""
      for(i in 0..5){
        insertMiddle += "${tokens[i].fixQuote()},"
      }
      insertMiddle = insertMiddle[0..-2] //strip off trailing comma
      outputFile.append("${insertStart}${insertMiddle}${insertEnd}\n")
    }
  }
}

outputFile.append("END;")

class Fixer{
  static String fixQuote(String self){
    if(self.startsWith("\"")){
      return "'" + self[1..-2] + "'"
    }
    else{
      return self
    }
  }
}
```

```
  static String[] getNext(String self, int numberOf){
    def list = []
    def st = new StringTokenizer(self, ",")
    numberOf.times{
      def thisToken = st.nextToken()
      while(thisToken.startsWith("\"") && !thisToken.endsWith("\"") ){
        thisToken += "," + st.nextToken()
      }
      list << thisToken
    }
    return list
  }
}
```

class Fixer now has a second method: getNext. You pass it an arbitrary number, and it returns an array with exactly that number of elements. If an element starts with a double quote, the while loop appends the next token in the list to it until it ends with a double quote as well. This code could still be more robust—it fails if you pass in a empty double quote (""). It also fails if you pass in a token that starts with a leading comma. But in true pragmatic (lazy?) fashion, this code works for the immediate data set, so I'll leave those additional enhancements for a rainy day.

Notice that inside the use(Fixer) block, we call inputFile.eachLine{ line -> instead of inputFile.splitEachLine(","){ tokens ->. Other than that and the very next line—String[] tokens = line.getNext(6)—the rest of the code remains unchanged. Run this latest revision, and insert the data into PostgreSQL:

```
INSERT 0 1
INSERT 0 1
psql:college.sql:165: ERROR:  syntax error at or near "Hall"
LINE 1: ...102614,'University of Alaska Fairbanks','Signers' Hall','Fai...
```

Of course—if embedded commas tripped us up, why not embedded single quotes as well? The good news is our final fix for parsing our persnickety CSV file is a single additional line of code:

```
static String fixQuote(String self){
  self = self[0] + self[1..-2].replaceAll("\'", "\'\'") + self[-1]

  if(self.startsWith("\"")){
    return "'" + self[1..-2] + "'"
  }
  else{
    return self
  }
}
```

Geocoders and Guesstimates

When you type a street address into your web browser and get a point back on a map, it seems so *definitive*. The reality is that most times the point on the map is nothing more than a "best guess."

The TIGER data set is good example of what most geocoders rely on. It contains street segments that represent a stretch of road. The important nonspatial attributes are the start and end addresses. In other words, a single POLYLINE might represent Main Street with addresses in the 100–200 range. When you search for "123 Main Street," the geocoder finds the road segment and then interpolates where 123 most likely is along the line segment. Only in rare cases do geocoders have actual point data. Even then, what does the point correspond to? The centroid of your tax lot? Your driveway? Your front door?

Let's add one more wrinkle: address normalization. Humans don't have any trouble recognizing that "123 Main Street" and "123 Main St" are the same address. But what about 123 Main? Is there a Main Street and a Main Boulevard in the same city? Is there an East Main Street and a West Main Street? Is East Main Street the same as plain old Main? And what about the cases where Main is also Highway 651 and Joe Football Star Memorial Blvd? It makes my teeth itch just talking about it—imagine if geocoding software had teeth.

When a website doesn't find the address I'm looking for, I don't blame it too much. I vary the words (East –> E). I drop words and add words in a friendly attempt to help the geocoder out. I try not to be like the ugly American in a foreign country who repeats the same unintelligible phrase over and over again, each time slower and more loudly. What is my other option? Picking up one of those analog dead-tree devices commonly known as the *Yellow Pages*? I'd rather take my horse-drawn carriage to my barber/doctor for a leaching.

Using the Java-native replaceAll method on the String does the trick. Yes, I am well aware that the first argument of replaceAll is a regular expression. Live long and prosper, my Vulcan friend.

9.2 Geocoding Your Data

So, in 65 lines of Groovy code we've gone from CSV data in a flat file to SQL statements and 7,018 records in a database. The problem with these records is that they are still just *nearly* spatial. Let's programmatically geocode the addresses to get lat/long points that we can actually map.

Remember the U.S. Census Bureau TIGER data set we talked about back in Section 2.8, *The Downloadable States of America*, on page 20? We've been working with the states' boundary shapefile ever since.

The U.S. Census Bureau data goes deeper than simple state outlines—much deeper. But rather than having to download the data and wrestle with those funky ASCII file formats yourself, what if someone had done all of the dirty work for you and exposed it as a friendly website. What if, indeed?

Fire up your web browser, and visit Geocoder.us.[3] This website, maintained by the authors of *Mapping Hacks* (O'Reilly), is the friendliest way to interact with the TIGER data set without having to actually download it. (See Figure 9.1, on the next page.)

Enter your street address—see whether the U.S. Census Bureau knew where you lived back in 2000. (Remember, the U.S. Census Bureau data is updated every ten years.)

Although working with the website interactively is fun, it would get less fun typing in 7,019 addresses by hand. Luckily, Geocoder.us offers web services as well as a website. Scroll to the bottom of the home page and look for the section titled "How Can I Use It?" It offers SOAP, XML-RPC, RESTful, and even CSV-based services.

---

3. http://geocoder.us

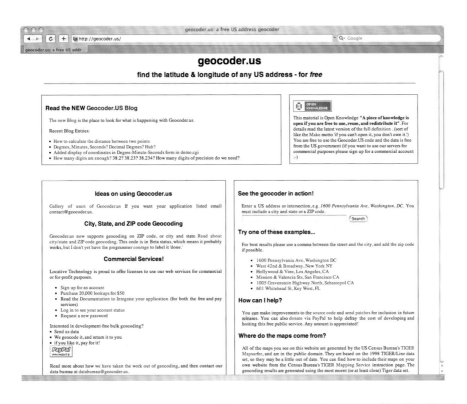

Figure 9.1: GEOCODER.US

Grab the first address from our sample.csv file, and give the RESTful web service a whirl:

```
$ wget -O result.xml
  http://rpc.geocoder.us/service/rest?
  address=130+W+Maxwell+Blvd,Montgomery,AL,36112-6613
```

```
$ cat result.xml
<?xml version="1.0"?>
<rdf:RDF
  xmlns:dc="http://purl.org/dc/elements/1.1/"
  xmlns:geo="http://www.w3.org/2003/01/geo/wgs84_pos#"
  xmlns:rdf="http://www.w3.org/1999/02/22-rdf-syntax-ns#"
>
<geo:Point rdf:nodeID="aid59839714">
    <dc:description>130 Maxwell Blvd E, Montgomery AL 36112</dc:description>
    <geo:long>-86.347754</geo:long>
    <geo:lat>32.379938</geo:lat>
</geo:Point>
</rdf:RDF>
```

Although it's cool that we can get the data back as XML, we're already pretty good at dealing with CSV data. Try this instead:

```
$ wget -O result.csv
  http://rpc.geocoder.us/service/csv?
  address=130+W+Maxwell+Blvd,Montgomery,AL,36112-6613

$ cat result.csv
32.379938,-86.347754,130 Maxwell Blvd E,Montgomery,AL,36112
```

We'll perform this query in code in just a moment. Before we move on, do you notice any subtle differences between the address that we submitted and the address that got returned? Our address got normalized. But are "W Maxwell Blvd" and "Maxwell Blvd E" truly the same location? Type the following into your web browser:

```
http://maps.google.com/maps?q=130+Maxwell+Blvd+E,Montgomery,AL,36112
```

On the resulting map, "E Maxwell" and "W Maxwell" fall on either side of the info window. I feel reasonably comfortable that the address got geocoded correctly. (Just for grins, try submitting it as "W Maxwell" to Google. Notice that it gets confused as well.)

OK, let's try the next address on the list:

```
$ wget -O result2.csv
  http://rpc.geocoder.us/service/csv?
  address=4107+Meridian+St,Normal,AL,35762

$ cat result2.csv
2: couldn't find this address! sorry
```

Curses! Foiled on our second attempt. What does Google have to say about that?

```
http://maps.google.com/maps?q=4107+Meridian+St,Normal,AL,35762
```

Google pulls it right up. Maybe we should just use Google's geocoder[4] then. The documentation shows examples of using it in JavaScript as well as an HTTP GET request. You can get the results back as CSV, XML, KML, or JSON. To use it, all you have to do is register for a free API key.[5] Here's the request to the Google geocoder:

```
wget -O google.csv
    "http://maps.google.com/maps/geo?q=4107+Meridian+St,Normal,AL,35762
    &output=csv&key=[YOUR KEY]"
```

---

4. http://www.google.com/apis/maps/documentation/#Geocoding_Examples
5. http://www.google.com/apis/maps/signup.html

And the response?

`602,0,0,0`

The first value is the return code. The second is the level of accuracy. The third is the latitude, and the fourth is the longitude. So, what does 602 mean? Address not found. Huh? But we found it on the map. Google *clearly knows where it is*. What gives?

I'll do the Internet research for you this time. In a knowledge base entry titled "Why does the API geocoder provide different locations than Google Maps?"[6] the first sentence says it all: "The API geocoder and Google Maps geocoder rely on two different data sources." (Feel free to mumble under your breath. I did....) This is pure conjecture on my part, but it sure sounds like a licensing issue to me. Google buys its geodata from commercial providers, and those providers most likely put some restrictions on how Google could expose the data. Google Maps? No problem. A programmatic API? Not so fast, Bub....

OK, let's give it one more try. Yahoo also offers a free geocoder.[7] Like Google, you must register for a free application ID. The results come back to you as XML or PHP:

```
$ wget -O yahoo.xml
  "http://api.local.yahoo.com/MapsService/V1/geocode?
   street=4107+Meridian+St&city=Normal&state=AL&zip=35762
   &appid=[YOUR KEY]"
```

```
$ tidy -i -xml yahoo.xml
<ResultSet xmlns:xsi="http://www.w3.org/2001/XMLSchema-instance"
xmlns="urn:yahoo:maps"
xsi:schemaLocation="urn:yahoo:maps
http://api.local.yahoo.com/MapsService/V1/GeocodeResponse.xsd">

  <Result precision="zip">
    <Latitude>34.7924</Latitude>
    <Longitude>-86.5718</Longitude>
    <Address></Address>
    <City>NORMAL</City>
    <State>AL</State>
    <Zip>35762</Zip>
    <Country>US</Country>
  </Result>
```

---

6. http://code.google.com/support/bin/answer.py?answer=60738\&topic=10946
7. http://developer.yahoo.com/maps/rest/V1/geocode.html

Aha! We got a hit this time. But wait a minute—where is the address? Notice the precision attribute in the result element? That means that Yahoo tried to geocode the address and failed, so it fell back to geocoding the ZIP code. If you go back and look more closely at the Google Maps result—the one that worked—notice anything different about the address? The address we submitted was "4107 Meridian St, Normal, AL 35762." The response we got back was "4107 Meridian St N, Huntsville, AL 35811." That's not only a different street address but a completely different city and ZIP code as well. The map shows the point right on the edge of campus, so it's mostly likely a good hit, but this demonstrates what a tricky game geocoding is.

As a last-ditch attempt, you could geocode the data by hand. InfoSports[8] provides an interesting service. They put up a Google Maps map and allow you to click the map to find the lat/long yourself. There is no way for you to enter an address, so it doesn't help us much. It is just an interesting example of a point-and-click geocoder.

Coding the Geocoding

Since there doesn't seem to be a silver bullet for our geocoding problems, let's use our first choice—Geocoder.us—on the full data set and see how many hits we get. I'm not expecting 100%, but I hope we'll do better than the 50% we got in two attempts.

Let's run our newly Geoserver.us-enabled Groovy script against our sample set and see how we do:

```
$ groovy csv2pgsql
1 'Community College of the Air Force'
        32.379938,-86.347754,130 Maxwell Blvd E,Montgomery,AL,36112
2 'Alabama A & M University'
        2: couldn't find this address! sorry
3 'University of Alabama at Birmingham'
        2: couldn't find this address! sorry
4 'Southern Christian University'
        32.382580,-86.172265,1200 Taylor Rd N,Montgomery,AL,36117
        32.365395,-86.171722,1200 Taylor Rd,Montgomery,AL,36117
5 'University of Alabama in Huntsville'
        34.723716,-86.644094,301 Sparkman Dr NW,Huntsville,AL,35805

Started: Sat Apr 07 13:17:02 MDT 2007
  Ended: Sat Apr 07 13:17:58 MDT 2007
Date: Sat Apr 07 13:17:58 MDT 2007
```

---

8. http://www.infosports.com/m/map.htm

```
Total: 5 Found: 3, 60.0% Not Found: 2, 40.0%
```

The good news is that our data now contains lat/long points. The bad news is that our script took a much longer time to run (averaging about ten to twelve seconds per request—the full run took me more than thirty hours). For the purposes of this chapter, let's stick with the sample.csv file. (You can find the full results from Geocoder.us in college-gecoder.us.sql.)

Let's look at the code that accomplished this. To start, we expanded the ddl statement to include the new fields: lat, long, and the normalized addresses returned from the geocoder. Not shown here, we also expanded the fields in the SQL INSERT statement:

```
outputFile = new File("college.sql")
if(outputFile.exists()){ outputFile.delete() }
ddl = """
BEGIN;
CREATE TABLE college (
"id" numeric PRIMARY KEY,
"name" varchar(255),
"address" varchar(255),
"city" varchar(255),
"state" varchar(255),
"zip" varchar(255),
"lat" varchar(255),
"lon" varchar(255),
"address_n" varchar(255),
"city_n" varchar(255),
"state_n" varchar(255),
"zip_n" varchar(255));
"""
```

The next thing we did was create an Addr class. This not only is a convenient place to store our values—we can also hang some Addr-specific functions off of it as well. It just didn't seem to make sense to bolt a geocode method onto everything using metaprogramming. Since we need to have specific fields named a specific way, it just made more sense to create a class. Here are the fields of the class. Notice that we created a constructor that pulls the values out of our existing tokens array and populates the class.

```
class Addr{
  String id
  String name
  String address
  String city
  String state
  String zip
```

```
String lat
String lon
String addressNormalized
String cityNormalized
String stateNormalized
String zipNormalized

public Addr(String[] tokens){
  id = tokens[0].noQuote()
  name = tokens[1].noQuote()
  address = tokens[2].noQuote()
  city = tokens[3].noQuote()
  state = tokens[4].noQuote()
  zip = tokens[5].noQuote()
}

  ...
}
```

And here is the geocode method that takes the values and sends them up to Geocoder.us:

```
public boolean geocode(){
  def urlStart = "http://rpc.geocoder.us/service/csv?address="
  def urlBody = "${address},${city},${state},${zip}"
  def urlEncoded = urlStart + URLEncoder.encode(urlBody, "UTF-8")
  new URL(urlEncoded).eachLine{ line ->
    println "\t${line}"
    if(line.startsWith("2")){
      addressNormalized = "NOT FOUND"
    }
    else{
      def tokens = line.getNext(6)
      lat = tokens[0]
      lon = tokens[1]
      addressNormalized = tokens[2].fixQuote()
      cityNormalized = tokens[3].fixQuote()
      stateNormalized = tokens[4].fixQuote()
      zipNormalized = tokens[5].fixQuote()
    }
  }

  return addressNormalized != "NOT FOUND"
}
```

urlStart should look familiar—that is the address of the web service. url-Body strings the variables together in the proper order. Before we can send it to Geocoder.us, we need to URLEncode[9] the string.

---

9. http://en.wikipedia.org/wiki/Urlencode

This converts spaces to +, commas to %2C, and so on. URLEncoder is a native Java class that takes care of the logistics for us.

```
BEFORE:
130 W Maxwell Blvd,Montgomery,AL,36112-6613

AFTER:
130+W+Maxwell+Blvd%2CMontgomery%2CAL%2C36112-6613
```

Once we have a well-formed URL, Groovy makes it easy for us to call the web service. new URL(urlEncoded) creates the call. eachLine makes the call and, as the name implies, allows us to iterate through the response line by line. You may have noticed earlier that the geocoder could potentially return more than one line. (See "Southern Christian University.") Our code traps for multiline responses, storing the last line in the Addr object.

Let's see all of this in action. We create a new Addr, passing in the tokens array. We call the geocode method. Finally, we call toSql and append it to the insertMiddle string:

```
use(Fixer){
  inputFile.eachLine{ line ->
    String[] tokens = line.getNext(6)
    if(counter == 0) {
      /* skip the headers */
      counter++
    }
    else{
      println "${counter++} ${tokens[1].fixQuote()}" //show what is going on
      addr = new Addr(tokens)
      addr.geocode() ? found++ : notFound++
      insertMiddle = ""
      for(i in 0..5){
        insertMiddle += "${tokens[i].fixQuote()},"
      }
      insertMiddle += addr.toSql()
      //insertMiddle = insertMiddle[0..-2] //strip off trailing comma
      outputFile.append("${insertStart}${insertMiddle}${insertEnd}\n")

      //write out current status
      statusFile = new File("status.txt")
      statusFile.append(new Status(counter, found, notFound).toString())
    }
  }
}
```

9.3 Adding PostGIS Fields

Our script is a whiz at creating String fields. Why don't we try creating the spatial fields now? Recall from Section 5.3, *Adding Geometric Columns by Hand*, on page 102, that AddGeometryColumn inserts the field into both your table and the geometry_columns table:

```
SELECT AddGeometryColumn('college','the_geom','4326','POINT',2);
```

Once we have the geometry column in place, we need to tweak our SQL INSERT statement to call GeomFromText:

```
GeomFromText('POINT(-104.98716 39.73909)', 4326)
```

Here is our new geocode method that creates a well-formed SQL string if the geocoder returns data, or otherwise it simply makes the field null:

```
public boolean geocode(){
  def urlStart = "http://rpc.geocoder.us/service/csv?address="
  def urlBody = "${address},${city},${state},${zip}"
  def urlEncoded = urlStart + URLEncoder.encode(urlBody, "UTF-8")
  new URL(urlEncoded).eachLine{ line ->
    println "\t${line}"
    if(line.startsWith("2")){
      addressNormalized = "NOT FOUND"
      theGeom = 'null'
    }
    else{
      def tokens = line.getNext(6)
      lat = tokens[0]
      lon = tokens[1]
      addressNormalized = tokens[2].fixQuote()
      cityNormalized = tokens[3].fixQuote()
      stateNormalized = tokens[4].fixQuote()
      zipNormalized = tokens[5].fixQuote()
      theGeom = "GeomFromText('POINT(${lon} ${lat})', ${epsg})"
    }
  }

  return addressNormalized != "NOT FOUND"
}
```

Run your code one last time. Type psql -U postgres -d g4wd -f college.sql to insert your data. It took less than 200 lines of Groovy to go from the raw data from the NCES to a fully populated PostGIS database. It would've been less than 150 lines if I hadn't been so chatty with all of the comments, printlns, and result files. Overall, that's not too shabby.

The final statistics for Geocoder.us aren't too shabby, either. Out of 7,018 records, it returned addresses for 5,103, or just shy of 75%. The downside is that the run took more than thirty hours to complete.

A Quick Look at Yahoo

Even though it is not open source (although it is free), here is the code to do the same thing using Yahoo's geocoder. Yahoo adds two fields to the results—precision and warning—that allow us to capture some additional metadata about the process. Since Yahoo returns XML instead of CSV, our geocode method changes slightly:

```
public boolean geocode(){
  def urlStart = "http://api.local.yahoo.com/MapsService/V1/geocode?appid=[YOUR KEY]"
  def urlBody = "&street=" + URLEncoder.encode(address, "UTF-8")
  urlBody += "&city=" + URLEncoder.encode(city, "UTF-8")
  urlBody += "&state=" + URLEncoder.encode(state, "UTF-8")
  urlBody += "&zip=" + URLEncoder.encode(zip, "UTF-8")
  def urlEncoded = urlStart + urlBody
  def queryResponse = new URL(urlEncoded).openConnection()

  if(queryResponse.responseCode == 200){
    def xml = queryResponse.content.text
    def ns = new groovy.xml.Namespace("urn:yahoo:maps");
    def resultSet = new XmlParser().parseText(xml)[ns.Result]
    resultSet.each{
      lat = it[ns.Latitude].text()
      lon = it[ns.Longitude].text()
      addressNormalized = it[ns.Address].text()
      cityNormalized = it[ns.City].text()
      stateNormalized = it[ns.State].text()
      zipNormalized = it[ns.Zip].text()
      precision = it['@precision']
      warning = it['@warning']
      theGeom = "GeomFromText('POINT(${lon} ${lat})', ${epsg})"
    }
    println "\t${precision}"
  }
  else{
    addressNormalized = "NOT FOUND"
    theGeom = 'null'
    warning = "${queryResponse.responseCode}:${queryResponse.responseMessage}"
  }

  return addressNormalized != "NOT FOUND"
}
```

More noteworthy are Yahoo's stats. The run took just more than thirty minutes, as opposed to thirty hours with Geocoder.us. Yahoo's geocoder limits you to roughly 5,000 requests a day, so that thirty minutes is split over two application IDs—I mean two days, of course. Yahoo gave us more hits compared to Geocoder.us as well. Yahoo matched 88% of the addresses compared to 73% for Geocoder.us. Rather than returning null when an address couldn't be matched, Yahoo usually

Figure 9.2: CREATING THE COLLEGE FEATURETYPE IN GEOSERVER

returned ZIP code data, which is better than nothing. The sixteen "null" values returned a "400: Bad Request." Those mostly are Puerto Rico addresses.

```
# select precision, count(*) as total, ( count(*) / 7018.0 ) * 100 as percent
  from college group by precision order by total desc;
 precision | total |         percent
-----------+-------+------------------------
 address   |  6174 | 87.97378170418922770000
 zip       |   476 | 6.78255913365631234000
 street    |   204 | 2.90681105728127671700
 zip+4     |   111 | 1.58164719293245939000
 zip+2     |    37 | 0.52721573097748646300
 null      |    16 | 0.22798518096323739000
(6 rows)
```

For legal reasons,[10] we can't distribute the Yahoo addresses. The addresses came from a variety of commercial data sets and are made available via the geocoder "for personal use only" and "not for resale or redistribution." Geocoder.us uses the U.S. Census Bureau data, which is in the public domain, which means we are free to distribute it as we like. Drop the colleges table one last time, and type psql -U postgres -d g4wd -f college-gecoder.us.sql.

---

10. http://help.yahoo.com/l/us/yahoo/maps/using/maps-24.html

And What About a Non-PostGIS Solution?

Of course, this isn't the only way we could've solved this problem. I like the fact that we ended up with an ASCII text file full of SQL INSERTs. That makes it easy to store the results in source control, it's fully language-independent, and it is consistent with our other familiar tool, shp2pgsql.

Given different requirements, I might have used the PostGIS JDBC driver[11] to insert the data directly into the database. Or perhaps our final destination wasn't PostGIS at all. If I needed to convert the data into a shapefile, I would've reached for GeoTools[12]—the Java API that powers many popular Java-based projects such as GeoServer and uDig. If I needed to pass the data off to a remote server, I could've used WFS-T. As you can see, having a variety of tools in your tool belt allows you to choose the proper one to get the job done.

9.4 Setting Up OGC Services

Getting the data into PostGIS was the hard part. Now that we have GeoServer installed and configured, adding one more FeatureType is a breeze. Click Config > Data > FeatureType. (See Figure 9.2, on the preceding page.) Generate the bounding box, and click Submit. Apply and save the server settings in the upper-left corner. Finally, visit the website[13] to see the magic dots appear. (See Figure 9.3, on the following page.)

Although setting up the raw data is easy, styling it will generally take up the lion's share of your time. And once you begin adding multiple map layers, styling them all so that they use complementary color schemes is no small task. In the final example, I use the US States layer, our newly created Colleges layer, and a number of layers from the Colorado Department of Transportation—highways, cities, and lakes. Each needs to be styled in a way that it blends with the other map layers. (As you'll see in just a moment, I actually create two styles per layer: one with labels and one without.)

For example, let's put together a nice, elegant style for the US States layer that displays the state name. For inspiration, we'll "borrow" (open source code word for "steal") an existing SLD from the GeoServer wiki:[14]

---

11. http://www.postgis.org/download/postgis.jar

12. http://geotools.codehaus.org/

13. http://localhost:8888/geoserver/preview/g4wd_college.html

14. http://docs.codehaus.org/display/GEOSDOC/ComplexLabelingExample

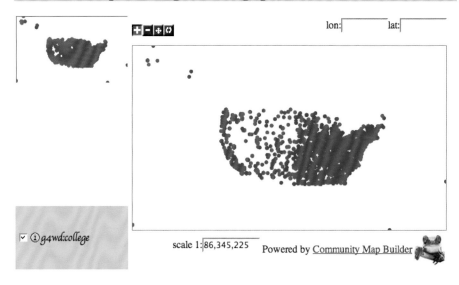

Figure 9.3: Previewing the College FeatureType in GeoServer

```xml
<StyledLayerDescriptor version="1.0.0"
  xsi:schemaLocation="http://www.opengis.net/sld StyledLayerDescriptor.xsd"
  xmlns="http://www.opengis.net/sld" xmlns:ogc="http://www.opengis.net/ogc"
  xmlns:xlink="http://www.w3.org/1999/xlink"
  xmlns:xsi="http://www.w3.org/2001/XMLSchema-instance">
<NamedLayer> <Name> us_states_labeled </Name>
  <UserStyle>
    <FeatureTypeStyle>
      <FeatureTypeName>Feature</FeatureTypeName>

      <!-- This rule fills in the Polygons -->
      <Rule>
        <PolygonSymbolizer>
          <Fill>
            <CssParameter name="fill">
              <ogc:Literal>#EBF8C4</ogc:Literal>
            </CssParameter>
            <CssParameter name="fill-opacity">
              <ogc:Literal>1.0</ogc:Literal>
            </CssParameter>
          </Fill>
          <Stroke><CssParameter name="fill">#A1CE18</CssParameter></Stroke>
        </PolygonSymbolizer>
      </Rule>
```

```
<!-- second rule is the state names
   a) we went them centered on the polygon centroid
   b) we want a 'halo' around them so they are easier to read
   c) we put a little space around them so the map isn't cluttered
-->
<Rule>
  <TextSymbolizer>
    <Label><ogc:PropertyName>name</ogc:PropertyName></Label>

    <Font>
      <CssParameter name="font-family">Times New Roman</CssParameter>
      <CssParameter name="font-style">Normal</CssParameter>
      <CssParameter name="font-size">18</CssParameter>
      <CssParameter name="font-weight">bold</CssParameter>
    </Font>

    <!-- this centers the label on the polygon's centroid-->
    <LabelPlacement>
      <PointPlacement>
        <AnchorPoint>
          <AnchorPointX>0.5</AnchorPointX>
          <AnchorPointY>0.5</AnchorPointY>
        </AnchorPoint>
      </PointPlacement>
    </LabelPlacement>

    <!--  make the label easy to read-->
    <Halo>
      <Radius>
            <ogc:Literal>2</ogc:Literal>
          </Radius>
      <Fill>
        <CssParameter name="fill">#FFFFFF</CssParameter>
        <CssParameter name="fill-opacity">0.85</CssParameter>
      </Fill>
    </Halo>

    <Fill><CssParameter name="fill">#749A00</CssParameter></Fill>

    <VendorOption name="group">yes</VendorOption>

    <!-- add a little extra space around the labels so the map
         isn't cluttered -->
    <VendorOption name="spaceAround">5</VendorOption>

  </TextSymbolizer>
</Rule>
      </FeatureTypeStyle>
    </UserStyle>
  </NamedLayer>
</StyledLayerDescriptor>
```

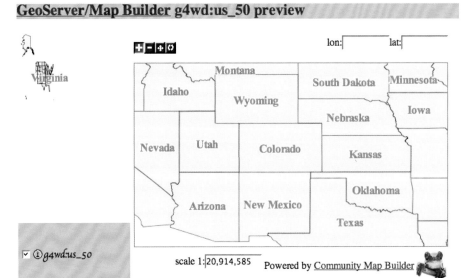

Figure 9.4: AN ELEGANT SLD STYLE FOR US_50

Applying this SLD to our us_50 layer in PostGIS yields a nice-looking map in Mapbuilder. (See Figure 9.4.) There aren't enough trees in the Amazon forest to print all of the SLDs for this example. The states SLD is representative of what is going on in the rest of 'em (including the Colleges layer), but just because we can't reproduce them here doesn't mean that you are off the hook. Your homework is to study the rest of them to make sure you understand how they are put together.

9.5 Tiling vs. Styling

So, the U.S. states looked pretty good in Mapbuilder. Since SLDs are a well-understood standard, this layer should look just as good in Open-Layers, right? (See Figure 9.5, on the facing page.) Uh, not so fast. Don't worry—I'll show you the code for this in the next section. I just want to focus on the portrayal issues for now.

The duplicate labels might make you scratch your head for a moment. How could they look so nice in Mapbuilder and so awful in OpenLayers? What was the killer feature that OpenLayers brought to the party?

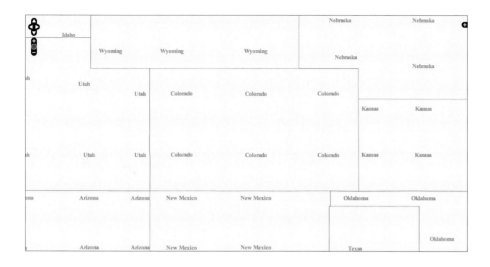

Figure 9.5: DUPLICATE LABELS IN OPENLAYERS?

Tessellation. Each map in OpenLayers is actually a series of individual WMS requests, each tile measuring 256 by 256 pixels. This view of the same map with the individual images outlined might help. (See Figure 9.6, on the next page.)

As you can see, the SLD labels get applied correctly to each tile. GeoServer (and the OGC standards in general) expect to render one big map. It has no idea that OpenLayers is doing the tessellation one request at a time, so there is no cross-tile optimization going on at all. Each tile, as far as GeoServer is concerned, is a one-of-a-kind masterpiece.

So, where does this leave us in the short term? It looks as if you have to choose between the convenience and performance of OpenLayers' tiling strategy over labeling issues. That's not really the truth, but that is where we are going to leave it in this chapter. If you install TileCache, mod_python, and mod_expires and you do a number of other tweaks as discussed in the GeoServer/TileCache tutorial,[15] you can overcome these issues and significantly increase your performance as well. The steps are well described on the wiki but are more involved than we have time to get into right now. They also target a single proprietary, albeit

---

15. http://docs.codehaus.org/display/GEOSDOC/TileCache+Tutorial

Figure 9.6: OpenLayer's Tiling Strategy Is the Culprit

open source, web framework—OpenLayers. Once WMS-T becomes a formal standard and there are more clients that can take advantage of it, you'll be pleased that you got some experience with it in the early days.

If you fall back on the "one big tile" strategy that Mapbuilder employs, your labeling will actually look pretty good. Since GeoServer has to compose just a single map, it will do the right thing when it comes to styling your map. The drawback is you won't get the full Google Maps slippy map effect. You can drag the map with your mouse, but you don't get a redraw until you release the mouse button.

Therein lies the rub. These two issues—styling and tiling—end up being the twin pillars of web mapping challenges. Current OGC standards favor the former, while popular web mapping sites such as Google and Yahoo favor the latter. The two aren't mutually exclusive. You *can* have a site that both looks good and performs well, but bear in mind that the two forces will pull you in opposite directions.

The "render on-the-fly" nature of WMS requests are simultaneously their biggest strength and their Achilles heel. By treating each map as a completely customizable entity, WMS gives you the ultimate in flexibility. Hey, don't like how that map turned out? No worries—throw it away, and ask me for a new one. What this solution lacks is any sense of reusability. Even if two people ask for the same map, at exactly the same resolution, in exactly the same file format, GeoServer won't cache the results and reserve them.

Rendering vector layers into rasters for the web browser is a computationally expensive operation. If your vector layers don't change often (like the US States layer), you are wasting precious CPU cycles redrawing the same lines over and over again. Multiply this by the millions of hits a popular website takes every day (if not every hour), and you can see that this solution simply won't scale for the masses. Think of it this way—is that search engine really scouring the Web for your answers in real time? Of course not. It precompiles the results and caches them. There might be a lag of an hour or even a day or two between the time a new website goes up and the search engine spider crawls the pages, analyzes them, and includes them in search results.

The big mapping websites work the same way. They prerender huge images so that the labels all look right. They then break those large images into bite-sized 256 by 256 pixels tiles. The tiles are small so that they download quickly. Their filenames don't change so that your browser will cache them up. Google Maps and similar websites actually get faster as you use them. The more tiles that end up in your local cache (or your router's, or your proxy server's, or your ISP server's), the fewer request actually have to go all the way back to Google. This is a classic win-win—your application is faster, and Google can serve more customer requests simultaneously. And all of this is simply leveraging the native functionality of the Web. Google didn't have to do anything more than just play by the rules.

But consider what you can't do with Google Maps. You can't turn individual layers on and off. (I'd like to see water but not roads.) You don't have infinite zoom levels. (Granted, twenty seems like more than enough.) Everything that can possibly be prerendered is already in place by the time you request the tile. The only thing that can't reasonably be prerendered—the driving directions from point A to point B—is created on the fly.

And that, my friends, is the solution to the tiling vs. styling conundrum. Prerender and tile everything that you possibly can. Create one big map (like the OGC prefers) so that your labels come out right, and then whack it up into tiny pieces (like Google prefers). The only thing that you should be rendering on the fly is the data that, for temporal reasons, can't be rendered ahead of time.

Unless, of course, you aren't Google. You've heard that "premature optimization is the root of all evil,"[16] haven't you? If you are building an intranet application that is meant to serve tens of users instead of tens of millions, then the OGC solution is more than adequate. You can still have Google-style fixed maps by including multiple map layers in a single request, or you can offer more flexibility because of the limited number of users you are serving.

The point is there is no one right answer. By understanding the strengths and weaknesses of both strategies, you can choose the right solution for the problem.

9.6 Creating a Slippy Map

Now that we have everything in place, we're finally ready to create a map. Because of the labeling issues we discussed in the previous section, we'll create a map in both Mapbuilder and OpenLayers. The Mapbuilder solution will work with nothing more than GeoServer in place. The OpenLayers solution will be lacking labels, but it will be ready for you if you decide to install Apache Web Server, TileCache, Python, and everything else necessary to go down that path.

Mapbuilder

Here is what our investment in Mapbuilder will yield. (See Figure 9.7, on page 226.)

Since all of the hard work is wrapped up in the SLDs, all we have to do here is assemble the layers. Look in the preview directory for the three required files (foo.html, foo.xml, and fooConfig.xml), and copy them up to our g4wd directory. Rename them to college*.

The foo.html and Config.xml files don't require many changes. The fooContext.xml file is where we'll assemble our layers:

```
<?xml version="1.0" encoding="ISO-8859-1" standalone="no"?>
<ViewContext version="1.0.0" id="atlas_world"
            xmlns="http://www.opengis.net/context"
            xmlns:xlink="http://www.w3.org/1999/xlink"
            xmlns:xsi="http://www.w3.org/2001/XMLSchema-instance"
            xsi:schemaLocation="http://www.opengis.net/context
              http://schemas.opengis.net/context/1.0.0/context.xsd">
```

---

16. http://en.wikipedia.org/wiki/Premature_optimization

```
<General>
  <!-- <Window width="500" height="250"/> -->
  <Window width="1000" height="500"/>

  <BoundingBox SRS="EPSG:4326" minx="-180" miny="-90" maxx="180" maxy="90"/>
  <Title>US Colleges</Title>
  <KeywordList>
    <Keyword>us colleges</Keyword>
  </KeywordList>
  <Abstract></Abstract>
</General>
<LayerList>

  <Layer queryable="1" hidden="0">
    <Server service="OGC:WMS" version="1.1.1" title="US States">
      <OnlineResource xlink:type="simple" xlink:href="../wms"/>
    </Server>
    <Name>g4wd:us_50</Name>
    <Title>US</Title>
    <SRS>EPSG:4326</SRS>
    <FormatList><Format current="1">image/png</Format></FormatList>
  </Layer>

  <Layer queryable="1" hidden="1">
    <Server service="OGC:WMS" version="1.1.1" title="g4wd:co_lake">
      <OnlineResource xlink:type="simple" xlink:href="../wms"/>
    </Server>
    <Name>g4wd:co_lake</Name>
    <Title>CO Lakes</Title>
    <SRS>EPSG:4326</SRS>
    <FormatList><Format current="1">image/png</Format></FormatList>
  </Layer>

  <Layer queryable="1" hidden="1">
    <Server service="OGC:WMS" version="1.1.1" title="g4wd:co_highway">
      <OnlineResource xlink:type="simple" xlink:href="../wms"/>
    </Server>
    <Name>g4wd:co_highway</Name>
    <Title>CO Highways</Title>
    <SRS>EPSG:4326</SRS>
    <FormatList><Format current="1">image/png</Format></FormatList>
  </Layer>

  <Layer queryable="1" hidden="1">
    <Server service="OGC:WMS" version="1.1.1" title="g4wd:co_city">
      <OnlineResource xlink:type="simple" xlink:href="../wms"/>
    </Server>
    <Name>g4wd:co_city</Name>
    <Title>CO Cities</Title>
    <SRS>EPSG:4326</SRS>
    <FormatList><Format current="1">image/png</Format></FormatList>
  </Layer>
```

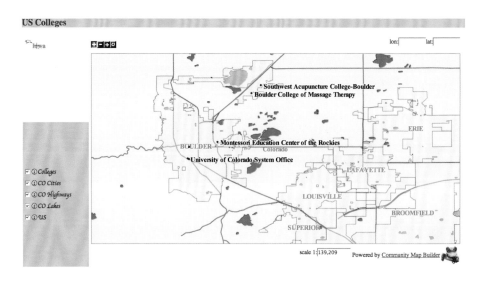

Figure 9.7: A FINISHED MAP IN MAPBUILDER

```
<Layer queryable="1" hidden="1">
  <Server service="OGC:WMS" version="1.1.1" title="g4wd:college">
    <OnlineResource xlink:type="simple" xlink:href="../wms"/>
  </Server>
  <Name>g4wd:college</Name>
  <Title>Colleges</Title>
  <SRS>EPSG:4326</SRS>
  <FormatList><Format current="1">image/png</Format></FormatList>
</Layer>

  </LayerList>
</ViewContext>
```

If you don't have all of these layers reprojected and imported into Post-GIS, don't worry. Remember the three steps to getting our UTM Colorado highways reprojected into WGS84 and imported into PostGIS?

```
ogr2ogr -t_srs EPSG:4326 co-hw.shp highways.shp
shp2pgsql -s 4326 co-hw.shp co_highway > co_highway.sql
psql -U postgres -d g4wd -f co_highway.sql
```

Performing these same three steps on the remaining CDOT shapefiles will have you all caught up. Once they are in GeoServer, don't forget to associate the SLD styles with the FeatureTypes.

OpenLayers

Adding these layers to an OpenLayers map is similarly easy. Change to the /opt/geoserver/webapps/geoserver/g4wd directory. Create ol4.html, and add the following:

```
<html xmlns="http://www.w3.org/1999/xhtml">
  <head>
    <style type="text/css">
      #map {
        width: 95%;
        height: 95%;
        border: 1px solid black;
      }
    </style>
    <script src="http://www.openlayers.org/api/OpenLayers.js"></script>
    <script type="text/javascript">
      //NOTE: geographic center of the US
      var lon = -98.583333;
      var lat = 39.833333;
      var zoom = 5;
      var map;
      var blueMarble, us_base;
      var colleges, highways, cities, water;

      function init(){
        map = new OpenLayers.Map( $('map') );

        //base layers
        us_base = new OpenLayers.Layer.WMS( "US",
                  "http://localhost:8888/geoserver/wms?",
                  {layers: 'g4wd:us_50', format: 'image/png',
                    transparent: true, styles:'us_states'},
                  {isBaseLayer:true} );
        map.addLayer(us_base);

        blueMarble = new OpenLayers.Layer.WMS( "Blue Marble",
                  "http://wms.jpl.nasa.gov/wms.cgi?",
                  {layers: 'BMNG', format: 'image/png'},
                  {isBaseLayer:true});
        map.addLayer(blueMarble);

        //feature layers
        colleges = new OpenLayers.Layer.WMS( "Colleges",
                  "http://localhost:8888/geoserver/wms?",
                  {layers: 'g4wd:college', format: 'image/png',
                    transparent: true, styles:'colleges'},
                  {isBaseLayer:false, opacity:0.5} );
        map.addLayer(colleges);
```

```
        highways = new OpenLayers.Layer.WMS( "Highways",
                   "http://localhost:8888/geoserver/wms?",
                   {layers: 'g4wd:co_highway', format: 'image/png',
                     transparent: true},
                   {isBaseLayer:false, opacity:0.5} );
        map.addLayer(highways);

        cities = new OpenLayers.Layer.WMS( "Cities",
                  "http://localhost:8888/geoserver/wms?",
                  {layers: 'g4wd:co_city', format: 'image/png',
                    transparent: true, style:'city'},
                  {isBaseLayer:false, opacity:0.5} );
        map.addLayer(cities);

        water = new OpenLayers.Layer.WMS( "Water",
                  "http://localhost:8888/geoserver/wms?",
                  {layers: 'g4wd:co_lake', format: 'image/png',
                    transparent: true},
                  {isBaseLayer:false, opacity:0.5} );
        map.addLayer(water);

        map.setCenter(new OpenLayers.LonLat(lon, lat), zoom);
        map.addControl( new OpenLayers.Control.LayerSwitcher() );
      }
    </script>
  </head>
  <body onload="init()">
    <div id="map"></div>
  </body>
</html>
```

Notice in the layer definition the style attribute. If you don't include a style attribute, OpenLayers chooses the default style associated with the layer. Since all of these default styles have labels that will look funny, we override the default, pointing the layer to the SLD of our choice. (I left the city labels in place because they didn't end up looking too bad.)

Once everything is all said and done, we end up with a similarly attractive map in OpenLayers. (See Figure 9.8, on the next page.)

9.7 Beyond the Web: 3D Viewers

Since we made it this far, we might as well end with a brief glimpse into the future of mapping. As exciting as slippy maps are, they still face the same problem that all paper maps face: portraying 3D information in only two dimensions.

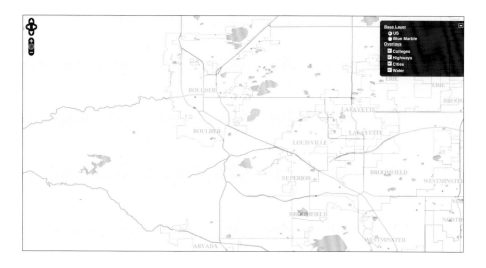

Figure 9.8: A FINISHED MAP IN OPENLAYERS

There are a couple of 3D viewers that allow us to see the world in its original shape. We'll take a look at an open source one (NASA World Wind) and a free one (Google Earth).

I call these viewers "the future of mapping," but really I think that they represent the future of computer programming in general. They are hybrid applications—rather than being confined to the browser, they are full executables that must be downloaded and installed locally. But they don't ship with the data. As we mentioned in Section 4.2, *Terraserver-USA: Another Source of Free Raster Imagery*, on page 62, terabytes of data won't fit comfortably onto most people's hard drives. So, these applications stream the data across the Web as needed. They act like a browser in this sense, but they aren't limited to HTML, CSS, and JavaScript.

Your operating system is installed locally, but it calls back to the mothership periodically for security patches and new features. Apple iTunes is another example of a hybrid application. You burn your CDs to disk locally, but you can also buy music across the Web. As you play your music, iTunes downloads the album art for you behind the scenes. Sun Microsystems famously said, "The network is the computer." At the time, most people scratched their heads and said, "Huh?" The network may not be the computer, but the computer isn't much fun without the network these days. More and more programs are built on the assumption that the Internet is available and ready to use.

NASA World Wind

NASA World Wind[17] is an open source 3D viewer. As of version 1.4, it is available only for the Windows platform. But a Java version is in the works, which should extend it to the Mac and Linux fans as well.

World Wind is a full-featured viewer out of the box. The Blue Marble imagery is spectacularly rendered—seeing it in three dimensions really brings it to life. World Wind comes with a rich set of data layers, from real-time weather to political boundaries.

Your welcome screen is a globe, suspended in space. You spin it by dragging it with your mouse. To zoom in, double-click an area of interest. As you zoom in, the imagery is streamed to your computer on the fly from NASA's servers across the Web.

So, what does any of that have to do with the GeoServer we have sitting idle at this point? Well, it just so happens that World Wind is a great WMS viewer. Oh sure, it'll read shapefiles from disk and put them up on the globe. But wiring it up to your OGC server, or for that matter any OGC server on the Web, is where the fun begins.

In the menu bar, choose Tools > Import WMS url to layer. (See Figure 9.9, on the next page.) The first text box asks you for an URL. You know what's going to happen—World Wind is about to perform a Get Capabilities request. Enter http://localhost:8888/geoserver/wms?. Click the Get WMS Tree button. Once it has a list of layers, you can preview any of them by clicking them. You can give the layer a custom title, or you can simply use the title suggested by the server. In the XML filename field, you can give the capabilities document an intuitive name and save it. Saving it to disk allows your server to show up in the Layers list. You are one check box away from seeing your colleges rendered on the globe. (See Figure 9.10, on the facing page.)

Flying across your data set like Superman, tilting the globe so that you can see the mountains rise up in the distance, is like nothing that can be offered by a browser-based slippy map today. You don't realize how much you miss that third dimension until you have it available to you. Orthorectified views of the earth are still nice, but getting the chance to look at the same features at an oblique angle really, no pun intended, adds a whole new dimension to your data.

---

17. http://worldwind.arc.nasa.gov/

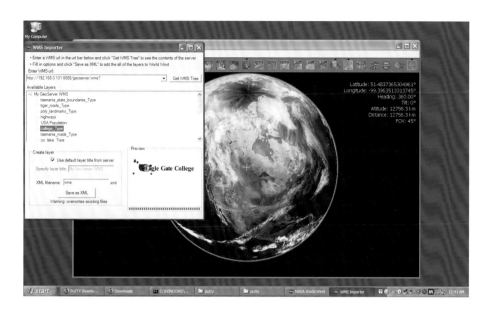

Figure 9.9: ADDING YOUR WMS SERVER TO NASA WORLD WIND

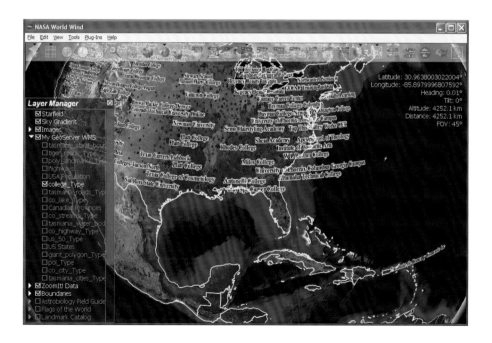

Figure 9.10: YOUR COLLEGES LAYER

Google Earth

As nice as World Wind is, there is another application to consider. Google Earth[18] is free but not open source. What it brings to the table is the full backing of a major web player with deep pockets. Google offers versions of Google Earth for Windows, Mac OS X, and Linux and fast servers with up-to-date commercial imagery and vector data.

A rabid community has sprouted up around this next generation map viewer. While Google Earth offers experimental WMS support, its lingua franca is *Keyhole Markup Language* (KML).[19] The name Keyhole comes from the original name of the product and the company that built it. Once Google acquired the company, the product was rebranded, but the original name still lingers.

KML is largely inspired by GML. The only difference is that GML is a pure data description language, leaving styling to SLDs and Context documents. KML merges both data and portrayal instructions into a single file. Although this riled many OGC purists, the file format has become wildly popular.

In a nod to the popularity of the format, GeoServer offers native KML support. From the Google Earth menu, choose Add > Network Link. Although you can experiment with trying to add your WMS layers, I've had better luck simply dealing with KML. Enter the following: http://localhost:8888/geoserver/wms/kml_reflect?layers=g4wd:college. Just as with NASA World Wind, your globe will come down with a case of red dot fever.

The free version of Google Earth is limited to KML data feeds. Yes, you can overlay images on the globe, but Google Earth doesn't pay attention to any geocoding. You simply import the image of your choices and snap it to a point on the globe. Hardly a feature for professionals, this rubbersheeting does make it trivially easy put anything you want onto a map. You can also create your own points and lines, annotate them, and save them to your own KML file. You can even email it directly from within the application. For a nominal fee, Google Earth Plus allows you to import your GPS data and Microsoft Excel spreadsheets. The top version, Google Earth Pro, allows you to overlay shapefiles on the globe and gives you access to premium data.

---

18. http://earth.google.com/
19. http://earth.google.com/kml/

But the real value of Google Earth is the community. On websites such as Vactionworld,[20] fans put together KML files showing everything from the Travels of Julius Caesar to a Da Vinci Code Tour, complete with timed flybys and text overlays. You can easily lose hours to looking at meteor craters, aircrafts in flight, and shipwrecks. Although Google Earth might lack sophisticated GIS features, it makes up for it in accessibility. It has turned thousands of people into map geeks, sharing mapping data as easily as they forward on the email joke of the day. Dare I say it? Google Earth made mapping cool.

9.8 Conclusion

Well, you made it. You now have your master's degree in neogeography. Unlike an expensive hobby such as golf or flying, mapping is something that you can do on the cheap with nothing but free and open source data and applications. Of course, the results are anything but cheap looking. They are every bit the world-class solution as the expensive ones. You just supply the time and the enthusiasm.

What was once the domain of a few specialists should now be commonplace. The address data that appears over and over in every business should no longer look like simple strings and numbers—it should now look like points, lines, and polygons just waiting to be mapped. I'm sure you'll see more and more spatial data everywhere you look without even trying. Databases and web services take on new meaning now that you know what they are *really* capable of.

But don't forget the cardinal rule of neogeography—you must pay it forward. The next time someone says, "Wow, that map is cool. I wonder how they did that?" your response should be, "Aw, that's easy. Let me show you. You see, there are two types of geospatial data: vectors and rasters...." And with that simple response, one more black box of geographic wonder will be pried open.

Thanks for sharing your time with me. I hope that you enjoyed yourself.

20. http://vacationworld.googlepages.com/files

Mac/Linux Installation

This appendix will walk you through the installation process for all the software mentioned in the book. These instructions apply to the Mac/Linux platform.

A.1 Installing GDAL/Proj/Geos

The foundation of nearly every other application discussed in this book is the "holy trinity" of GDAL, Proj, and GEOS. Linux and Windows users can download precompiled binaries from the web.[1] If you're a Mac user, many of these libraries are available from DarwinPorts.[2] Even if precompiled binaries are available for your platform, your best bet is still to build them from source. Thankfully, if you have Xcode installed (or the GCC compiler), they are pretty easy to compile.

Proj

Description: PROJ.4 is a library that allows you to reproject geographic data.

Version: 4.5.0   *Source*: http://proj.maptools.org

To build, follow these steps:

1. Download the source, and unzip.
2. (optional) Download and unzip proj-datumgrid-1.3.zip into the nad directory. This allows you to reproject NAD27, NAD83, and New Zealand NZGD49 datums.

---

1. http://fwtools.maptools.org/ (named for and supported by Frank Warmerdam, the creator of GDAL and Proj).
2. http://darwinports.opendarwin.org/

3. Run configure.

4. Run make.

5. Run sudo make install.

Verify by following these steps:

1. Enter which proj. It should return /usr/local/bin/proj.

2. Enter proj. It should return 4.5.0.

3. You should see libproj.* in /usr/local/lib.

GEOS

Description: Geometry Engine Open Source (GEOS) is a library of geo-metric/spatial functions. It is a C++ port of the Java Topology Suite (JTS); see http://www.jump-project.org/project.php?PID=JTS&SID=OVER). GEOS is maintained by Refractions Research, the same company that maintains PostGIS.

Version: 2.2.3 *Source*: http://geos.refractions.net/

To build, follow these steps:

1. Download the source, and unzip.

2. Run configure.

3. Run make.

4. Run sudo make install.

Verify by following these steps:

1. Enter which geos-config. It should return /usr/local/bin/geos-config.

2. Enter geos-config --version. It should return 2.2.3.

3. You should see libgeos.* in /usr/local/lib.

GDAL

Description: Geospatial Data Abstraction Library (GDAL) is a raster library that allows you to gather metadata and reproject imagery. OGR is an included library that allows you to do the same thing to vector data.

Version: 1.4.0 *Source*: http://gdal.maptools.org

To build, follow these steps:

1. Download the source, and unzip.

2. Run configure.

3. Run make.

4. Run sudo make install.

Verify by following these steps:

1. Enter which gdal-config. It should return /usr/local/bin/gdal-config.
2. Enter gdal-config --version. It should return 1.4.0.
3. You should see libgdal.* in /usr/local/lib.

A.2 Installing PostgreSQL and PostGIS

I recommend building these two projects from source. Assuming that you have successfully built Proj and GEOS (both recommended for PostGIS but not required), the only additional requirement for PostgreSQL is the Readline library. Readline provides nice command-line history, but it is completely optional. Use configure --without-readline on PostgreSQL if you choose not to download and install it.

Readline

Description: Readline provides a command-line history for PostgreSQL. It is completely optional.

Version: 5.2   *Source*: http://tiswww.case.edu/~chet/readline/rltop.html

To build, follow these steps:

1. Download the source, and unzip.
2. Run configure.
3. Run make.
4. Run sudo make install.

Verify by following these steps:

1. You should see libreadline.* in /usr/local/lib.

PostgreSQL

Description: PostgreSQL is a database that, in conjunction with PostGIS, allows you to store and manipulate vector data.

Version: 8.2.1   *Source*: http://www.postgresql.org

To build, follow these steps:

1. Download the source, and unzip.
2. Run configure.
3. Run make.
4. Run sudo make install.

Verify by following these steps:

1. Enter which psql. It should return /usr/local/bin/psql.
2. Enter psql --version. It should return 8.2.1.

Here are the post-installation steps:

To use PostgreSQL, you should create a user account. In OS X, go to System Preferences > Accounts and create a user named *postgres*. Assign a password.

To create a new database, follow these steps:

1. Run cd /usr/local/pgsql.
2. Run sudo mkdir data.
3. Run sudo mkdir log.
4. Run sudo chown postgres data log.
5. Run su - postgres.
6. Run cd /usr/local/pgsql/bin.
7. Run initdb -D /usr/local/pgsql/data.
8. Run pg_ctl -D /usr/local/pgsql/data -l /usr/local/pgsql/log/logfile start.
9. Run createdb g4wd.

Verify by following these steps:

1. Enter netstat -an |more. You should see a service running on port 5432.
2. Enter psql g4wd. You should seeWelcome to psql 8.2.1, the PostgreSQL interactive terminal.
3. Enter create table test (id int, name varchar(25));. Enter \d test.
4. Enter \q to quit.

PostGIS

Description: PostGIS is a spatial extension that allows you to store GIS data in PostgreSQL.

Version: 1.2.1   *Source*: http://postgis.refractions.net

To build, follow these steps:

1. Download the source, and unzip.
2. Run configure --with-pgsql=/usr/local/pgsql/bin/pg_config.
3. Run make.
4. Run sudo make install.

Verify by following these steps:

1. Enter which pgsql2shp. It should return /usr/local/bin/pgsql2shp.
2. Enter psql. It should return usage instructions.

Here are the post-installation steps:

Before you can add geographic data to your database, you must spatially enable it. These steps must be done on each new database you create.

To spatially enable a new database, follow these steps:

1. Run su - postgres.
2. Run cd /usr/local/pgsql/bin.
3. Run createlang plpgsql g4wd.
4. Run cd /usr/local/pgsql/share.
5. Run psql -d g4wd -f lwpostgis.sql.
6. Run psql -d g4wd -f spatial_ref_sys.sql.

Verify by following these steps:

1. Run psql g4wd.
2. Run \d.
3. Run \d geometry_columns.
4. Run \d spatial_ref_sys.
5. Run select postgis_full_version();.
6. Run \q.

GDAL (Again)

The last time we compiled GDAL, we didn't have PostGIS installed. Let's add support for it back into GDAL.

To build, follow these steps:

1. Change back to the source directory for GDAL.
2. Run configure --with-pg=/usr/local/pgsql/bin/pg_config.
3. Run make.
4. Run sudo make install.

Verify by following these steps:

1. Enter ogrinfo --formats. You should see PostgreSQL listed.

A.3   LibTIFF and LibGeoTIFF

To create GeoTIFFs, you should have both LibTIFF and LibGeoTIFF installed.

LibTIFF

Description: LibTIFF allows you to manipulate TIFFs.

Version: 3.8.2   *Source*: http://www.remotesensing.org/libtiff/

To build, follow these steps:

1. Download the source, and unzip.
2. Run configure.
3. Run make.
4. Run sudo make install.

Verify by following these steps:

1. Enter which tiffinfo. It should return /usr/local/bin/tiffinfo.
2. Enter tiffinfo. It should return usage instructions.

LibGeoTIFF

Description: LibGeoTIFF allows you to create true GeoTIFFs by combining world files and TIFFs.

Version: 1.2.3   *Source*: ftp://ftp.remotesensing.org/pub/geotiff/

To build, follow these steps:

1. Download the source, and unzip.
2. Run configure.
3. Run make.
4. Run sudo make install.

Verify by following these steps:

1. Enter which geotifcp. It should return /usr/local/bin/geotifcp.
2. Enter geotifcp. It should return usage instructions.

Appendix B

Installing Groovy

Everything you need to run Groovy is included in the single download—well, everything except the JDK, that is. (Groovy runs on JDK 1.4, 1.5, and 1.6.) This appendix contains platform-specific installation instructions.

B.1   Unix, Linux, and Mac OS X

Download the latest version of Groovy from http://groovy.codehaus.org. Unzip it to the directory of your choice. I prefer /opt. You will end up with a groovy directory that has the version number on the end of it: groovy-1.0, for example. I like creating a simply named symlink: ln -s groovy-1.0 groovy. This allows me to switch between versions cleanly and easily.

Once the directory is in place, the next thing you need to do is create a GROOVY_HOME environment variable. This varies from shell to shell. For Bash, edit either .bash_profile or .bash_rc in your home directory. Add the following:

```
### Groovy
GROOVY_HOME=/opt/groovy
PATH=$PATH:$GROOVY_HOME/bin
export GROOVY_HOME PATH
```

For these changes to take effect, you need to exit or restart your terminal session. Alternately, you can type source .bash_profile to load the changes in the current session. Type echo $GROOVY_HOME to confirm that your changes took effect.

To verify that the Groovy command is in the path, type groovy. If you see a message similar to the following, you have successfully installed Groovy:

```
$ groovy
error: neither -e or filename provided
usage: groovy
 -a,--autosplit <splitPattern>    automatically split current line
                                  (defaults to '\s'
 -c,--encoding <charset>          specify the encoding of the files
 -d,--debug                       debug mode will print out full stack
                                  traces
 -e <script>                      specify a command line script
 -h,--help                        usage information
 -i <extension>                   modify files in place, create backup if
                                  extension is given (e.g. '.bak')
 -l <port>                        listen on a port and process inbound
                                  lines
 -n                               process files line by line
 -p                               process files line by line and print
                                  result
 -v,--version                     display the Groovy and JVM versions
```

B.2 Windows

Download the latest version of Groovy from http://groovy.codehaus.org. Unzip it to the directory of your choice. I prefer c:\opt. You will end up with a groovy directory that has the version number on the end of it: groovy-1.0, for example. Although you can rename it to something simpler—groovy—I've found that maintaining the version number helps upgrades and future migrations.

Once the directory is in place, next create a GROOVY_HOME environment variable. For Windows XP, go to the Control Panel, and double-click System. Click the Advanced tab, and then click Environment Variables at the bottom of the window. In the new window, click New under System Variables. Use GROOVY_HOME for the variable name and c:\opt\groovy-1.0 for the variable value. (See Figure B.1, on the next page.)

To add Groovy to the path, find the PATH variable, and double-click it. Add ;%GROOVY_HOME%\bin to the end of the variable. (Don't forget the leading semicolon.) Click OK to back your way out of all the dialog boxes.

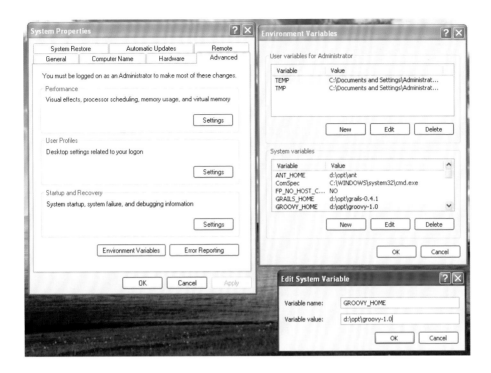

Figure B.1: CREATING THE GROOVY_HOME ENVIRONMENT VARIABLE IN WINDOWS

For these changes to take effect, you need to exit or restart any command prompts you have open. Open a new command prompt, and type set to display a list of all environment variables. Make sure that GROOVY_HOME appears.

To verify that the Groovy command is in the path, type groovy. If you see a message similar to the following, you have successfully installed Groovy:

```
c:\> groovy
error: neither -e or filename provided
usage: groovy
 -a,--autosplit <splitPattern>    automatically split current line
                                  (defaults to '\s'
 -c,--encoding <charset>          specify the encoding of the files
 -d,--debug                       debug mode will print out full stack
                                  traces
 -e <script>                      specify a command line script
```

-h,--help	usage information
-i <extension>	modify files in place, create backup if extension is given (e.g. '.bak')
-l <port>	listen on a port and process inbound lines
-n	process files line by line
-p	process files line by line and print result
-v,--version	display the Groovy and JVM versions

Index

Pragmatic Tools

You may be interested in other Pragmatic Bookshelf titles that look at pragmatic tools, techniques, your team and your own career.

For a full list of our current titles, as well as announcements of new titles, please visit www.pragmaticprogrammer.com.

Pragmatic Ajax

AJAX redefines the user experience for web applications, providing compelling user interfaces. Now you can dig deeper into AJAX itself as this book shows you how to make AJAX magic. Explore both the fundamental technologies and the emerging frameworks that make it easy.

From Google Maps to Ajaxified Java, .NET, and Ruby on Rails applications, this Pragmatic guide strips away the mystery and shows you the easy way to make Ajax work for you.

Pragmatic Ajax: A Web 2.0 Primer
Justin Gehtland, Ben Galbraith, Dion Almaer
(296 pages) ISBN: 0-9766940-8-5. $29.95
http://pragmaticprogrammer.com/titles/ajax

TextMate

If you're coding Ruby or Rails on a Mac, then you owe it to yourself to get the TextMate editor. And, once you're using TextMate, you owe it to yourself to pick up this book. It's packed with information which will help you automate all your editing tasks, saving you time to concentrate on the important stuff. Use snippets to insert boilerplate code and refactorings to move stuff around. Learn how to write your own extensions to customize it to the way you work.

TextMate: Power Editing for the Mac
James Edward Gray II
(200 pages) ISBN: 0-9787392-3-X. $29.95
http://pragmaticprogrammer.com/titles/textmate

Agile Techniques

Learn about all the *Practices of an Agile Developer*, and especially how to get a team together by using *Agile Retrospectives*.

Practices of an Agile Developer

Agility is all about using feedback to respond to change. Learn how to apply the principles of agility throughout the software development process • Establish and maintain an agile working environment • Deliver what users really want • Use personal agile techniques for better coding and debugging • Use effective collaborative techniques for better teamwork • Move to an agile approach

Practices of an Agile Developer: Working in the Real World
Venkat Subramaniam and Andy Hunt
(189 pages) ISBN: 0-9745140-8-X. $29.95
http://pragmaticprogrammer.com/titles/pad

Agile Retrospectives

Mine the experience of your software development team continually throughout the life of the project. Rather than waiting until the end of the project—as with a traditional retrospective, when it's too late to help—agile retrospectives help you adjust to change *today*.

The tools and recipes in this book will help you uncover and solve hidden (and not-so-hidden) problems with your technology, your methodology, and those difficult "people issues" on your team.

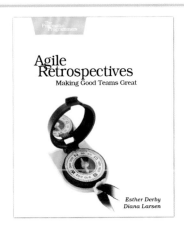

Agile Retrospectives: Making Good Teams Great
Esther Derby and Diana Larsen
(170 pages) ISBN: 0-9776166-4-9. $29.95
http://pragmaticprogrammer.com/titles/dlret

A Pragmatic Career

Being a Pragmatic Programmer is just the beginning—there's a lot more to architecting your career than just slinging code. Learn how to grow into a technical lead or manager by learning the secrets from *Behind Closed Doors*.

And when you're ready to take that to the next level, see how to *Manage It!*, also by author Johanna Rothman.

Behind Closed Doors

You can learn to be a better manager—even a great manager—with this guide. You'll find powerful tips covering:

- Delegating effectively • Using feedback and goal-setting • Developing influence • Handling one-on-one meetings • Coaching and mentoring
- Deciding what work to do-and what not to do
- . . . and more!

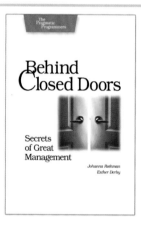

Behind Closed Doors Secrets of Great Management
Johanna Rothman and Esther Derby
(192 pages) ISBN: 0-9766940-2-6. $24.95
http://pragmaticprogrammer.com/titles/rdbcd

Manage It!

Manage It! is a risk-based guide to making good decisions about how to plan and guide your projects. Author Johanna Rothman shows you how to beg, borrow, and steal from the best methodologies to fit your particular project. You'll find what works best for *you*.

- Learn all about different project lifecycles • See how to organize a project • Compare sample project dashboards • See how to staff a project
- Know when you're done—and what that means.

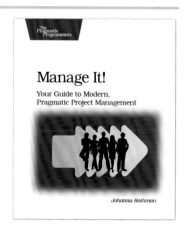

Your Guide to Modern, Pragmatic Project Management
Johanna Rothman
(360 pages) ISBN: 0-9787392-4-8. $34.95
http://pragmaticprogrammer.com/titles/jrpm

For the Whole Team

You'll find Pragmatic titles for everyone on the team: from developers to managers, testers to admins. Looking for ways to migrate your organization to new technology? Then check out *From Java To Ruby: Things Every Manager Should Know*.

Do you have people near your team who'd like to *Learn to Program*? This guide for non-programmers can teach testers, database administrators, and even your kids how to program using Ruby, no previous experience required.

From Java To Ruby

How can you justify the move away from established platforms such as J2EE? Bruce Tate's *From Java to Ruby* has the answers, and it expresses them in a language that'll help persuade managers and executives who've seen it all. See when and where the switch makes sense, and see how to make it work.

From Java To Ruby: Things Every Manager Should Know
Bruce Tate
(160 pages) ISBN: 0-9766940-9-3. $29.95
http://pragmaticprogrammer.com/titles/fr_j2r

Learn to Program

Now everyone can learn to write programs for themselves—no experience required! Chris Pine takes a thorough but light-hearted approach that teaches how to program with a minimum of fuss or bother. Learn to write programs using Ruby, a modern, fully object-oriented programming language. • Learn to program with no previous experience necessary • Create utilities and applications • Take control of the computer • Build a foundation to understand large, professional applications

Learn to Program
Chris Pine
(175 pages) ISBN: 0-9766940-4-2. $19.95
http://pragmaticprogrammer.com/titles/fr_ltp

For the Whole Team

Do you have Java developers on your team who would like to learn Rails? They can leverage their existing knowledge of Java and learn Rails more quickly with Stuart Halloway and Justin Gehtland's *Rails for Java Developers*.

Is you application ready for the real world? Find out if you're really ready to *Release It!* or not.

Rails for Java Developers

Enterprise Java developers already have most of the skills needed to create Rails applications. They just need a guide which shows how their Java knowledge maps to the Rails world. That's what this book does. It covers: • The Ruby language • Building MVC Applications • Unit and Functional Testing • Security • Project Automation • Configuration • Web Services This book is the fast track for Java programmers who are learning or evaluating Ruby on Rails.

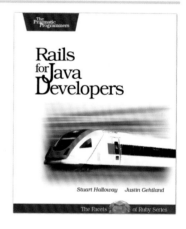

Rails for Java Developers
Stuart Halloway and Justin Gehtland
(300 pages) ISBN: 0-9776166-9-X. $34.95
http://pragmaticprogrammer.com/titles/fr_r4j

Release It!

Whether it's in Java, .NET, or Ruby on Rails, getting your application ready to ship is only half the battle. Did you design your system to survive a sudden rush of visitors from Digg or Slashdot? Or an influx of real world customers from 100 different countries? Are you ready for a world filled with flakey networks, tangled databases, and impatient users?

If you're a developer and don't want to be on call at 3AM for the rest of your life, this book will help.

Design and Deploy Production-Ready Software
Michael T. Nygard
(368 pages) ISBN: 0-9787392-1-3. $34.95
http://pragmaticprogrammer.com/titles/mnee

The Pragmatic Bookshelf

The Pragmatic Bookshelf features books written by developers for developers. The titles continue the well-known Pragmatic Programmer style, and continue to garner awards and rave reviews. As development gets more and more difficult, the Pragmatic Programmers will be there with more titles and products to help you stay on top of your game.

Visit Us Online

GIS for Web Developers Home Page
http://pragmaticprogrammer.com/titles/sdgis
Source code from this book, errata, and other resources. Come give us feedback, too!

Register for Updates
http://pragmaticprogrammer.com/updates
Be notified when updates and new books become available.

Join the Community
http://pragmaticprogrammer.com/community
Read our weblogs, join our online discussions, participate in our mailing list, interact with our wiki, and benefit from the experience of other Pragmatic Programmers.

New and Noteworthy
http://pragmaticprogrammer.com/news
Check out the latest pragmatic developments in the news.

Save on the PDF

Save big on the PDF version of this book. Owning the paper version of this book entitles you to purchase the PDF version at a great discount. The PDF is great for carrying around on your laptop. It's hyperlinked, has color, and is fully searchable. Buy it now at pragmaticprogrammer.com/coupon.

Contact Us

Phone Orders:	1-800-699-PROG (+1 919 847 3884)
Online Orders:	www.pragmaticprogrammer.com/catalog
Customer Service:	orders@pragmaticprogrammer.com
Non-English Versions:	translations@pragmaticprogrammer.com
Pragmatic Teaching:	academic@pragmaticprogrammer.com
Author Proposals:	proposals@pragmaticprogrammer.com